Undergraduate Topics in Computer Science

'Undergraduate Topics in Computer Science' (UTiCS) delivers high-quality instructional content for undergraduates studying in all areas of computing and information science. From core foundational and theoretical material to final-year topics and applications, UTiCS books take a fresh, concise, and modern approach and are ideal for self-study or for a one- or two-semester course. The texts are all authored by established experts in their fields, reviewed by an international advisory board, and contain numerous examples and problems, many of which include fully worked solutions.

The UTiCS concept relies on high-quality, concise books in softback format, and generally a maximum of 275–300 pages. For undergraduate textbooks that are likely to be longer, more expository, Springer continues to offer the highly regarded Texts in Computer Science series, to which we refer potential authors.

More information about this series at http://www.springer.com/series/7592

Antti Laaksonen

Guide to Competitive Programming

Learning and Improving Algorithms
Through Contests

Second Edition

Antti Laaksonen
Department of Computer Science
University of Helsinki
Helsinki, Finland

ISSN 1863-7310   ISSN 2197-1781   (electronic)
Undergraduate Topics in Computer Science
ISBN 978-3-030-39356-4   ISBN 978-3-030-39357-1   (eBook)
https://doi.org/10.1007/978-3-030-39357-1

This Springer imprint is published by the registered company Springer Nature Switzerland AG
The registered company address is: Gewerbestrasse 11, 6330 Cham, Switzerland

Preface to the Second Edition

This second edition of the book contains several new sections that discuss advanced topics, such as calculating the Fourier transform, finding minimum cost flows in graphs, and using automata in string problems.

I am grateful to Olli Matilainen for reading through most of the new material and giving many useful comments and suggestions.

Helsinki, Finland
February 2020

Antti Laaksonen

Preface to the First Edition

The purpose of this book is to give you a comprehensive introduction to modern competitive programming. It is assumed that you already know the basics of programming, but previous background in algorithm design or programming contests is not necessary. Since the book covers a wide range of topics of various difficulty, it suits both for beginners and more experienced readers.

Programming contests already have a quite long history. The *International Collegiate Programming Contest* for university students started during the 1970s, and the first *International Olympiad in Informatics* for secondary school students was organized in 1989. Both competitions are now established events with a large number of participants from all around the world.

Today, competitive programming is more popular than ever. The Internet has played a significant role in this progress. There is now an active online community of competitive programmers, and many contests are organized every week. At the same time, the difficulty of contests is increasing. Techniques that only the very best participants mastered some years ago are now standard tools known by a large number of people.

Competitive programming has its roots in the scientific study of algorithms. However, while a computer scientist writes a proof to show that their algorithm works, a competitive programmer *implements* their algorithm and submits it to a contest system. Then, the algorithm is tested using a set of test cases, and if it passes all of them, it is accepted. This is an essential element in competitive programming, because it provides a way to *automatically* get strong evidence that an algorithm works. In fact, competitive programming has proved to be an excellent way to learn algorithms, because it encourages to design algorithms that really work, instead of sketching ideas that may work or not.

Another benefit of competitive programming is that contest problems require *thinking*. In particular, there are no spoilers in problem statements. This is actually a severe problem in many algorithms courses. You are given a nice problem to solve, but then the last sentence says, for example: "*Hint*: modify Dijkstra's algorithm to solve the problem." After reading this, there is not much thinking needed, because you already know how to solve the problem. This never happens in competitive programming. Instead, you have a full set of tools available, and you have to figure out *yourself* which of them to use.

Solving competitive programming problems also improves one's programming and debugging skills. Typically, a solution is awarded points only if it correctly solves all test cases, so a successful competitive programmer has to be able to implement programs that do not have bugs. This is a valuable skill in software engineering, and it is not a coincidence that IT companies are interested in people who have background in competitive programming.

It takes a long time to become a good competitive programmer, but it is also an opportunity to learn a lot. You can be sure that you will get a good general understanding of algorithms if you spend time reading the book, solving problems and taking part in contests.

If you have any feedback, I would like to hear it! You can always send me a message to `ahslaaks@cs.helsinki.fi`.

I am very grateful to a large number of people who have sent me feedback on draft versions of this book. This feedback has greatly improved the quality of the book. I especially thank Mikko Ervasti, Janne Junnila, Janne Kokkala, Tuukka Korhonen, Patric Östergård, and Roope Salmi for giving detailed feedback on the manuscript. I also thank Simon Rees and Wayne Wheeler for excellent collaboration when publishing this book with Springer.

Helsinki, Finland   Antti Laaksonen
October 2017

Contents

Introduction

1

This chapter shows what competitive programming is about, outlines the contents of the book, and discusses additional learning resources.

Section 1.1 goes through the elements of competitive programming, introduces a selection of popular programming contests, and gives advice on how to practice competitive programming.

Section 1.2 discusses the goals and topics of this book and briefly describes the contents of each chapter.

Section 1.3 presents the CSES Problem Set, which contains a collection of practice problems. Solving the problems while reading the book is a good way to learn competitive programming.

Section 1.4 discusses other books related to competitive programming and the design of algorithms.

1.1 What Is Competitive Programming?

Competitive programming combines two topics: the design of algorithms and the implementation of algorithms.

Design of Algorithms The core of competitive programming is about inventing efficient algorithms that solve well-defined computational problems. The design of algorithms requires problem-solving and mathematical skills. Often a solution to a problem is a combination of well-known methods and new insights.

Mathematics plays an important role in competitive programming. Actually, there are no clear boundaries between algorithm design and mathematics. This book has been written so that not much background in mathematics is needed. The appendix of the book reviews some mathematical concepts that are used throughout the book, such as sets, logic, and functions, and the appendix can be used as a reference when reading the book.

© Springer Nature Switzerland AG 2020
A. Laaksonen, *Guide to Competitive Programming*, Undergraduate Topics in Computer Science, https://doi.org/10.1007/978-3-030-39357-1_1

Implementation of Algorithms In competitive programming, the solutions to problems are evaluated by testing an implemented algorithm using a set of test cases. Thus, after coming up with an algorithm that solves the problem, the next step is to correctly implement it, which requires good programming skills. Competitive programming greatly differs from traditional software engineering: Programs are short (usually at most some hundreds of lines), they should be written quickly, and it is not needed to maintain them after the contest.

At the moment, the most popular programming languages used in contests are C++, Python, and Java. For example, in Google Code Jam 2019, among the best 4500 participants, 71% used C++, 21% used Python and 8% used Java. Many people regard C++ as the best choice for a competitive programmer. The benefits of using C++ are that it is a very efficient language and its standard library contains a large collection of data structures and algorithms.

All example programs in this book are written in C++, and the standard library's data structures and algorithms are often used. The programs follow the C++11 standard, which can be used in most contests nowadays. If you cannot program in C++ yet, now is a good time to start learning.

1.1.1 Programming Contests

IOI The *International Olympiad in Informatics* is an annual programming contest for secondary school students. Each country is allowed to send a team of four students to the contest. There are usually about 300 participants from 80 countries.

The IOI consists of two five-hour-long contests. In both contests, the participants are asked to solve three difficult programming tasks. The tasks are divided into subtasks, each of which has an assigned score. While the contestants are divided into teams, they compete as individuals.

Participants for the IOI are selected through national contests. Before the IOI, many regional contests are organized, such as the Baltic Olympiad in Informatics (BOI), the Central European Olympiad in Informatics (CEOI), and the Asia-Pacific Informatics Olympiad (APIO).

ICPC The *International Collegiate Programming Contest* is an annual programming contest for university students. Each team in the contest consists of three students, and unlike in the IOI, the students work together; there is only one computer available for each team.

The ICPC consists of several stages, and finally the best teams are invited to the World Finals. While there are tens of thousands of participants in the contest, there are only a small number[1] of final slots available, so even advancing to the finals is a great achievement.

In each ICPC contest, the teams have five hours of time to solve about ten algorithm problems. A solution to a problem is accepted only if it solves all test cases efficiently.

---

[1]The exact number of final slots varies from year to year; in 2019, there were 135 final slots.

During the contest, competitors may view the results of other teams, but for the last hour the scoreboard is frozen, and it is not possible to see the results of the last submissions.

Online Contests There are also many online contests that are open for everybody. At the moment, the most active contest site is Codeforces, which organizes contests about weekly. Other popular contest sites include AtCoder, CodeChef, CS Academy, HackerRank, and Topcoder.

Some companies organize online contests with onsite finals. Examples of such contests are Facebook Hacker Cup, Google Code Jam, and Yandex.Algorithm. Of course, companies also use those contests for recruiting: Performing well in a contest is a good way to prove one's skills in programming.

1.1.2 Tips for Practicing

Learning competitive programming requires a great amount of work. However, there are many ways to practice, and some of them are better than others.

When solving problems, one should keep in mind that the *number* of solved problems is not as important as the *quality* of the problems. It is tempting to select problems that look nice and easy and solve them, and skip problems that look hard and tedious. However, the way to really improve one's skills is to focus on the latter type of problems.

Another important observation is that most programming contest problems can be solved using simple and short algorithms, but the difficult part is to invent the algorithm. Competitive programming is not about learning complex and obscure algorithms by heart, but rather about learning problem solving and ways to approach difficult problems using simple tools.

Finally, some people despise the implementation of algorithms: It is fun to design algorithms but boring to implement them. However, the ability to quickly and correctly implement algorithms is an important asset, and this skill can be practiced. It is a bad idea to spend most of the contest time for writing code and finding bugs, instead of thinking of how to solve problems.

1.2 About This Book

The *IOI Syllabus* [17] regulates the topics that may appear at the International Olympiad in Informatics, and the syllabus has been a starting point when selecting topics for this book. However, the book also discusses some advanced topics that are (as of 2019) excluded from the IOI but may appear in other contests. Examples of such topics are maximum flows, Nim theory, and suffix structures.

While many competitive programming topics are discussed in standard algorithms textbooks, there are also differences. For example, many textbooks focus on implementing sorting algorithms and fundamental data structures from scratch, but this knowledge is not very relevant in competitive programming, because standard library functionality can be used. Then, there are topics that are well known in the competitive programming community but rarely discussed in textbooks. An example of such a topic is the segment tree data structure that can be used to solve a large number of problems that would otherwise require tricky algorithms.

One of the purposes of this book has been to *document* competitive programming techniques that are usually only discussed in online forums and blog posts. Whenever possible, scientific references have been given for methods that are specific to competitive programming. However, this has not often been possible, because many techniques are now part of competitive programming *folklore* and nobody knows who has originally discovered them.

The structure of the book is as follows:

- Chapter 2 reviews features of the C++ programming language and then discusses recursive algorithms and bit manipulation.
- Chapter 3 focuses on efficiency: how to create algorithms that can quickly process large data sets.
- Chapter 4 discusses sorting algorithms and binary search, focusing on their applications in algorithm design.
- Chapter 5 goes through a selection of data structures of the C++ standard library, such as vectors, sets, and maps.
- Chapter 6 introduces an algorithm design technique called dynamic programming and presents examples of problems that can be solved using it.
- Chapter 7 discusses elementary graph algorithms, such as finding shortest paths and minimum spanning trees.
- Chapter 8 deals with some advanced algorithm design topics, such as bit-parallelism and amortized analysis.
- Chapter 9 focuses on efficiently processing array range queries, such as calculating sums of values and determining minimum values.
- Chapter 10 presents specialized algorithms for trees, including methods for processing tree queries.
- Chapter 11 discusses mathematical topics that are relevant in competitive programming.
- Chapter 12 presents advanced graph techniques, such as strongly connected components and maximum flows.
- Chapter 13 focuses on geometric algorithms and presents techniques using which geometric problems can be solved conveniently.
- Chapter 14 deals with string techniques, such as string hashing, the Z-algorithm, and using suffix arrays.
- Chapter 15 discusses a selection of more advanced topics, such as square root algorithms and dynamic programming optimization.

1.3 CSES Problem Set

The *CSES Problem Set* provides a collection of problems that can be used to practice competitive programming. The problems have been arranged in the order of difficulty, and many of the techniques needed for solving the problems are discussed in this book. The problem set is available at the following address:

https://cses.fi/problemset/

Let us see how to solve the first problem in the problem set, called *Weird Algorithm*. The problem statement is as follows:

Consider an algorithm that takes as input a positive integer n. If n is even, the algorithm divides it by two, and if n is odd, the algorithm multiplies it by three and adds one. The algorithm repeats this, until n is one. For example, the sequence for $n = 3$ is as follows:

$$3 \rightarrow 10 \rightarrow 5 \rightarrow 16 \rightarrow 8 \rightarrow 4 \rightarrow 2 \rightarrow 1$$

Your task is to simulate the execution of the algorithm for a given value of n.

Input

The only input line contains an integer n.

Output

Print a line that contains all values of n during the algorithm.

Constraints

- $1 \leq n \leq 10^6$

Example

Input:

3

Output:

3 10 5 16 8 4 2 1

This problem is connected to the famous *Collatz conjecture* which states that the above algorithm terminates for every value of n. However, nobody has been able to prove it. In this problem, though, we know that the initial value of n will be at most one million, which makes the problem much easier to solve.

This problem is a simple simulation problem, which does not require much thinking. Here is a possible way to solve the problem in C++:

```
#include <iostream>

using namespace std;

int main() {
    int n;
    cin >> n;
    while (true) {
        cout << n << " ";
        if (n == 1) break;
        if (n%2 == 0) n /= 2;
        else n = n*3+1;
    }
    cout << "\n";
}
```

The code first reads in the input number n, then simulates the algorithm, and prints the value of n after each step. It is easy to test that the algorithm correctly handles the example case $n = 3$ given in the problem statement.

Now is the time to *submit* the code to CSES. Then the code will be compiled and tested using a set of test cases. For each test case, CSES will tell us whether our code passed it or not, and we can also examine the input, the expected output, and the output produced by our code.

After testing our code, CSES gives the following report[2]:

Test	Verdict	Time (s)
#1	ACCEPTED	0.06 / 1.00
#2	ACCEPTED	0.06 / 1.00
#3	ACCEPTED	0.07 / 1.00
#4	ACCEPTED	0.06 / 1.00
#5	ACCEPTED	0.06 / 1.00
#6	TIME LIMIT EXCEEDED	– / 1.00
#7	TIME LIMIT EXCEEDED	– / 1.00
#8	WRONG ANSWER	0.07 / 1.00
#9	TIME LIMIT EXCEEDED	– / 1.00
#10	ACCEPTED	0.06 / 1.00

This means that our code passed some of the test cases (ACCEPTED), was sometimes too slow (TIME LIMIT EXCEEDED), and also produced an incorrect output (WRONG ANSWER). This is quite surprising!

The first test case that fails has $n = 138367$. If we test our code locally using this input, it turns out that the code is indeed slow. In fact, it never terminates.

---

[2]Note that if you try to submit this code to CSES, you may get a slightly different result because there may be new features and test cases in the judging environment.

The reason why our code fails is that n can become quite large during the simulation. In particular, it can become larger than the upper limit of an `int` variable. To fix the problem, it suffices to change our code so that the type of n is `long long`. Then we will get the desired result:

Test	Verdict	Time (s)
#1	ACCEPTED	0.05 / 1.00
#2	ACCEPTED	0.06 / 1.00
#3	ACCEPTED	0.07 / 1.00
#4	ACCEPTED	0.06 / 1.00
#5	ACCEPTED	0.06 / 1.00
#6	ACCEPTED	0.05 / 1.00
#7	ACCEPTED	0.06 / 1.00
#8	ACCEPTED	0.05 / 1.00
#9	ACCEPTED	0.07 / 1.00
#10	ACCEPTED	0.06 / 1.00

As this example shows, even very simple algorithms may contain subtle bugs. Competitive programming teaches how to write algorithms that really work.

1.4   Other Resources

Besides this book, there are already several other books on competitive programming. Skiena's and Revilla's *Programming Challenges* [32] is a pioneering book in the field published in 2003. A more recent book is *Competitive Programming 3* [16] by Halim and Halim. Both the above books are intended for readers with no background in competitive programming.

Looking for a Challenge? [8] is an advanced book, which presents a collection of difficult problems from Polish programming contests. The most interesting feature of the book is that it provides detailed analyses of how to solve the problems. The book is intended for experienced competitive programmers.

Of course, general algorithms books are also good reads for competitive programmers. The most comprehensive of them is *Introduction to Algorithms* [7] written by Cormen, Leiserson, Rivest, and Stein, also called the *CLRS*. This book is a good resource if you want to check all details concerning an algorithm and how to rigorously prove that it is correct.

Kleinberg's and Tardos's *Algorithm Design* [22] focuses on algorithm design techniques and thoroughly discusses the divide and conquer method, greedy algorithms, dynamic programming, and maximum flow algorithms. Skiena's *The Algorithm Design Manual* [31] is a more practical book which includes a large catalog of computational problems and describes ways how to solve them.

Programming Techniques

2

This chapter presents some of the features of the C++ programming language that are useful in competitive programming and gives examples of how to use recursion and bit operations in programming.

Section 2.1 discusses a selection of topics related to C++, including input and output methods, working with numbers, and how to shorten code.

Section 2.2 focuses on recursive algorithms. First we will learn an elegant way to generate all subsets and permutations of a set using recursion. After this, we will use backtracking to count the number of ways to place n non-attacking queens on an $n \times n$ chessboard.

Section 2.3 discusses the basics of bit operations and shows how to use them to represent subsets of sets.

2.1 Language Features

A typical C++ code template for competitive programming looks like this:

```cpp
#include <bits/stdc++.h>

using namespace std;

int main() {
    // solution comes here
}
```

© Springer Nature Switzerland AG 2020
A. Laaksonen, *Guide to Competitive Programming*, Undergraduate Topics in Computer Science, https://doi.org/10.1007/978-3-030-39357-1_2

The #include line at the beginning of the code is a feature of the g++ compiler that allows us to include the entire standard library. Thus, it is not needed to separately include libraries such as iostream, vector, and algorithm, but rather they are available automatically.

The using line declares that the classes and functions of the standard library can be used directly in the code. Without the using line we would have to write, for example, std::cout, but now it suffices to write cout.

The code can be compiled using the following command:

```
g++ -std=c++11 -O2 -Wall test.cpp -o test
```

This command produces a binary file test from the source code test.cpp. The compiler follows the C++11 standard (-std=c++11), optimizes the code (-O2), and shows warnings about possible errors (-Wall).

2.1.1   Input and Output

In most contests, standard streams are used for reading input and writing output. In C++, the standard streams are cin for input and cout for output. Also C functions, such as scanf and printf, can be used.

The input for the program usually consists of numbers and strings separated with spaces and newlines. They can be read from the cin stream as follows:

```
int a, b;
string x;
cin >> a >> b >> x;
```

This kind of code always works, assuming that there is at least one space or newline between each element in the input. For example, the above code can read both the following inputs:

```
123 456 monkey
```

```
123     456
monkey
```

The cout stream is used for output as follows:

```
int a = 123, b = 456;
string x = "monkey";
cout << a << " " << b << " " << x << "\n";
```

Input and output are sometimes a bottleneck in the program. The following lines at the beginning of the code make input and output more efficient:

```
ios::sync_with_stdio(0);
cin.tie(0);
```

Note that the newline "\n" works faster than endl, because endl always causes a flush operation.

The C functions scanf and printf are an alternative to the C++ standard streams. They are usually slightly faster, but also more difficult to use. The following code reads two integers from the input:

```
int a, b;
scanf("%d %d", &a, &b);
```

The following code prints two integers:

```
int a = 123, b = 456;
printf("%d %d\n", a, b);
```

Sometimes the program should read a whole input line, possibly containing spaces. This can be accomplished by using the getline function:

```
string s;
getline(cin, s);
```

If the amount of data is unknown, the following loop is useful:

```
while (cin >> x) {
    // code
}
```

This loop reads elements from the input one after another, until there is no more data available in the input.

In some contest systems, files are used for input and output. An easy solution for this is to write the code as usual using standard streams, but add the following lines to the beginning of the code:

```
freopen("input.txt", "r", stdin);
freopen("output.txt", "w", stdout);
```

After this, the program reads the input from the file "input.txt" and writes the output to the file "output.txt."

2.1.2 Working with Numbers

Integers The most used integer type in competitive programming is int, which is a 32-bit type[1] with a value range of $-2^{31} \ldots 2^{31} - 1$ (about $-2 \cdot 10^9 \ldots 2 \cdot 10^9$). If the type int is not enough, the 64-bit type long long can be used. It has a value range of $-2^{63} \ldots 2^{63} - 1$ (about $-9 \cdot 10^{18} \ldots 9 \cdot 10^{18}$).

The following code defines a long long variable:

```
long long x = 123456789123456789LL;
```

The suffix LL means that the type of the number is long long.

A common mistake when using the type long long is that the type int is still used somewhere in the code. For example, the following code contains a subtle error:

```
int a = 123456789;
long long b = a*a;
cout << b << "\n"; // -1757895751
```

Even though the variable b is of type long long, both numbers in the expression a*a are of type int and the result is also of type int. Because of this, the variable b will have a wrong result. The problem can be solved by changing the type of a to long long or by changing the expression to (long long)a*a.

Usually contest problems are set so that the type long long is enough. Still, it is good to know that the g++ compiler also provides a 128-bit type __int128_t with a value range of $-2^{127} \ldots 2^{127} - 1$ (about $-10^{38} \ldots 10^{38}$). However, this type is not available in all contest systems.

Modular Arithmetic Sometimes, the answer to a problem is a very large number but it is enough to output it "modulo m," i.e., the remainder when the answer is divided by m (e.g., "modulo $10^9 + 7$"). The idea is that even if the actual answer is very large, it suffices to use the types int and long long.

We denote by $x \bmod m$ the remainder when x is divided by m. For example, $17 \bmod 5 = 2$, because $17 = 3 \cdot 5 + 2$. An important property of remainders is that the following formulas hold:

$$(a + b) \bmod m = (a \bmod m + b \bmod m) \bmod m$$
$$(a - b) \bmod m = (a \bmod m - b \bmod m) \bmod m$$
$$(a \cdot b) \bmod m = (a \bmod m \cdot b \bmod m) \bmod m$$

Thus, we can take the remainder after every operation and the numbers will never become too large.

---

[1] In fact, the C++ standard does not exactly specify the sizes of the number types, and the bounds depend on the compiler and platform. The sizes given in this section are those you will very likely see when using modern systems.

For example, the following code calculates $n!$, the factorial of n, modulo m:

```
long long x = 1;
for (int i = 1; i <= n; i++) {
    x = (x*i)%m;
}
cout << x << "\n";
```

Usually we want the remainder to always be between $0 \ldots m - 1$. However, in C++ and other languages, the remainder of a negative number is either zero or negative. An easy way to make sure there are no negative remainders is to first calculate the remainder as usual and then add m if the result is negative:

```
x = x%m;
if (x < 0) x += m;
```

However, this is only needed when there are subtractions in the code and the remainder may become negative.

Floating Point Numbers In most competitive programming problems it suffices to use integers, but sometimes floating point numbers are needed. The most useful floating point types in C++ are the 64-bit double and, as an extension in the g++ compiler, the 80-bit long double. In most cases, double is enough, but long double is more accurate.

The required precision of the answer is usually given in the problem statement. An easy way to output the answer is to use the printf function and give the number of decimal places in the formatting string. For example, the following code prints the value of x with 9 decimal places:

```
printf("%.9f\n", x);
```

A difficulty when using floating point numbers is that some numbers cannot be represented accurately as floating point numbers, and there will be rounding errors. For example, in the following code, the value of x is slightly smaller than 1, while the correct value would be 1.

```
double x = 0.3*3+0.1;
printf("%.20f\n", x); // 0.99999999999999988898
```

It is risky to compare floating point numbers with the == operator, because it is possible that the values should be equal but they are not because of precision errors. A better way to compare floating point numbers is to assume that two numbers are equal if the difference between them is less than ε, where ε is a small number. For example, in the following code $\varepsilon = 10^{-9}$:

```
if (abs(a-b) < 1e-9) {
    // a and b are equal
}
```

Note that while floating point numbers are inaccurate, integers up to a certain limit can still be represented accurately. For example, using `double`, it is possible to accurately represent all integers whose absolute value is at most 2^{53}.

2.1.3 Shortening Code

Type Names The command `typedef` can be used to give a short name to a data type. For example, the name `long long` is long, so we can define a short name `ll` as follows:

```
typedef long long ll;
```

After this, the code

```
long long a = 123456789;
long long b = 987654321;
cout << a*b << "\n";
```

can be shortened as follows:

```
ll a = 123456789;
ll b = 987654321;
cout << a*b << "\n";
```

The command `typedef` can also be used with more complex types. For example, the following code gives the name `vi` for a vector of integers and the name `pi` for a pair that contains two integers.

```
typedef vector<int> vi;
typedef pair<int,int> pi;
```

Macros Another way to shorten code is to define *macros*. A macro specifies that certain strings in the code will be changed before the compilation. In C++, macros are defined using the `#define` keyword.

For example, we can define the following macros:

```
#define F first
#define S second
#define PB push_back
#define MP make_pair
```

After this, the code

```
v.push_back(make_pair(y1,x1));
v.push_back(make_pair(y2,x2));
int d = v[i].first+v[i].second;
```

can be shortened as follows:

```
v.PB(MP(y1,x1));
v.PB(MP(y2,x2));
int d = v[i].F+v[i].S;
```

A macro can also have parameters, which makes it possible to shorten loops and other structures. For example, we can define the following macro:

```
#define REP(i,a,b) for (int i = a; i <= b; i++)
```

After this, the code

```
for (int i = 1; i <= n; i++) {
    search(i);
}
```

can be shortened as follows:

```
REP(i,1,n) {
    search(i);
}
```

2.2 Recursive Algorithms

Recursion often provides an elegant way to implement an algorithm. In this section, we discuss recursive algorithms that systematically go through candidate solutions to a problem. First, we focus on generating subsets and permutations and then discuss the more general backtracking technique.

2.2.1 Generating Subsets

Our first application of recursion is generating all subsets of a set of n elements. For
example, the subsets of $\{1, 2, 3\}$ are $\emptyset, \{1\}, \{2\}, \{3\}, \{1, 2\}, \{1, 3\}, \{2, 3\}$, and $\{1, 2, 3\}$.
The following recursive function `search` can be used to generate the subsets. The
function maintains a vector

```
vector<int> subset;
```

that will contain the elements of each subset. The search begins when the function
is called with parameter 1.

```
void search(int k) {
    if (k == n+1) {
        // process subset
    } else {
        // include k in the subset
        subset.push_back(k);
        search(k+1);
        subset.pop_back();
        // don't include k in the subset
        search(k+1);
    }
}
```

When the function `search` is called with parameter k, it decides whether to
include the element k in the subset or not, and in both cases, then calls itself with
parameter $k + 1$ Then, if $k = n + 1$, the function notices that all elements have been
processed and a subset has been generated.

Figure 2.1 illustrates the generation of subsets when $n = 3$. At each function call,
either the upper branch (k is included in the subset) or the lower branch (k is not
included in the subset) is chosen.

Fig. 2.1 Recursion tree
when generating the subsets
of the set $\{1, 2, 3\}$

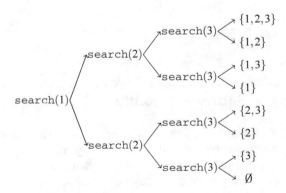

2.2.2 Generating Permutations

Next we consider the problem of generating all permutations of a set of n elements. For example, the permutations of $\{1, 2, 3\}$ are $(1, 2, 3)$, $(1, 3, 2)$, $(2, 1, 3)$, $(2, 3, 1)$, $(3, 1, 2)$, and $(3, 2, 1)$. Again, we can use recursion to perform the search. The following function search maintains a vector

```
vector<int> permutation;
```

that will contain each permutation, and an array

```
bool chosen[n+1];
```

which indicates for each element if it has been included in the permutation. The search begins when the function is called without parameters.

```
void search() {
    if (permutation.size() == n) {
        // process permutation
    } else {
        for (int i = 1; i <= n; i++) {
            if (chosen[i]) continue;
            chosen[i] = true;
            permutation.push_back(i);
            search();
            chosen[i] = false;
            permutation.pop_back();
        }
    }
}
```

Each function call appends a new element to permutation and records that it has been included in chosen. If the size of permutation equals the size of the set, a permutation has been generated.

Note that the C++ standard library also has the function next_permutation that can be used to generate permutations. The function is given a permutation, and it produces the next permutation in lexicographic order. The following code goes through the permutations of $\{1, 2, \ldots, n\}$:

```
for (int i = 1; i <= n; i++) {
    permutation.push_back(i);
}
do {
    // process permutation
} while (next_permutation(permutation.begin(),
                          permutation.end()));
```

2.2.3 Backtracking

A *backtracking* algorithm begins with an empty solution and extends the solution step by step. The search recursively goes through all different ways how a solution can be constructed.

As an example, consider the problem of calculating the number of ways n queens can be placed on an $n \times n$ chessboard so that no two queens attack each other. For example, Fig. 2.2 shows the two possible solutions for $n = 4$.

The problem can be solved using backtracking by placing queens on the board row by row. More precisely, exactly one queen will be placed on each row so that no queen attacks any of the queens placed before. A solution has been found when all n queens have been placed on the board.

For example, Fig. 2.3 shows some partial solutions generated by the backtracking algorithm when $n = 4$. At the bottom level, the three first configurations are illegal, because the queens attack each other. However, the fourth configuration is valid, and it can be extended to a complete solution by placing two more queens on the board. There is only one way to place the two remaining queens.

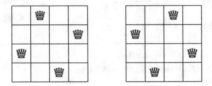

Fig. 2.2 Possible ways to place 4 queens on a 4 × 4 chessboard

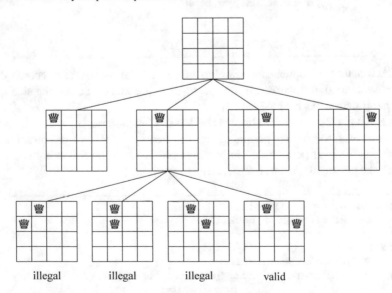

Fig. 2.3 Partial solutions to the queen problem using backtracking

Fig. 2.4 Numbering of the arrays when counting the combinations on the 4 × 4 board

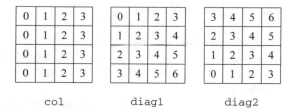

col   diag1   diag2

The algorithm can be implemented as follows:

```
void search(int y) {
    if (y == n) {
        count++;
        return;
    }
    for (int x = 0; x < n; x++) {
        if (col[x] || diag1[x+y] || diag2[x-y+n-1]) continue;
        col[x] = diag1[x+y] = diag2[x-y+n-1] = 1;
        search(y+1);
        col[x] = diag1[x+y] = diag2[x-y+n-1] = 0;
    }
}
```

The search begins by calling `search(0)`. The size of the board is n, and the code calculates the number of solutions to `count`. The code assumes that the rows and columns of the board are numbered from 0 to $n - 1$. When `search` is called with parameter y, it places a queen on row y and then calls itself with parameter $y + 1$. Then, if $y = n$, a solution has been found, and the value of `count` is increased by one.

The array `col` keeps track of the columns that contain a queen, and the arrays `diag1` and `diag2` keep track of the diagonals. It is not allowed to add another queen to a column or diagonal that already contains a queen. For example, Fig. 2.4 shows the numbering of columns and diagonals of the 4 × 4 board.

The above backtracking algorithm tells us that there are 92 ways to place 8 queens on the 8 × 8 board. When n increases, the search quickly becomes slow, because the number of solutions grows exponentially. For example, it takes already about a minute on a modern computer to calculate that there are 14772512 ways to place 16 queens on the 16 × 16 board.

In fact, nobody knows an *efficient* way to count the number of queen combinations for larger values of n. Currently, the largest value of n for which the result is known is 27: There are 234907967154122528 combinations in this case. This was discovered in 2016 by a group of researchers who used a cluster of computers to calculate the result [29].

2.3 Bit Manipulation

In programming, an n bit integer is internally stored as a binary number that consists of n bits. For example, the C++ type int is a 32-bit type, which means that every int number consists of 32 bits. For example, the bit representation of the int number 43 is

$$00000000000000000000000000101011.$$

The bits in the representation are indexed from right to left. To convert a bit representation $b_k \ldots b_2 b_1 b_0$ into a number, the formula

$$b_k 2^k + \cdots + b_2 2^2 + b_1 2^1 + b_0 2^0.$$

can be used. For example,

$$1 \cdot 2^5 + 1 \cdot 2^3 + 1 \cdot 2^1 + 1 \cdot 2^0 = 43.$$

The bit representation of a number is either *signed* or *unsigned*. Usually a signed representation is used, which means that both negative and positive numbers can be represented. A signed variable of n bits can contain any integer between -2^{n-1} and $2^{n-1} - 1$. For example, the int type in C++ is a signed type, so an int variable can contain any integer between -2^{31} and $2^{31} - 1$.

The first bit in a signed representation is the sign of the number (0 for nonnegative numbers and 1 for negative numbers), and the remaining $n - 1$ bits contain the magnitude of the number. *Two's complement* is used, which means that the opposite of a number is calculated by first inverting all the bits in the number, and then increasing the number by one. For example, the bit representation of the int number -43 is

$$11111111111111111111111111010101.$$

In an unsigned representation, only nonnegative numbers can be used, but the upper bound for the values is larger. An unsigned variable of n bits can contain any integer between 0 and $2^n - 1$. For example, in C++, an unsigned int variable can contain any integer between 0 and $2^{32} - 1$.

There is a connection between the representations: A signed number $-x$ equals an unsigned number $2^n - x$. For example, the following code shows that the signed number $x = -43$ equals the unsigned number $y = 2^{32} - 43$:

```
int x = -43;
unsigned int y = x;
cout << x << "\n"; // -43
cout << y << "\n"; // 4294967253
```

If a number is larger than the upper bound of the bit representation, the number will overflow. In a signed representation, the next number after $2^{n-1} - 1$ is -2^{n-1}, and in an unsigned representation, the next number after 2^{n-1} is 0. For example, consider the following code:

```
int x = 2147483647;
cout << x << "\n"; // 2147483647
x++;
cout << x << "\n"; // -2147483648
```

Initially, the value of x is $2^{31} - 1$. This is the largest value that can be stored in an int variable, so the next number after $2^{31} - 1$ is -2^{31}.

2.3.1 Bit Operations

AND Operation The *AND* operation $x \& y$ produces a number that has one bits in positions where both x and y have one bits. For example, $22 \& 26 = 18$, because

$$
\begin{array}{r}
10110\ (22) \\
\&\ 11010\ (26) \\
\hline
=\ 10010\ (18)\ .
\end{array}
$$

Using the AND operation, we can check if a number x is even because $x \& 1 = 0$ if x is even, and $x \& 1 = 1$ if x is odd. More generally, x is divisible by 2^k exactly when $x \& (2^k - 1) = 0$.

OR Operation The *OR* operation $x \mid y$ produces a number that has one bits in positions where at least one of x and y have one bits. For example, $22 \mid 26 = 30$, because

$$
\begin{array}{r}
10110\ (22) \\
\mid\ 11010\ (26) \\
\hline
=\ 11110\ (30)\ .
\end{array}
$$

XOR Operation The *XOR* operation $x \char`^ y$ produces a number that has one bits in positions where exactly one of $x$ and $y$ have one bits. For example, $22 \char`^ 26 = 12$, because

$$
\begin{array}{r}
10110\ (22) \\
\char`^\ 11010\ (26) \\
\hline
=\ 01100\ (12)\ .
\end{array}
$$

NOT Operation The *NOT* operation $\sim x$ produces a number where all the bits of x have been inverted. The formula $\sim x = -x - 1$ holds, for example, $\sim 29 = -30$. The result of the NOT operation at the bit level depends on the length of the bit representation, because the operation inverts all bits. For example, if the numbers are 32-bit int numbers, the result is as follows:

$$x = \quad 29 \quad 00000000000000000000000000011101$$
$$\sim x = -30 \quad 11111111111111111111111111100010$$

Bit Shifts The *left bit shift* $x << k$ appends k zero bits to the number, and the *right bit shift* $x >> k$ removes the k last bits from the number. For example, $14 << 2 = 56$, because 14 and 56 correspond to 1110 and 111000. Similarly, $49 >> 3 = 6$, because 49 and 6 correspond to 110001 and 110. Note that $x << k$ corresponds to multiplying x by 2^k, and $x >> k$ corresponds to dividing x by 2^k rounded down to an integer.

Bit Masks A *bit mask* of the form $1 << k$ has a one bit in position k and all other bits are zero, so we can use such masks to access single bits of numbers. In particular, the kth bit of a number is one exactly when $x \& (1 << k)$ is not zero. The following code prints the bit representation of an int number x:

```
for (int k = 31; k >= 0; k--) {
    if (x&(1<<k)) cout << "1";
    else cout << "0";
}
```

It is also possible to modify single bits of numbers using similar ideas. The formula $x \mid (1 << k)$ sets the kth bit of x to one, the formula $x \& \sim(1 << k)$ sets the kth bit of x to zero, and the formula $x \,\hat{}\, (1 << k)$ inverts the kth bit of x. Then, the formula $x \& (x - 1)$ sets the last one bit of x to zero, and the formula $x \& -x$ sets all the one bits to zero, except for the last one bit. The formula $x \mid (x - 1)$ inverts all the bits after the last one bit. Finally, a positive number x is a power of two exactly when $x \& (x - 1) = 0$.

One pitfall when using bit masks is that $1 << k$ is always an int bit mask. An easy way to create a long long bit mask is 1LL $<< k$.

Additional Functions The g++ compiler also provides the following functions for counting bits:

- __builtin_clz(x): the number of zeros at the beginning of the bit representation
- __builtin_ctz(x): the number of zeros at the end of the bit representation
- __builtin_popcount(x): the number of ones in the bit representation
- __builtin_parity(x): the parity (even or odd) of the number of ones in the bit representation.

The functions can be used as follows:

```
int x = 5328; // 00000000000000000001010011010000
cout << __builtin_clz(x) << "\n"; // 19
cout << __builtin_ctz(x) << "\n"; // 4
cout << __builtin_popcount(x) << "\n"; // 5
cout << __builtin_parity(x) << "\n"; // 1
```

Note that the above functions only support `int` numbers, but there are also `long long` versions of the functions available with the suffix `ll`.

2.3.2 Representing Sets

Every subset of a set $\{0, 1, 2, \ldots, n-1\}$ can be represented as an n bit integer whose one bits indicate which elements belong to the subset. This is an efficient way to represent sets, because every element requires only one bit of memory, and set operations can be implemented as bit operations.

For example, since `int` is a 32-bit type, an `int` number can represent any subset of the set $\{0, 1, 2, \ldots, 31\}$. The bit representation of the set $\{1, 3, 4, 8\}$ is

$$00000000000000000000000100011010,$$

which corresponds to the number $2^8 + 2^4 + 2^3 + 2^1 = 282$.

The following code declares an `int` variable x that can contain a subset of $\{0, 1, 2, \ldots, 31\}$. After this, the code adds the elements 1, 3, 4, and 8 to the set and prints the size of the set.

```
int x = 0;
x |= (1<<1);
x |= (1<<3);
x |= (1<<4);
x |= (1<<8);
cout << __builtin_popcount(x) << "\n"; // 4
```

Then, the following code prints all elements that belong to the set:

```
for (int i = 0; i < 32; i++) {
    if (x&(1<<i)) cout << i << " ";
}
// output: 1 3 4 8
```

Set Operations Table 2.1 shows how set operations can be implemented as bit operations. For example, the following code first constructs the sets $x = \{1, 3, 4, 8\}$ and $y = \{3, 6, 8, 9\}$ and then constructs the set $z = x \cup y = \{1, 3, 4, 6, 8, 9\}$:

Table 2.1 Implementing set operations as bit operations

Operation	Set syntax	Bit syntax
Intersection	$a \cap b$	$a \,\&\, b$
Union	$a \cup b$	$a \mid b$
Complement	$\bar{a}$	~a
Difference	$a \setminus b$	$a \,\&\, (\text{~}b)$

```
int x = (1<<1)|(1<<3)|(1<<4)|(1<<8);
int y = (1<<3)|(1<<6)|(1<<8)|(1<<9);
int z = x|y;
cout << __builtin_popcount(z) << "\n"; // 6
```

The following code goes through the subsets of $\{0, 1, \ldots, n - 1\}$:

```
for (int b = 0; b < (1<<n); b++) {
    // process subset b
}
```

Then, the following code goes through the subsets with exactly k elements:

```
for (int b = 0; b < (1<<n); b++) {
    if (__builtin_popcount(b) == k) {
        // process subset b
    }
}
```

Finally, the following code goes through the subsets of a set x:

```
int b = 0;
do {
    // process subset b
} while (b=(b-x)&x);
```

Why does the above code work? The idea is that the formula $b - x$ detects the rightmost one bit in x that is zero in b. This bit becomes one, and all bits after it become zero. Then the AND operation ensures that the resulting value is a subset of x. Note that $b - x$ equals $-(x - b)$ so we can think that we first remove all one bits that appear in b and then invert the value and add one.

C++ Bitsets The C++ standard library also provides the `bitset` structure, which corresponds to an array whose each value is either 0 or 1. For example, the following code creates a bitset of 10 elements:

```
bitset<10> s;
s[1] = 1;
s[3] = 1;
s[4] = 1;
s[7] = 1;
cout << s[4] << "\n"; // 1
cout << s[5] << "\n"; // 0
```

The function count returns the number of one bits in the bitset:

```
cout << s.count() << "\n"; // 4
```

Also bit operations can be directly used to manipulate bitsets:

```
bitset<10> a, b;
// ...
bitset<10> c = a&b;
bitset<10> d = a|b;
bitset<10> e = a^b;
```

Efficiency

3

The efficiency of algorithms plays a central role in competitive programming. In this chapter, we learn tools that make it easier to design efficient algorithms.

Section 3.1 introduces the concept of time complexity, which allows us to estimate running times of algorithms without implementing them. The time complexity of an algorithm shows how quickly its running time increases when the size of the input grows.

Section 3.2 presents two algorithm design problems which can be solved in many ways. In both problems, we can easily design a slow brute force solution, but it turns out that we can also create much more efficient algorithms.

Section 3.3 discusses code optimization. First we learn how we can examine machine code produced by a compiler and see some optimization tricks. After this, we focus on how modern processors use caches and parallelism to speed up code execution.

3.1 Time Complexity

The *time complexity* of an algorithm estimates how much time the algorithm will use for a given input. By calculating the time complexity, we can often find out whether the algorithm is fast enough for solving a problem—without implementing it.

A time complexity is denoted $O(\cdots)$ where the three dots represent some function. Usually, the variable n denotes the input size. For example, if the input is an array of numbers, n will be the size of the array, and if the input is a string, n will be the length of the string.

© Springer Nature Switzerland AG 2020

A. Laaksonen, *Guide to Competitive Programming*, Undergraduate Topics in Computer Science, https://doi.org/10.1007/978-3-030-39357-1_3

3.1.1 Calculation Rules

If a code consists of single commands, its time complexity is $O(1)$. For example, the time complexity of the following code is $O(1)$.

```
a++;
b++;
c = a+b;
```

The time complexity of a loop estimates the number of times the code inside the loop is executed. For example, the time complexity of the following code is $O(n)$, because the code inside the loop is executed n times. We assume that ". . ." denotes a code whose time complexity is $O(1)$.

```
for (int i = 1; i <= n; i++) {
    . . .
}
```

Then, the time complexity of the following code is $O(n^2)$:

```
for (int i = 1; i <= n; i++) {
    for (int j = 1; j <= n; j++) {
        . . .
    }
}
```

In general, if there are k nested loops and each loops goes through n values, the time complexity is $O(n^k)$.

A time complexity does not tell us the exact number of times the code inside a loop is executed, because it only shows the order of growth and ignores the constant factors. In the following examples, the code inside the loop is executed $3n$, $n + 5$, and $\lceil n/2 \rceil$ times, but the time complexity of each code is $O(n)$.

```
for (int i = 1; i <= 3*n; i++) {
    . . .
}
```

```
for (int i = 1; i <= n+5; i++) {
    . . .
}
```

```
for (int i = 1; i <= n; i += 2) {
    ...
}
```

As another example, the time complexity of the following code is $O(n^2)$, because the code inside the loop is executed $1 + 2 + \cdots + n = \frac{1}{2}(n^2 + n)$ times.

```
for (int i = 1; i <- n; i++) {
    for (int j = 1; j <= i; j++) {
        ...
    }
}
```

If an algorithm consists of consecutive phases, the total time complexity is the largest time complexity of a single phase. The reason for this is that the slowest phase is the bottleneck of the algorithm. For example, the following code consists of three phases with time complexities $O(n)$, $O(n^2)$, and $O(n)$. Thus, the total time complexity is $O(n^2)$.

```
for (int i = 1; i <= n; i++) {
    ...
}
for (int i = 1; i <= n; i++) {
    for (int j = 1; j <= n; j++) {
        ...
    }
}
for (int i = 1; i <= n; i++) {
    ...
}
```

Sometimes the time complexity depends on several factors, and the time complexity formula contains several variables. For example, the time complexity of the following code is $O(nm)$:

```
for (int i = 1; i <= n; i++) {
    for (int j = 1; j <= m; j++) {
        ...
    }
}
```

The time complexity of a recursive function depends on the number of times the function is called and the time complexity of a single call. The total time complexity is the product of these values. For example, consider the following function:

```
void f(int n) {
    if (n == 1) return;
    f(n-1);
}
```

The call $f(n)$ causes n function calls, and the time complexity of each call is $O(1)$, so the total time complexity is $O(n)$.

As another example, consider the following function:

```
void g(int n) {
    if (n == 1) return;
    g(n-1);
    g(n-1);
}
```

What happens when the function is called with a parameter n? First, there are two calls with parameter $n - 1$, then four calls with parameter $n - 2$, then eight calls with parameter $n - 3$, and so on. In general, there will be 2^k calls with parameter $n - k$ where $k = 0, 1, \ldots, n - 1$. Thus, the time complexity is

$$1 + 2 + 4 + \cdots + 2^{n-1} = 2^n - 1 = O(2^n).$$

3.1.2 Common Time Complexities

The following list contains common time complexities of algorithms:

$O(1)$ The running time of a *constant-time* algorithm does not depend on the input size. A typical constant-time algorithm is a direct formula that calculates the answer.

$O(\log n)$ A *logarithmic* algorithm often halves the input size at each step. The running time of such an algorithm is logarithmic, because $\log_2 n$ equals the number of times n must be divided by 2 to get 1. Note that the base of the logarithm is not shown in the time complexity.

$O(\sqrt{n})$ A *square root algorithm* is slower than $O(\log n)$ but faster than $O(n)$. A special property of square roots is that $\sqrt{n} = n/\sqrt{n}$, so n elements can be divided into $O(\sqrt{n})$ blocks of $O(\sqrt{n})$ elements.

$O(n)$ A *linear* algorithm goes through the input a constant number of times. This is often the best possible time complexity, because it is usually necessary to access each input element at least once before reporting the answer.

$O(n \log n)$ This time complexity often indicates that the algorithm sorts the input, because the time complexity of efficient sorting algorithms is $O(n \log n)$. Another possibility is that the algorithm uses a data structure where each operation takes $O(\log n)$ time.

$O(n^2)$ A *quadratic* algorithm often contains two nested loops. It is possible to go
through all pairs of the input elements in $O(n^2)$ time.

$O(n^3)$ A *cubic* algorithm often contains three nested loops. It is possible to go
through all triplets of the input elements in $O(n^3)$ time.

$O(2^n)$ This time complexity often indicates that the algorithm iterates through all
subsets of the input elements. For example, the subsets of $\{1, 2, 3\}$ are $\emptyset$, $\{1\}$, $\{2\}$,
$\{3\}$, $\{1, 2\}$, $\{1, 3\}$, $\{2, 3\}$, and $\{1, 2, 3\}$.

$O(n!)$ This time complexity often indicates that the algorithm iterates through all
permutations of the input elements. For example, the permutations of $\{1, 2, 3\}$ are
$(1, 2, 3)$, $(1, 3, 2)$, $(2, 1, 3)$, $(2, 3, 1)$, $(3, 1, 2)$, and $(3, 2, 1)$.

An algorithm is *polynomial* if its time complexity is at most $O(n^k)$ where k is a
constant. All the above time complexities except $O(2^n)$ and $O(n!)$ are polynomial. In
practice, the constant k is usually small, and therefore a polynomial time complexity
roughly means that the algorithm can process large inputs.

Most algorithms in this book are polynomial. Still, there are many important
problems for which no polynomial algorithm is known, i.e., nobody knows how to
solve them efficiently. *NP-hard* problems are an important set of problems, for which
no polynomial algorithm is known.

3.1.3 Estimating Efficiency

By calculating the time complexity of an algorithm, it is possible to check, before
implementing the algorithm, that it is efficient enough for solving a problem. The
starting point for estimations is the fact that a modern computer can perform some
hundreds of millions of simple operations in a second.

For example, assume that the time limit for a problem is one second and the
input size is $n = 10^5$. If the time complexity is $O(n^2)$, the algorithm will perform
about $(10^5)^2 = 10^{10}$ operations. This should take at least some tens of seconds, so
the algorithm seems to be too slow for solving the problem. However, if the time
complexity is $O(n \log n)$, there will be only about $10^5 \log 10^5 \approx 1.6 \cdot 10^6$ operations,
and the algorithm will surely fit the time limit.

On the other hand, given the input size, we can try to *guess* the required time
complexity of the algorithm that solves the problem. Table 3.1 contains some useful
estimates assuming a time limit of one second.

For example, if the input size is $n = 10^5$, it is probably expected that the time
complexity of the algorithm is $O(n)$ or $O(n \log n)$. This information makes it easier
to design the algorithm, because it rules out approaches that would yield an algorithm
with a worse time complexity.

Still, it is important to remember that a time complexity is only an estimate of
efficiency, because it hides the constant factors. For example, an algorithm that runs
in $O(n)$ time may perform $n/2$ or $5n$ operations, which has an important effect on
the actual running time of the algorithm.

Table 3.1 Estimating time complexity from input size

Input size	Expected time complexity
$n \le 10$	$O(n!)$
$n \le 20$	$O(2^n)$
$n \le 500$	$O(n^3)$
$n \le 5000$	$O(n^2)$
$n \le 10^6$	$O(n \log n)$ or $O(n)$
n is large	$O(1)$ or $O(\log n)$

3.1.4 Formal Definitions

What does it *exactly* mean that an algorithm works in $O(f(n))$ time? It means that there are constants c and n_0 such that the algorithm performs *at most* $cf(n)$ operations for all inputs where $n \ge n_0$. Thus, the O notation gives an *upper bound* for the running time of the algorithm for sufficiently large inputs.

For example, it is technically correct to say that the time complexity of the following algorithm is $O(n^2)$.

```
for (int i = 1; i <= n; i++) {
    ...
}
```

However, a better bound is $O(n)$, and it would be very misleading to give the bound $O(n^2)$, because everybody actually assumes that the O notation is used to give an accurate estimate of the time complexity.

There are also two other common notations. The Ω notation gives a *lower bound* for the running time of an algorithm. The time complexity of an algorithm is $\Omega(f(n))$, if there are constants c and n_0 such that the algorithm performs *at least* $cf(n)$ operations for all inputs where $n \ge n_0$. Finally, the Θ notation gives an *exact bound*: The time complexity of an algorithm is $\Theta(f(n))$ if it is both $O(f(n))$ and $\Omega(f(n))$. For example, since the time complexity of the above algorithm is both $O(n)$ and $\Omega(n)$, it is also $\Theta(n)$.

We can use the above notations in many situations, not only for referring to time complexities of algorithms. For example, we might say that an array contains $O(n)$ values, or that an algorithm consists of $O(\log n)$ rounds.

3.2 Algorithm Design Examples

This section presents two algorithm design examples where a problem can be solved in several different ways. We start with simple brute force algorithms and then create more efficient solutions by using various algorithm design ideas.

Fig. 3.1 Maximum sum
subarray of this array is
$[2, 4, -3, 5, 2]$, whose sum
is 10

3.2.1 Maximum Subarray Sum

Given an array of n numbers, our first task is to calculate the *maximum subarray sum*,
i.e., the largest possible sum of a sequence of consecutive values in the array. The
problem is interesting when there may be negative values in the array. For example,
Fig. 3.1 shows an array and its maximum sum subarray.

$O(n^3)$ **Time Solution** A straightforward way to solve the problem is to go through
all possible subarrays, calculate the sum of values in each subarray, and maintain the
maximum sum. The following code implements this algorithm:

```
int best = 0;
for (int a = 0; a < n; a++) {
    for (int b = a; b < n; b++) {
        int sum = 0;
        for (int k = a; k <= b; k++) {
            sum += array[k];
        }
        best = max(best,sum);
    }
}
cout << best << "\n";
```

The variables a and b fix the first and last index of the subarray, and the sum of
values is calculated to the variable sum. The variable best contains the maximum
sum found during the search. The time complexity of the algorithm is $O(n^3)$, because
it consists of three nested loops that go through the input.

$O(n^2)$ **Time Solution** It is easy to make the algorithm more efficient by removing
one loop from it. This is possible by calculating the sum at the same time when the
right end of the subarray moves. The result is the following code:

```
int best = 0;
for (int a = 0; a < n; a++) {
    int sum = 0;
    for (int b = a; b < n; b++) {
        sum += array[b];
        best = max(best,sum);
    }
}
cout << best << "\n";
```

Table 3.2 Comparing running times of the maximum subarray sum algorithms

Array size n	$O(n^3)$ (s)	$O(n^2)$ (s)	$O(n)$ (s)
10^2	0.0	0.0	0.0
10^3	0.1	0.0	0.0
10^4	> 10.0	0.1	0.0
10^5	> 10.0	5.3	0.0
10^6	> 10.0	> 10.0	0.0
10^7	> 10.0	> 10.0	0.0

After this change, the time complexity is $O(n^2)$.

$O(n)$ **Time Solution** It turns out that it is possible to solve the problem in $O(n)$ time, which means that just one loop is enough. The idea is to calculate for each array position the maximum sum of a subarray that ends at that position. After this, the answer to the problem is the maximum of those sums.

Consider the subproblem of finding the maximum sum subarray that ends at position k. There are two possibilities:

1. The subarray only contains the element at position k.
2. The subarray consists of a subarray that ends at position $k - 1$, followed by the element at position k.

In the latter case, since we want to find a subarray with maximum sum, the subarray that ends at position $k - 1$ should also have the maximum sum. Thus, we can solve the problem efficiently by calculating the maximum subarray sum for each ending position from left to right.

The following code implements the algorithm:

```
int best = 0, sum = 0;
for (int k = 0; k < n; k++) {
    sum = max(array[k],sum+array[k]);
    best = max(best,sum);
}
cout << best << "\n";
```

The algorithm only contains one loop that goes through the input, so the time complexity is $O(n)$. This is also the best possible time complexity, because any algorithm for the problem has to examine all array elements at least once.

Efficiency Comparison How efficient are the above algorithms in practice? Table 3.2 shows the running times of the above algorithms for different values of n on a modern computer. In each test, the input was generated randomly, and the time needed for reading the input was not measured.

Fig. 3.2 All possible ways to place two non-attacking queens on the 3 × 3 chessboard

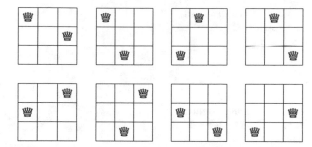

Table 3.3 First values of the function $q(n)$: the number of ways to place two non-attacking queens on an $n \times n$ chessboard

Board size n	Number of ways $q(n)$
1	0
2	0
3	8
4	44
5	140
6	340
7	700
8	1288
9	2184
10	3480

The comparison shows that all algorithms work quickly when the input size is small, but larger inputs bring out remarkable differences in the running times. The $O(n^3)$ algorithm becomes slow when $n = 10^4$, and the $O(n^2)$ algorithm becomes slow when $n = 10^5$. Only the $O(n)$ algorithm is able to process even the largest inputs instantly.

3.2.2 Two Queens Problem

Given an $n \times n$ chessboard, our next problem is to count the number of ways we can place *two* queens on the board in such a way that they do not attack each other. For example, as Fig. 3.2 shows, there are eight ways to place two queens on the 3 × 3 board. Let $q(n)$ denote the number of valid combinations for an $n \times n$ board. For example, $q(3) = 8$, and Table 3.3 shows the values of $q(n)$ for $1 \le n \le 10$.

To start with, a simple way to solve the problem is to go through all possible ways to place two queens on the board and count the combinations where the queens do not attack each other. Such an algorithm works in $O(n^4)$ time, because there are n^2 ways to choose the position of the first queen, and for each such position, there are $n^2 - 1$ ways to choose the position of the second queen.

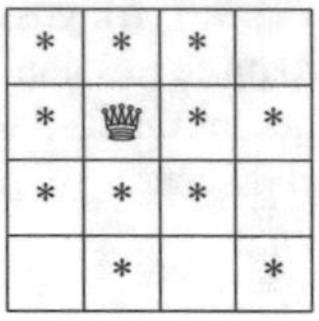

Fig. 3.3 Queen attacks all squares marked with "*" on the board

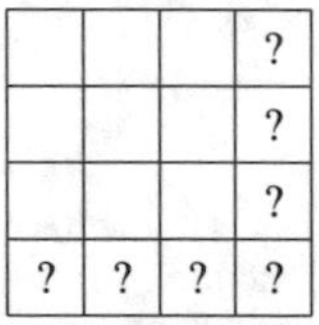

Fig. 3.4 Possible positions for queens on the last row and column

Since the number of combinations grows fast, an algorithm that counts combinations one by one will certainly be too slow for processing larger values of n. Thus, to create an efficient algorithm, we need to find a way to count combinations in *groups*. One useful observation is that it is quite easy to calculate the number of squares that a single queen attacks (Fig. 3.3). First, it always attacks $n - 1$ squares horizontally and $n - 1$ squares vertically. Then, for both diagonals, it attacks $d - 1$ squares where d is the number of squares on the diagonal. Using this information, we can calculate in $O(1)$ time the number of squares where the other queen can be placed, which yields an $O(n^2)$ time algorithm.

Another way to approach the problem is to try to formulate a recursive function that counts the number of combinations. The question is: If we know the value of $q(n)$, how can we use it to calculate the value of $q(n + 1)$?

To get a recursive solution, we may focus on the last row and last column of the $n \times n$ board (Fig. 3.4). First, if there are no queens on the last row or column, the number of combinations is simply $q(n - 1)$. Then, there are $2n - 1$ positions for a queen on the last row or column. It attacks $3(n - 1)$ squares, so there are $n^2 - 3(n - 1) - 1$ positions for the other queen. Finally, there are $(n - 1)(n - 2)$ combinations where both queens are on the last row or column. Since we counted those combinations twice, we have to remove this number from the result. By combining all this, we get a recursive formula

$$q(n) = q(n - 1) + (2n - 1)(n^2 - 3(n - 1) - 1) - (n - 1)(n - 2)$$
$$= q(n - 1) + 2(n - 1)^2(n - 2),$$

which provides an $O(n)$ solution to the problem.

Finally, it turns out that there is also a closed-form formula

$$q(n) = \frac{n^4}{2} - \frac{5n^3}{3} + \frac{3n^2}{2} - \frac{n}{3},$$

which can be proved using induction and the recursive formula. Using this formula, we can solve the problem in $O(1)$ time.

3.3   Code Optimization

While the time complexity of an algorithm tells a lot about its efficiency, implementation details are also important. For example, here are two codes that check if an array has an element x:

```
bool ok = false;
for (int i = 0; i < n; i++) {
    if (a[i] == x) ok = true;
}
```

```
bool ok = false;
for (int i = 0; i < n; i++) {
    if (a[i] == x) {ok = true; break;}
}
```

Both codes work in $O(n)$ time, but the second code can be much more efficient in practice, because it immediately stops when x has been found. This is a useful optimization, because it really improves the performance of the code, and it is also easy to implement.

Could we further improve the code? There is one classic trick that we can try: We can use a *sentinel value*, i.e., append a new array element whose value is x. Then we do not have to do the test $i < n$ in the loop:

```
a[n] = x;
int i;
bool ok = false;
for (i = 0; a[i] != x; i++);
if (i < n) ok = true;
```

This is a nice trick but does not seem very useful in practice: It turns out that the test $i < n$ is not the real bottleneck in the algorithm, because accessing array elements takes much more time. Thus, not all optimizations are useful—they may only make the code more difficult to understand.

3.3.1   Compiler Output

A C++ compiler converts C++ code into machine code that the processor can execute. An important task of the compiler is to *optimize* the code. The resulting machine code should correspond to the C++ code but also be as fast as possible. There are often a large number of possible optimizations.

We can get the machine code (in assembly form) produced by the g++ compiler using the flag -S as follows:

```
g++ -S test.cpp -o test.out
```

This command creates a file test.out that contains the assembly code. There is also a useful online tool *Compiler Explorer*[1] that can be used to examine outputs of various compilers, including g++.

Compiler Optimizations For example, consider the following C++ code:

```
int collatz(int n) {
    if (n%2 == 0) return n/2;
    else return 3*n+1;
}
```

The assembly output of g++ (using the -O2 optimization flag) can be as follows:

```
        test    dil, 1
        jne     .L2
        mov     eax, edi
        shr     eax, 31
        add     eax, edi
        sar     eax
        ret
.L2:
        lea     eax, [rdi+1+rdi*2]
        ret
```

Even this small assembly output has many optimizations. The instruction test checks if the rightmost bit of n is 1, i.e., it is an odd number, which is faster than a modulo operation. Then, the instruction sar performs a right bit shift that calculates the value of $n/2$, which is faster than a division operation. Finally, the value of $3n + 1$ is calculated using an additional trick: The purpose of the instruction lea is actually to determine the *memory address* of an array element, but it can also be used for simple calculations.

It is often not necessary to use optimization tricks (like prefer bit operations to modulo and division) in C++, because the compiler also knows the tricks and can apply them. The compiler can also detect unnecessary code and remove it. For example, consider the following function:

---

[1]https://godbolt.org/.

```
void test(int n) {
    int s = 0;
    for (int i = 1; i <= n; i++) {
        s += i;
    }
}
```

The corresponding assembly output is simply

```
        ret
```

meaning that we return from the function. Since the value of s is not used, the variable and the loop can be removed and the code works in $O(1)$ time. For this reason, when measuring the running time of a code, it is important that the result of the code is used (e.g., we can print it), so that the compiler cannot optimize away all the code.

Hardware-Specific Optimizations The g++ flag -march=native turns on hardware-specific optimizations. For example, some processors have special instructions that other processors do not have. Here native means that the compiler automatically detects the actual architecture of the processor and uses hardware-specific optimizations if possible.

For example, consider the following code that calculates the sum of one bits using the g++ function __builtin_popcount:

```
c = 0;
for (int i - 1; i <= n; i++) {
    c += __builtin_popcount(i);
}
```

Many processors have a special instruction popcnt that efficiently performs the bit count operation. However, since not all processors support it, g++ does not automatically use it and we need to use the -march=native flag to enable it. The above code can be two or three times faster using the flag.

The -march=native flag is not often set in contest systems, but we can specify the architecture in our code using a #pragma directive. However, in this context, the value native is not supported but we have to name the architecture. For example, the following directive (assuming the Sandy Bridge architecture) can work:

```
#pragma GCC target ("arch=sandybridge")
```

3.3.2 Processor Features

When processors execute code, they also try to do it as fast as possible. There are caches that speed up memory accesses, and it may also be possible to execute several instructions in parallel. Modern processors are very complex, and not many people actually understand how they work.

Caches As using the main memory is relatively slow, processors have caches that contain small parts of the memory and can be accessed faster. The caches are automatically used when nearby memory contents are read or written. In particular, scanning array elements from left to right is fast, while inspecting random array positions is slow.

As an example, consider the following codes:

```
for (int i = 0; i < n; i++) {
    for (int j = 0; j < n; j++) {
        s += x[i][j];
    }
}
```

```
for (int i = 0; i < n; i++) {
    for (int j = 0; j < n; j++) {
        s += x[j][i];
    }
}
```

Both codes calculate the sum of values in a two-dimensional array, but the first code can be much more efficient, because it is *cache-friendly*. The elements of the array are stored in the memory in the following order:

$$x[0][0], x[0][1], \ldots, x[0][n-1], x[1][0], x[1][1], \ldots$$

Thus, it is better that the outermost loop handles the first dimension, and the innermost loop handles the second dimension.

Parallelism Modern processors can execute multiple instructions at the same time, and this happens automatically in many situations. In general, two consecutive instructions can be executed in parallel if they do not depend on each other. For example, consider the following code:

```
ll f = 1;
for (int i = 1; i <= n; i++) {
    f = (f*i)%M;
}
```

The code computes the factorial of n modulo M using a loop. We can try to make the code more efficient as follows (assuming that n is even):

```
ll f1 = 1;
ll f2 = 1;
for (int i = 1; i <= n; i += 2) {
    f1 = (f1*i)%M;
    f2 = (f2*(i+1))%M;
}
ll f = f1*f2%M;
```

The idea is that we use two independent variables: f_1 will contain the product $1 \cdot 3 \cdot 5 \cdots \cdot n - 1$, and f_2 will contain the product $2 \cdot 4 \cdot 6 \cdots \cdot n$. After the loop, the results are combined. Surprisingly, this code typically works about twice as fast as the first code, because the processor is able to parallelly execute the instructions that modify the variables f_1 and f_2 in the loop. We can even try to use more variables (like four or eight) to further speed up the code.

Sorting and Searching

4

Many efficient algorithms are based on sorting the input data, because sorting often makes solving the problem easier. This chapter discusses the theory and practice of sorting as an algorithm design tool.

Section 4.1 first discusses three important sorting algorithms: bubble sort, merge sort, and counting sort. After this, we will learn how to use the sorting algorithm available in the C++ standard library.

Section 4.2 shows how sorting can be used as a subroutine to create efficient algorithms. For example, to quickly determine if all array elements are unique, we can first sort the array and then simply check all pairs of consecutive elements.

Section 4.3 presents the binary search algorithm, which is another important building block of efficient algorithms.

4.1 Sorting Algorithms

The basic problem in sorting is as follows: Given an array that contains n elements, sort the elements in increasing order. For example, Fig. 4.1 shows an array before and after sorting.

In this section we will go through some fundamental sorting algorithms and examine their properties. It is easy to design an $O(n^2)$ time sorting algorithm, but there are also more efficient algorithms. After discussing the theory of sorting, we will focus on using sorting in practice in C++.

© Springer Nature Switzerland AG 2020
A. Laaksonen, *Guide to Competitive Programming*, Undergraduate Topics in Computer Science, https://doi.org/10.1007/978-3-030-39357-1_4

Fig. 4.1 Array before and after sorting

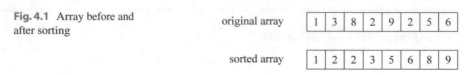

original array

1	3	8	2	9	2	5	6

sorted array

1	2	2	3	5	6	8	9

4.1.1 Bubble Sort

Bubble sort is a simple sorting algorithm that works in $O(n^2)$ time. The algorithm consists of n rounds, and on each round, it iterates through the elements of the array. Whenever two consecutive elements are found that are in wrong order, the algorithm swaps them. The algorithm can be implemented as follows:

```
for (int i = 0; i < n; i++) {
    for (int j = 0; j < n-1; j++) {
        if (array[j] > array[j+1]) {
            swap(array[j],array[j+1]);
        }
    }
}
```

After the first round of bubble sort, the largest element will be in the correct position, and more generally, after k rounds, the k largest elements will be in the correct positions. Thus, after n rounds, the whole array will be sorted.

For example, Fig. 4.2 shows the first round of swaps when bubble sort is used to sort an array.

Bubble sort is an example of a sorting algorithm that always swaps *consecutive* elements in the array. It turns out that the time complexity of such an algorithm

Fig. 4.2 First round of bubble sort

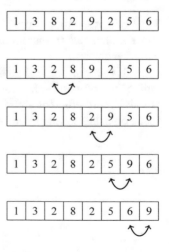

Fig. 4.3 This array has three inversions: $(3, 4)$, $(3, 5)$, and $(6, 7)$

0	1	2	3	4	5	6	7
1	2	2	6	3	5	9	8

is *always* at least $O(n^2)$, because in the worst case, $O(n^2)$ swaps are required for sorting the array.

Inversions A useful concept when analyzing sorting algorithms is an *inversion*: a pair of array indices (a, b) such that $a < b$ and array[a] > array[b], i.e., the elements are in wrong order. For example, the array in Fig. 4.3 has three inversions: $(3, 4)$, $(3, 5)$, and $(6, 7)$.

The number of inversions indicates how much work is needed to sort the array. An array is completely sorted when there are no inversions. On the other hand, if the array elements are in the reverse order, the number of inversions is

$$1 + 2 + \cdots + (n - 1) = \frac{n(n - 1)}{2} = O(n^2),$$

which is the largest possible.

Swapping a pair of consecutive elements that are in the wrong order removes exactly one inversion from the array. Hence, if a sorting algorithm can only swap consecutive elements, each swap removes at most one inversion, and the time complexity of the algorithm is at least $O(n^2)$.

4.1.2 Merge Sort

If we want to create an efficient sorting algorithm, we have to be able to reorder elements that are in different parts of the array. There are several such sorting algorithms that work in $O(n \log n)$ time. One of them is *merge sort*, which is based on recursion. Merge sort sorts a subarray array[$a \ldots b$] as follows:

1. If $a = b$, do not do anything, because a subarray that only contains one element is already sorted.
2. Calculate the position of the middle element: $k = \lfloor (a + b)/2 \rfloor$.
3. Recursively sort the subarray array[$a \ldots k$].
4. Recursively sort the subarray array[$k + 1 \ldots b$].
5. *Merge* the sorted subarrays array[$a \ldots k$] and array[$k + 1 \ldots b$] into a sorted subarray array[$a \ldots b$].

For example, Fig. 4.4 shows how merge sort sorts an array of eight elements. First, the algorithm divides the array into two subarrays of four elements. Then, it sorts these subarrays recursively by calling itself. Finally, it merges the sorted subarrays into a sorted array of eight elements.

Merge sort is an efficient algorithm, because it halves the size of the subarray at each step. Then, merging the sorted subarrays is possible in linear time, because they

Fig. 4.4 Sorting an array
using merge sort

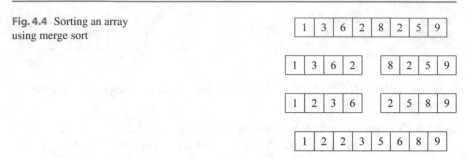

are already sorted. Since there are $O(\log n)$ recursive levels, and processing each
level takes a total of $O(n)$ time, the algorithm works in $O(n \log n)$ time.

4.1.3   Sorting Lower Bound

Is it possible to sort an array faster than in $O(n \log n)$ time? It turns out that this
is *not* possible when we restrict ourselves to sorting algorithms that are based on
comparing array elements.

The lower bound for the time complexity can be proved by considering sorting as
a process where each comparison of two elements gives more information about the
contents of the array. Figure 4.5 illustrates the tree created in this process.

Here "$x < y$?" means that some elements x and y are compared. If $x < y$, the
process continues to the left, and otherwise to the right. The results of the process
are the possible ways to sort the array, a total of $n!$ ways. For this reason, the height
of the tree must be at least

$$\log_2(n!) = \log_2(1) + \log_2(2) + \cdots + \log_2(n).$$

We get a lower bound for this sum by choosing the last $n/2$ elements and changing
the value of each element to $\log_2(n/2)$. This yields an estimate

$$\log_2(n!) \geq (n/2) \cdot \log_2(n/2),$$

Fig. 4.5 Progress of a
sorting algorithm that
compares array elements

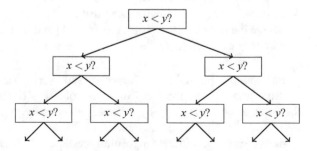

so the height of the tree and the worst-case number of steps in a sorting algorithm are $\Omega(n \log n)$.

4.1.4 Counting Sort

The lower bound $\Omega(n \log n)$ does not apply to algorithms that do not compare array elements but use some other information. An example of such an algorithm is *counting sort* that sorts an array in $O(n)$ time assuming that every element in the array is an integer between $0 \ldots c$ and $c = O(n)$.

The algorithm creates a bookkeeping array, whose indices are elements of the original array. The algorithm iterates through the original array and calculates how many times each element appears in the array. As an example, Fig. 4.6 shows an array and the corresponding bookkeeping array. For example, the value at position 3 is 2, because the value 3 appears 2 times in the original array.

The construction of the bookkeeping array takes $O(n)$ time. After this, the sorted array can be created in $O(n)$ time, because the number of occurrences of each element can be retrieved from the bookkeeping array. Thus, the total time complexity of counting sort is $O(n)$.

Counting sort is a very efficient algorithm but it can only be used when the constant c is small enough, so that the array elements can be used as indices in the bookkeeping array.

4.1.5 Sorting in Practice

In practice, it is almost never a good idea to implement a homemade sorting algorithm, because all modern programming languages have good sorting algorithms in their standard libraries. There are many reasons to use a library function: It is certainly correct and efficient, and also easy to use.

Fig. 4.6 Sorting an array using counting sort

1	3	6	9	9	3	5	9

0	1	2	3	4	5	6	7	8	9
0	1	0	2	0	1	1	0	0	3

In C++, the function `sort` efficiently[1] sorts the contents of a data structure. For example, the following code sorts the elements of a vector in increasing order:

```
vector<int> v = {4,2,5,3,5,8,3};
sort(v.begin(),v.end());
```

After the sorting, the contents of the vector will be $[2, 3, 3, 4, 5, 5, 8]$. The default sorting order is increasing, but a reverse order is possible as follows:

```
sort(v.rbegin(),v.rend());
```

An ordinary array can be sorted as follows:

```
int n = 7; // array size
int a[] = {4,2,5,3,5,8,3};
sort(a,a+n);
```

Then, the following code sorts the string s:

```
string s = "monkey";
sort(s.begin(), s.end());
```

Sorting a string means that the characters of the string are sorted. For example, the string "monkey" becomes "ekmnoy".

Comparison Operators The `sort` function requires that a *comparison operator* is defined for the data type of the elements to be sorted. When sorting, this operator will be used whenever it is necessary to find out the order of two elements.

Most C++ data types have a built-in comparison operator, and elements of those types can be sorted automatically. Numbers are sorted according to their values, and strings are sorted in alphabetical order. Pairs are sorted primarily according to their first elements and secondarily according to their second elements:

```
vector<pair<int,int>> v;
v.push_back({1,5});
v.push_back({2,3});
v.push_back({1,2});
sort(v.begin(), v.end());
// result: [(1,2),(1,5),(2,3)]
```

---

[1]The C++11 standard requires that the `sort` function works in $O(n \log n)$ time; the exact implementation depends on the compiler.

In a similar way, tuples are sorted primarily by the first element, secondarily by the second element, etc.[2]:

```
vector<tuple<int,int,int>> v;
v.push_back({2,1,4});
v.push_back({1,5,3});
v.push_back({2,1,3});
sort(v.begin(), v.end());
// result: [(1,5,3),(2,1,3),(2,1,4)]
```

User-defined structs do not have a comparison operator automatically. The operator should be defined inside the struct as a function `operator<`, whose parameter is another element of the same type. The operator should return `true` if the element is smaller than the parameter, and `false` otherwise.

For example, the following struct `point` contains the x- and y-coordinates of a point. The comparison operator is defined so that the points are sorted primarily by the x-coordinate and secondarily by the y-coordinate.

```
struct point {
    int x, y;
    bool operator<(const point &p) {
        if (x == p.x) return y < p.y;
        else return x < p.x;
    }
};
```

Comparison Functions It is also possible to give an external *comparison function* to the `sort` function as a callback function. For example, the following comparison function `comp` sorts strings primarily by length and secondarily by alphabetical order:

```
bool comp(string a, string b) {
    if (a.size() == b.size()) return a < b;
    else return a.size() < b.size();
}
```

Now a vector of strings can be sorted as follows:

```
sort(v.begin(), v.end(), comp);
```

---

[2]Note that in some older compilers, the function `make_tuple` has to be used to create a tuple instead of braces (for example, `make_tuple(2,1,4)` instead of `{2,1,4}`).

4.2 Solving Problems by Sorting

Often, we can easily solve a problem in $O(n^2)$ time using a brute force algorithm, but such an algorithm is too slow if the input size is large. In fact, a frequent goal in algorithm design is to find $O(n)$ or $O(n \log n)$ time algorithms for problems that can be trivially solved in $O(n^2)$ time. Sorting is one way to achieve this goal.

For example, suppose that we want to check if all elements in an array are unique. A brute force algorithm goes through all pairs of elements in $O(n^2)$ time:

```
bool ok = true;
for (int i = 0; i < n; i++) {
    for (int j = i+1; j < n; j++) {
        if (array[i] == array[j]) ok = false;
    }
}
```

However, we can solve the problem in $O(n \log n)$ time by first sorting the array. Then, if there are equal elements, they are next to each other in the sorted array, so they are easy to find in $O(n)$ time:

```
bool ok = true;
sort(array, array+n);
for (int i = 0; i < n-1; i++) {
    if (array[i] == array[i+1]) ok = false;
}
```

Several other problems can be solved in a similar way in $O(n \log n)$ time, such as counting the number of distinct elements, finding the most frequent element, and finding two elements whose difference is minimum.

4.2.1 Sweep Line Algorithms

A *sweep line* algorithm models a problem as a set of events that are processed in a sorted order. For example, suppose that there is a restaurant and we know the arriving and leaving times of all customers on a certain day. Our task is to find out the maximum number of customers who visited the restaurant at the same time.

For example, Fig. 4.7 shows an instance of the problem where there are four customers A, B, C, and D. In this case, the maximum number of simultaneous customers is three between A's arrival and B's leaving.

To solve the problem, we create two events for each customer: one event for arrival and another event for leaving. Then, we sort the events and go through them according to their times. To find the maximum number of customers, we maintain a counter whose value increases when a customer arrives and decreases when a customer leaves. The largest value of the counter is the answer to the problem.

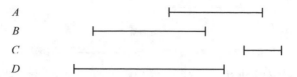

Fig. 4.7 Instance of the restaurant problem

Fig. 4.8 Solving the restaurant problem using a sweep line algorithm

Figure 4.8 shows the events in our example scenario. Each customer is assigned two events: "+" denotes an arriving customer, and "−" denotes a leaving customer. The resulting algorithm works in $O(n \log n)$ time, because sorting the events takes $O(n \log n)$ time and the sweep line part takes $O(n)$ time.

4.2.2 Scheduling Events

Many scheduling problems can be solved by sorting the input data and then using a *greedy* strategy to construct a solution. A greedy algorithm always makes a choice that looks the best at the moment and never takes back its choices.

As an example, consider the following problem: Given n events with their starting and ending times, find a schedule that includes as many events as possible. For example, Fig. 4.9 shows an instance of the problem where an optimal solution is to select two events.

In this problem, there are several ways how we could sort the input data. One strategy is to sort the events according to their *lengths* and select as *short* events as possible. However, this strategy does not always work, as shown in Fig. 4.10. Then, another idea is to sort the events according to their *starting times* and always select the next possible event that *begins* as *early* as possible. However, we can find a counterexample also for this strategy, shown in Fig. 4.11.

A third idea is to sort the events according to their *ending times* and always select the next possible event that *ends* as *early* as possible. It turns out that this algorithm *always* produces an optimal solution. To justify this, consider what happens if we

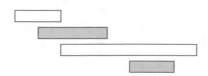

Fig. 4.9 Instance of the scheduling problem and an optimal solution with two events

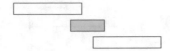

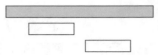

Fig. 4.10 If we select the short event, we can only select one event, but we could select both long events

Fig. 4.11 If we select the first event, we cannot select any other events, but we could to select the other two events

first select an event that ends later than the event that ends as early as possible. Now, we will have at most an equal number of choices left how we can select the next event. Hence, selecting an event that ends later can never yield a better solution, and the greedy algorithm is correct.

4.2.3 Tasks and Deadlines

Finally, consider a problem where we are given n tasks with durations and deadlines, and our task is to choose an order to perform the tasks. For each task, we earn $d - x$ points where d is the task's deadline and x is the moment when we finish the task. What is the largest possible total score we can obtain?

For example, suppose that the tasks are as follows:

Task	Duration	Deadline
A	4	2
B	3	10
C	2	8
D	4	15

Figure 4.12 shows an optimal schedule for the tasks in our example scenario. Using this schedule, C yields 6 points, B yields 5 points, A yields -7 points, and D yields 2 points, so the total score is 6.

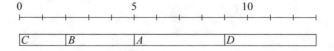

Fig. 4.12 Optimal schedule for the tasks

Fig. 4.13 Improving the solution by swapping tasks X and Y

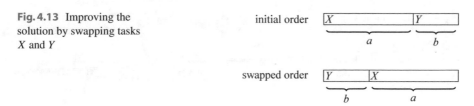

It turns out that the optimal solution to the problem does not depend on the deadlines at all, but a correct greedy strategy is to simply perform the tasks *sorted by their durations* in increasing order. The reason for this is that if we ever perform two tasks one after another such that the first task takes longer than the second task, we can obtain a better solution if we swap the tasks.

For example, in Fig. 4.13, there are two tasks X and Y with durations a and b. Initially, X is scheduled before Y. However, since $a > b$, the tasks should be swapped. Now X gives b points less and Y gives a points more, so the total score increases by $a - b > 0$. Thus, in an optimal solution, a shorter task must always come before a longer task, and the tasks must be sorted by their durations.

4.3 Binary Search

Binary search is an $O(\log n)$ time algorithm that can be used, for example, to efficiently check whether a sorted array contains a given element. In this section, we first focus on the implementation of binary search, and after that, we will see how binary search can be used to find optimal solutions for problems.

4.3.1 Implementing the Search

Suppose that we are given a sorted array of n elements and we want to check if the array contains an element with a target value x. Next we discuss two ways to implement a binary search algorithm for this problem.

First Method The most common way to implement binary search resembles looking for a word in a dictionary.[3] The search maintains an active subarray in the array, which initially contains all array elements. Then, a number of steps are performed, each of which halves the search range. At each step, the search checks the middle element of the active subarray. If the middle element has the target value, the search terminates. Otherwise, the search recursively continues to the left or right half of the subarray,

---

[3] Some people, including the author of this book, still use printed dictionaries. Another example is finding a phone number in a printed phone book, which is even more obsolete.

Fig. 4.14 Traditional way to
implement binary search. At
each step we check the
middle element of the active
subarray and proceed to the
left or right part

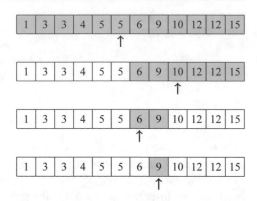

depending on the value of the middle element. For example, Fig. 4.14 shows how an
element with value 9 is found in the array.

The search can be implemented as follows:

```
int a = 0, b = n-1;
while (a <= b) {
    int k = (a+b)/2;
    if (array[k] == x) {
        // x found at index k
    }
    if (array[k] < x) a = k+1;
    else b = k-1;
}
```

In this implementation, the range of the active subarray is $a \ldots b$, and the initial
range is $0 \ldots n - 1$. The algorithm halves the size of the subarray at each step, so
the time complexity is $O(\log n)$.

Second Method Another way to implement binary search is to go through the array
from left to right making *jumps*. The initial jump length is $n/2$, and the jump length
is halved on each round: first $n/4$, then $n/8$, then $n/16$, etc., until finally the length
is 1. On each round, we make jumps until we would end up outside the array or in
an element whose value exceeds the target value. After the jumps, either the desired
element has been found or we know that it does not appear in the array. Figure 4.15
illustrates the technique in our example scenario.

The following code implements the search:

```
int k = 0;
for (int b = n/2; b >= 1; b /= 2) {
    while (k+b < n && array[k+b] <= x) k += b;
}
if (array[k] == x) {
    // x found at index k
}
```

Fig. 4.15 Alternative way to implement binary search. We scan the array from left to right jumping over elements

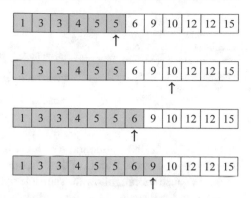

During the search, the variable b contains the current jump length. The time complexity of the algorithm is $O(\log n)$, because the code in the while loop is performed at most twice for each jump length.

4.3.2 Finding Optimal Solutions

Suppose that we are solving a problem and have a function valid(x) that returns true if x is a valid solution and false otherwise. In addition, we know that valid(x) is false when $x < k$ and true when $x \geq k$. In this situation, we can use binary search to efficiently find the value of k.

The idea is to binary search for the largest value of x for which valid(x) is false. Thus, the next value $k = x + 1$ is the smallest possible value for which valid(k) is true. The search can be implemented as follows:

```
int x = -1;
for (int b = z; b >= 1; b /= 2) {
    while (!valid(x+b)) x += b;
}
int k = x+1;
```

The initial jump length z has to be an upper bound for the answer, i.e., any value for which we surely know that valid(z) is true. The algorithm calls the function valid $O(\log z)$ times, so the running time depends on the function valid. For example, if the function works in $O(n)$ time, the running time is $O(n \log z)$.

Example Consider a problem where our task is to process k jobs using n machines. Each machine i is assigned an integer p_i: the time to process a single job. What is the minimum time to process all the jobs?

For example, suppose that $k = 8$, $n = 3$ and the processing times are $p_1 = 2$, $p_2 = 3$, and $p_3 = 7$. In this case, the minimum total processing time is 9, by following the schedule in Fig. 4.16.

Fig. 4.16 Optimal processing schedule: machine 1 processes four jobs, machine 2 processes three jobs, and machine 3 processes one job

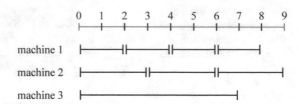

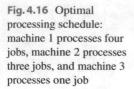

Let valid(x) be a function that finds out whether it is possible to process all the jobs using at most x units of time. In our example scenario, clearly valid(9) is true, because we can follow the schedule in Fig. 4.16. On the other hand, valid(8) must be false, because the minimum processing time is 9.

Calculating the value of valid(x) is easy, because each machine i can process at most $\lfloor x/p_i \rfloor$ jobs in x units of time. Thus, if the sum of all $\lfloor x/p_i \rfloor$ values is k or more, x is a valid solution. Then, we can use binary search to find the minimum value of x for which valid(x) is true.

How efficient is the resulting algorithm? The function valid takes $O(n)$ time, so the algorithm works in $O(n \log z)$ time, where z is an upper bound for the answer. One possible value for z is kp_1 which corresponds to a solution where only the first machine is used to process all the jobs. This is surely a valid upper bound.

Data Structures

5

This chapter introduces the most important data structures of the C++ standard library. In competitive programming, it is crucial to know which data structures are available in the standard library and how to use them. This often saves a large amount of time when implementing an algorithm.

Section 5.1 first describes the vector structure which is an efficient dynamic array. After this, we will focus on using iterators and ranges with data structures and briefly discuss deques, stacks, and queues.

Section 5.2 discusses sets, maps, and priority queues. Those data structures are often used as building blocks of efficient algorithms, because they allow us to maintain dynamic structures that support both efficient searches and updates.

Section 5.3 shows some results about the efficiency of data structures in practice. As we will see, there are important performance differences that cannot be detected by only looking at time complexities.

5.1 Dynamic Arrays

In C++, ordinary arrays are fixed-size structures, and it is not possible to change the size of an array after creating it. For example, the following code creates an array which contains n integer values:

```
int array[n];
```

A *dynamic array* is an array whose size can be changed during the execution of the program. The C++ standard library provides several dynamic arrays, most useful of them being the vector structure.

© Springer Nature Switzerland AG 2020
A. Laaksonen, *Guide to Competitive Programming*, Undergraduate Topics
in Computer Science, https://doi.org/10.1007/978-3-030-39357-1_5

5.1.1 Vectors

A *vector* is a dynamic array that allows us to efficiently add and remove elements
at the end of the structure. For example, the following code creates an empty vector
and adds three elements to it:

```
vector<int> v;
v.push_back(3); // [3]
v.push_back(2); // [3,2]
v.push_back(5); // [3,2,5]
```

Then, the elements can be accessed like in an ordinary array:

```
cout << v[0] << "\n"; // 3
cout << v[1] << "\n"; // 2
cout << v[2] << "\n"; // 5
```

Another way to create a vector is to give a list of its elements:

```
vector<int> v = {2,4,2,5,1};
```

We can also give the number of elements and their initial values:

```
vector<int> a(8); // size 8, initial value 0
vector<int> b(8,2); // size 8, initial value 2
```

The function `size` returns the number of elements in the vector. For example,
the following code iterates through the vector and prints its elements:

```
for (int i = 0; i < v.size(); i++) {
    cout << v[i] << "\n";
}
```

A shorter way to iterate through a vector is as follows:

```
for (auto x : v) {
    cout << x << "\n";
}
```

The function `back` returns the last element of a vector, and the function
`pop_back` removes the last element:

```
vector<int> v = {2,4,2,5,1};
cout << v.back() << "\n"; // 1
v.pop_back();
cout << v.back() << "\n"; // 5
```

Vectors are implemented so that the `push_back` and `pop_back` operations work in $O(1)$ time on average. In practice, using a vector is almost as fast as using an ordinary array.

5.1.2 Iterators and Ranges

An *iterator* is a variable that points to an element of a data structure. The iterator `begin` points to the first element of a data structure, and the iterator `end` points to the position *after* the last element. For example, the situation can look as follows in a vector v that consists of eight elements:

$$[5, 2, 3, 1, 2, 5, 7, 1]$$
$$\uparrow \qquad\qquad \uparrow$$
$$\texttt{v.begin()} \qquad \texttt{v.end()}$$

Note the asymmetry in the iterators: `begin()` points to an element in the data structure, while `end()` points *outside* the data structure.

A *range* is a sequence of consecutive elements in a data structure. The usual way to specify a range is to give iterators to its first element and the position after its last element. In particular, the iterators `begin()` and `end()` define a range that contains all elements in a data structure.

The C++ standard library functions typically operate with ranges. For example, the following code first sorts a vector, then reverses the order of its elements, and finally shuffles its elements.

```
sort(v.begin(),v.end());
reverse(v.begin(),v.end());
random_shuffle(v.begin(),v.end());
```

The element to which an iterator points can be accessed using the * syntax. For example, the following code prints the first element of a vector:

```
cout << *v.begin() << "\n";
```

To give a more useful example, `lower_bound` gives an iterator to the first element in a sorted range whose value is *at least* x, and `upper_bound` gives an iterator to the first element whose value is *larger than* x:

```
vector<int> v = {2,3,3,5,7,8,8,8};
auto a = lower_bound(v.begin(),v.end(),5);
auto b = upper_bound(v.begin(),v.end(),5);
cout << *a << " " << *b << "\n"; // 5 7
```

Note that the above functions only work correctly when the given range is sorted. The functions use binary search and find the requested element in logarithmic time.

If there is no such element, the functions return an iterator to the element after the last element in the range.

The C++ standard library contains a large number of useful functions that are worth exploring. For example, the following code creates a vector that contains the unique elements of the original vector in a sorted order:

```
sort(v.begin(),v.end());
v.erase(unique(v.begin(),v.end()),v.end());
```

5.1.3 Other Structures

A *deque* is a dynamic array that can be efficiently manipulated at both ends of the structure. Like a vector, a deque provides the functions push_back and pop_back, but it also provides the functions push_front and pop_front which are not available in a vector. A deque can be used as follows:

```
deque<int> d;
d.push_back(5); // [5]
d.push_back(2); // [5,2]
d.push_front(3); // [3,5,2]
d.pop_back(); // [3,5]
d.pop_front(); // [5]
```

The operations of a deque also work in $O(1)$ average time. However, deques have larger constant factors than vectors, so deques should be used only if there is a need to manipulate both ends of the array.

C++ also provides two specialized data structures that are, by default, based on a deque. A *stack* has the functions push and pop for inserting and removing elements at the end of the structure, and the function top that retrieves the last element:

```
stack<int> s;
s.push(2); // [2]
s.push(5); // [2,5]
cout << s.top() << "\n"; // 5
s.pop(); // [2]
cout << s.top() << "\n"; // 2
```

Then, in a *queue*, elements are inserted at the end of the structure and removed from the front of the structure. Both the functions front and back are provided for accessing the first and last element.

```
queue<int> q;
q.push(2); // [2]
q.push(5); // [2,5]
cout << q.front() << "\n"; // 2
q.pop(); // [5]
cout << q.back() << "\n"; // 5
```

5.2   Set Structures

A *set* is a data structure that maintains a collection of elements. The basic operations of sets are element insertion, search, and removal. Sets are implemented so that all the above operations are efficient, which often allows us to improve on running times of algorithms using sets.

5.2.1   Sets and Multisets

The C++ standard library contains two set structures:

- set is based on a balanced binary search tree and its operations work in $O(\log n)$ time.
- unordered_set is based on a hash table and its operations work, on average,[1] in $O(1)$ time.

Both structures are efficient, and often either of them can be used. Since they are used in the same way, we focus on the set structure in the following examples.

The following code creates a set that contains integers and shows some of its operations. The function insert adds an element to the set, the function count returns the number of occurrences of an element in the set, and the function erase removes an element from the set.

---

[1] The worst-case time complexity of the operations is $O(n)$, but this is very unlikely to occur.

```
set<int> s;
s.insert(3);
s.insert(2);
s.insert(5);
cout << s.count(3) << "\n"; // 1
cout << s.count(4) << "\n"; // 0
s.erase(3);
s.insert(4);
cout << s.count(3) << "\n"; // 0
cout << s.count(4) << "\n"; // 1
```

An important property of sets is that all their elements are *distinct*. Thus, the function count always returns either 0 (the element is not in the set) or 1 (the element is in the set), and the function insert never adds an element to the set if it is already there. The following code illustrates this:

```
set<int> s;
s.insert(3);
s.insert(3);
s.insert(3);
cout << s.count(3) << "\n"; // 1
```

A set can be used mostly like a vector, but it is not possible to access the elements using the [] notation. The following code prints the number of elements in a set and then iterates through the elements:

```
cout << s.size() << "\n";
for (auto x : s) {
    cout << x << "\n";
}
```

The function find(x) returns an iterator that points to an element whose value is x. However, if the set does not contain x, the iterator will be end().

```
auto it = s.find(x);
if (it == s.end()) {
    // x is not found
}
```

Ordered Sets The main difference between the two C++ set structures is that set is *ordered*, while unordered_set is not. Thus, if we want to maintain the order of the elements, we have to use the set structure.

For example, consider the problem of finding the smallest and largest value in a set. To do this efficiently, we need to use the set structure. Since the elements are sorted, we can find the smallest and largest value as follows:

```
auto first = s.begin();
auto last = s.end(); last--;
cout << *first << " " << *last << "\n";
```

Note that since `end()` points to an element after the last element, we have to decrease the iterator by one.

The `set` structure also provides the functions `lower_bound(x)` and `upper_bound(x)` that return an iterator to the smallest element in a `set` whose value is *at least* or *larger than x*, respectively. In both the functions, if the requested element does not exist, the return value is `end()`.

```
cout << *s.lower_bound(x) << "\n";
cout << *s.upper_bound(x) << "\n";
```

Multisets A *multiset* is a set that can have several copies of the same value. C++ has the structures `multiset` and `unordered_multiset` that resemble `set` and `unordered_set`. For example, the following code adds three copies of the value 5 to a multiset.

```
multiset<int> s;
s.insert(5);
s.insert(5);
s.insert(5);
cout << s.count(5) << "\n"; // 3
```

The function `erase` removes all copies of a value from a multiset:

```
s.erase(5);
cout << s.count(5) << "\n"; // 0
```

Often, only one value should be removed, which can be done as follows:

```
s.erase(s.find(5));
cout << s.count(5) << "\n"; // 2
```

Note that the functions `count` and `erase` have an additional $O(k)$ factor where k is the number of elements counted/removed. In particular, it is *not* efficient to count the number of copies of a value in a multiset using the `count` function.

5.2.2 Maps

A *map* is a set that consists of key-value pairs. A map can also be seen as a generalized array. While the keys in an ordinary array are always consecutive integers

$0, 1, \ldots, n - 1$, where n is the size of the array, the keys in a map can be of any data type and they do not have to be consecutive values.

The C++ standard library contains two map structures that correspond to the set structures: `map` is based on a balanced binary search tree and accessing elements takes $O(\log n)$ time, while `unordered_map` uses hashing and accessing elements take $O(1)$ time on average.

The following code creates a map whose keys are strings and values are integers:

```
map<string,int> m;
m["monkey"] = 4;
m["banana"] = 3;
m["harpsichord"] = 9;
cout << m["banana"] << "\n"; // 3
```

If the value of a key is requested but the map does not contain it, the key is automatically added to the map with a default value. For example, in the following code, the key "aybabtu" with value 0 is added to the map.

```
map<string,int> m;
cout << m["aybabtu"] << "\n"; // 0
```

The function `count` checks if a key exists in a map:

```
if (m.count("aybabtu")) {
    // key exists
}
```

Then, the following code prints all keys and values in a map:

```
for (auto x : m) {
    cout << x.first << " " << x.second << "\n";
}
```

5.2.3 Priority Queues

A *priority queue* is a multiset that supports element insertion and, depending on the type of the queue, retrieval and removal of either the minimum or maximum element. Insertion and removal take $O(\log n)$ time, and retrieval takes $O(1)$ time.

A priority queue is usually based on a heap structure, which is a special binary tree. While a `multiset` provides all the operations of a priority queue and more, the benefit of using a priority queue is that it has smaller constant factors. Thus, if we only need to efficiently find minimum or maximum elements, it is a good idea to use a priority queue instead of a set or multiset.

By default, the elements in a C++ priority queue are sorted in decreasing order, and it is possible to find and remove the largest element in the queue. The following code illustrates this:

```
priority_queue<int> q;
q.push(3);
q.push(5);
q.push(7);
q.push(2);
cout << q.top() << "\n"; // 7
q.pop();
cout << q.top() << "\n"; // 5
q.pop();
q.push(6);
cout << q.top() << "\n"; // 6
q.pop();
```

If we want to create a priority queue that supports finding and removing the smallest element, we can do it as follows:

```
priority_queue<int,vector<int>,greater<int>> q;
```

5.2.4   Policy-Based Sets

The g++ compiler also provides some data structures that are not part of the C++ standard library. Such structures are called *policy-based* structures. To use these structures, the following lines must be added to the code:

```
#include <ext/pb_ds/assoc_container.hpp>
using namespace __gnu_pbds;
```

After this, we can define a data structure indexed_set that is like set but can be indexed like an array. The definition for int values is as follows:

```
typedef tree<int,null_type,less<int>,rb_tree_tag,
             tree_order_statistics_node_update> indexed_set;
```

Then, we can create a set as follows:

```
indexed_set s;
s.insert(2);
s.insert(3);
s.insert(7);
s.insert(9);
```

The speciality of this set is that we have access to the indices that the elements would have in a sorted array. The function `find_by_order` returns an iterator to the element at a given position:

```
auto x = s.find_by_order(2);
cout << *x << "\n"; // 7
```

Then, the function `order_of_key` returns the position of a given element:

```
cout << s.order_of_key(7) << "\n"; // 2
```

If the element does not appear in the set, we get the position that the element would have in the set:

```
cout << s.order_of_key(6) << "\n"; // 2
cout << s.order_of_key(8) << "\n"; // 3
```

Both the functions work in logarithmic time.

5.3   Experiments

In this section, we present some results concerning the *practical* efficiency of the data structures presented in this chapter. While time complexities are a great tool, they do not always tell the whole truth about the efficiency, so it is worthwhile to also do experiments with real implementations and data sets.

5.3.1   Set Versus Sorting

Many problems can be solved using either sets or sorting. It is important to realize that algorithms that use sorting are usually much faster, even if this is not evident by just looking at the time complexities.

As an example, consider the problem of calculating the number of unique elements in a vector. One way to solve the problem is to add all the elements to a set and return the size of the set. Since it is not needed to maintain the order of the elements, we may use either a `set` or an `unordered_set`. Then, another way to solve the problem is to first sort the vector and then go through its elements. It is easy to count the number of unique elements after sorting the vector.

Table 5.1 shows the results of an experiment where the above algorithms were tested using random vectors of `int` values. It turns out that the `unordered_set` algorithm is about two times faster than the `set` algorithm, and the sorting algorithm is more than ten times faster than the `set` algorithm. Note that both the `set` algorithm and the sorting algorithm work in $O(n \log n)$ time; still the latter is much faster. The

Table 5.1 Results of an experiment where the number of unique elements in a vector was calculated. The first two algorithms insert the elements to a set structure, while the last algorithm sorts the vector and inspects consecutive elements

Input size n	set (s)	unordered_set (s)	Sorting (s)
10^6	0.65	0.34	0.11
$2 \cdot 10^6$	1.50	0.76	0.18
$4 \cdot 10^6$	3.38	1.63	0.33
$8 \cdot 10^6$	7.57	3.45	0.68
$16 \cdot 10^6$	17.35	7.18	1.38

Table 5.2 Results of an experiment where the most frequent value in a vector was determined. The two first algorithms use map structures, and the last algorithm uses an ordinary array

Input size n	map (s)	unordered_map (s)	Array (s)
10^6	0.55	0.23	0.01
$2 \cdot 10^6$	1.14	0.39	0.02
$4 \cdot 10^6$	2.34	0.73	0.03
$8 \cdot 10^6$	4.68	1.46	0.06
$16 \cdot 10^6$	9.57	2.83	0.11

reason for this is that sorting is a simple operation, while the balanced binary search tree used in set is a complex data structure.

5.3.2 Map Versus Array

Maps are convenient structures compared to arrays, because any indices can be used, but they also have large constant factors. In our next experiment, we created a vector of n random integers between 1 and 10^6 and then determined the most frequent value by counting the number of each element. First we used maps, but since the upper bound 10^6 is quite small, we were also able to use arrays.

Table 5.2 shows the results of the experiment. While unordered_map is about three times faster than map, an array is almost a hundred times faster. Thus, arrays should be used whenever possible instead of maps. Especially, note that while unordered_map provides $O(1)$ time operations, there are large constant factors hidden in the data structure.

5.3.3 Priority Queue Versus Multiset

Are priority queues really faster than multisets? To find this out, we conducted another experiment where we created two vectors of n random int numbers. First, we added

Table 5.3 Results of an experiment where elements were added and removed using a multiset and a priority queue

Input size n	multiset (s)	priority_queue (s)
10^6	1.17	0.19
$2 \cdot 10^6$	2.77	0.41
$4 \cdot 10^6$	6.10	1.05
$8 \cdot 10^6$	13.96	2.52
$16 \cdot 10^6$	30.93	5.95

all elements of the first vector to a data structure. Then, we went through the second vector and repeatedly removed the smallest element from the data structure and added the new element to it.

Table 5.3 shows the results of the experiment. It turns out that in this problem a priority queue is about five times faster than a multiset.

Dynamic Programming

6

Dynamic programming is an algorithm design technique that can be used to find optimal solutions to problems and to count the number of solutions. This chapter is an introduction to dynamic programming, and the technique will be used many times later in the book when designing algorithms.

Section 6.1 discusses the basic elements of dynamic programming in the context of a coin change problem. In this problem we are given a set of coin values, and our task is to construct a sum of money using as few coins as possible. There is a simple greedy algorithm for the problem, but as we will see, it does not always produce an optimal solution. However, using dynamic programming, we can create an efficient algorithm that always finds an optimal solution.

Section 6.2 presents a selection of problems that show some of the possibilities of dynamic programming. The problems include determining the longest increasing subsequence in an array, finding an optimal path in a two-dimensional grid, and generating all possible weight sums in a knapsack problem.

6.1 Basic Concepts

In this section, we go through the basic concepts of dynamic programming in the context of a coin change problem. First we present a greedy algorithm for the problem, which does not always produce an optimal solution. After this, we show how the problem can be efficiently solved using dynamic programming.

6.1.1 When Greedy Fails

Suppose that we are given a set of coin values $\texttt{coins} = \{c_1, c_2, \ldots, c_k\}$ and a target sum of money n, and we are asked to construct the sum n using as few coins as possible. There are no restrictions on how many times we can use each coin value. For

© Springer Nature Switzerland AG 2020
A. Laaksonen, *Guide to Competitive Programming*, Undergraduate Topics
in Computer Science, https://doi.org/10.1007/978-3-030-39357-1_6

example, if $coins = \{1, 2, 5\}$ and $n = 12$, the optimal solution is $5 + 5 + 2 = 12$, which requires three coins.

There is a natural greedy algorithm for solving the problem: Always select the largest possible coin so that the sum of coin values does not exceed the target sum. For example, if $n = 12$, we first select two coins of value 5 and then one coin of value 2, which completes the solution. This looks like a reasonable strategy, but is it always optimal?

It turns out that this strategy does *not* always work. For example, if $coins = \{1, 3, 4\}$ and $n = 6$, the optimal solution has only two coins ($3 + 3 = 6$) but the greedy strategy produces a solution with three coins ($4 + 1 + 1 = 6$). This simple counterexample shows that the greedy algorithm is not correct.[1]

How could we solve the problem, then? Of course, we could try to find another greedy algorithm, but there are no other obvious strategies that we could consider. Another possibility would be to create a brute force algorithm that goes through all possible ways to select coins. Such an algorithm would surely give correct results, but it would be very slow on large inputs.

However, using dynamic programming, we can create an algorithm that is almost like a brute force algorithm but it is also *efficient*. Thus, we can both be sure that the algorithm is correct and use it for processing large inputs. Furthermore, we can use the same technique for solving a large number of other problems.

6.1.2   Finding an Optimal Solution

To use dynamic programming, we should formulate the problem recursively so that the solution to the problem can be calculated from solutions to smaller subproblems. In the coin problem, a natural recursive problem is to calculate values of a function $solve(x)$: What is the minimum number of coins required to form a sum x? Clearly, the values of the function depend on the values of the coins. For example, if $coins = \{1, 3, 4\}$, the first values of the function are as follows:

$$
\begin{aligned}
solve(0) &= 0 \\
solve(1) &= 1 \\
solve(2) &= 2 \\
solve(3) &= 1 \\
solve(4) &= 1 \\
solve(5) &= 2 \\
solve(6) &= 2 \\
solve(7) &= 2 \\
solve(8) &= 2 \\
solve(9) &= 3 \\
solve(10) &= 3
\end{aligned}
$$

[1]It is an interesting question when exactly does the greedy algorithm work. Pearson [28] describes an efficient algorithm for testing this.

For example, `solve(10) = 3`, because at least 3 coins are needed to form the sum 10. The optimal solution is $3 + 3 + 4 = 10$.

The essential property of `solve` is that its values can be recursively calculated from its smaller values. The idea is to focus on the *first* coin that we choose for the sum. For example, in the above scenario, the first coin can be either 1, 3, or 4. If we first choose coin 1, the remaining task is to form the sum 9 using the minimum number of coins, which is a subproblem of the original problem. Of course, the same applies to coins 3 and 4. Thus, we can use the following recursive formula to calculate the minimum number of coins:

$$\begin{aligned} \text{solve}(x) = \min(&\text{solve}(x-1)+1, \\ &\text{solve}(x-3)+1, \\ &\text{solve}(x-4)+1). \end{aligned}$$

The base case of the recursion is `solve(0) = 0`, because no coins are needed to form an empty sum. For example,

$$\text{solve}(10) = \text{solve}(7) + 1 = \text{solve}(4) + 2 = \text{solve}(0) + 3 = 3.$$

Now we are ready to give a general recursive function that calculates the minimum number of coins needed to form a sum x:

$$\text{solve}(x) = \begin{cases} \infty & x < 0 \\ 0 & x = 0 \\ \min_{c \in \text{coins}} \text{solve}(x - c) + 1 & x > 0 \end{cases}$$

First, if $x < 0$, the value is infinite, because it is impossible to form a negative sum of money. Then, if $x = 0$, the value is zero, because no coins are needed to form an empty sum. Finally, if $x > 0$, the variable c goes through all possibilities how to choose the first coin of the sum.

Once a recursive function that solves the problem has been found, we can directly implement a solution in C++ (the constant `INF` denotes infinity):

```cpp
int solve(int x) {
    if (x < 0) return INF;
    if (x == 0) return 0;
    int best = INF;
    for (auto c : coins) {
        best = min(best, solve(x-c)+1);
    }
    return best;
}
```

Still, this function is not efficient, because there may be a large number of ways to construct the sum and the function checks all of them. Fortunately, it turns out that there is a simple way to make the function efficient.

Memoization The key idea in dynamic programming is *memoization*, which means that we store each function value in an array directly after calculating it. Then, when the value is needed again, it can be retrieved from the array without recursive calls. To do this, we create arrays

```
bool ready[N];
int value[N];
```

where ready[x] indicates whether the value of solve(x) has been calculated, and if it is, value[x] contains this value. The constant N has been chosen so that all required values fit in the arrays.

After this, the function can be efficiently implemented as follows:

```
int solve(int x) {
    if (x < 0) return INF;
    if (x == 0) return 0;
    if (ready[x]) return value[x];
    int best = INF;
    for (auto c : coins) {
        best = min(best, solve(x-c)+1);
    }
    ready[x] = true;
    value[x] = best;
    return best;
}
```

The function handles the base cases $x < 0$ and $x = 0$ as previously. Then it checks from ready[x] if solve(x) has already been stored in value[x], and if it is, the function directly returns it. Otherwise the function calculates the value of solve(x) recursively and stores it in value[x].

This function works efficiently, because the answer for each parameter x is calculated recursively only once. After a value of solve(x) has been stored in value[x], it can be efficiently retrieved whenever the function will be called again with the parameter x. The time complexity of the algorithm is $O(nk)$, where n is the target sum and k is the number of coins.

Iterative Implementation Note that we can also *iteratively* construct the array value using a loop as follows:

```
value[0] = 0;
for (int x = 1; x <= n; x++) {
    value[x] = INF;
    for (auto c : coins) {
        if (x-c >= 0) {
            value[x] = min(value[x], value[x-c]+1);
        }
    }
}
```

In fact, most competitive programmers prefer this implementation, because it is shorter and has smaller constant factors. From now on, we also use iterative implementations in our examples. Still, it is often easier to think about dynamic programming solutions in terms of recursive functions.

Constructing a Solution Sometimes we are asked both to find the value of an optimal solution and to give an example how such a solution can be constructed. To construct an optimal solution in our coin problem, we can declare a new array that indicates for each sum of money the first coin in an optimal solution:

```
int first[N];
```

Then, we can modify the algorithm as follows:

```
value[0] = 0;
for (int x = 1; x <= n; x++) {
    value[x] = INF;
    for (auto c : coins) {
        if (x-c >= 0 && value[x-c]+1 < value[x]) {
            value[x] = value[x-c]+1;
            first[x] = c;
        }
    }
}
```

After this, the following code prints the coins that appear in an optimal solution for the sum n:

```
while (n > 0) {
    cout << first[n] << "\n";
    n -= first[n];
}
```

6.1.3 Counting Solutions

Let us now consider another variant of the coin problem where our task is to calculate the total number of ways to produce a sum x using the coins. For example, if coins = $\{1, 3, 4\}$ and $x = 5$, there are a total of 6 ways:

- $1 + 1 + 1 + 1 + 1$
- $1 + 1 + 3$
- $1 + 3 + 1$

- $3 + 1 + 1$
- $1 + 4$
- $4 + 1$

Again, we can solve the problem recursively. Let solve(x) denote the number of ways we can form the sum x. For example, if coins $= \{1, 3, 4\}$, then solve(5) $= 6$ and the recursive formula is

$$
\begin{aligned}
\text{solve}(x) = &\text{solve}(x - 1) + \\
&\text{solve}(x - 3) + \\
&\text{solve}(x - 4).
\end{aligned}
$$

Then, the general recursive function is as follows:

$$
\text{solve}(x) = \begin{cases} 0 & x < 0 \\ 1 & x = 0 \\ \sum_{c \in \text{coins}} \text{solve}(x - c) & x > 0 \end{cases}
$$

If $x < 0$, the value is zero, because there are no solutions. If $x = 0$, the value is one, because there is only one way to form an empty sum. Otherwise we calculate the sum of all values of the form solve($x - c$) where c is in coins.

The following code constructs an array count such that count[x] equals the value of solve(x) for $0 \le x \le n$:

```
count[0] = 1;
for (int x = 1; x <= n; x++) {
    for (auto c : coins) {
        if (x-c >= 0) {
            count[x] += count[x-c];
        }
    }
}
```

Often the number of solutions is so large that it is not required to calculate the exact number but it is enough to give the answer modulo m where, for example, $m = 10^9 + 7$. This can be done by changing the code so that all calculations are done modulo m. In the above code, it suffices to add the line

```
count[x] %= m;
```

after the line

```
count[x] += count[x-c];
```

6.2 Further Examples

After having discussed the basic concepts of dynamic programming, we are now ready to go through a set of problems that can be efficiently solved using dynamic programming. As we will see, dynamic programming is a versatile technique that has many applications in algorithm design.

6.2.1 Longest Increasing Subsequence

The *longest increasing subsequence* in an array of n elements is a maximum length sequence of array elements that goes from left to right, and each element in the sequence is larger than the previous element. For example, Fig. 6.1 shows the longest increasing subsequence in an array of eight elements.

We can efficiently find the longest increasing subsequence in an array using dynamic programming. Let $\texttt{length}(k)$ denote the length of the longest increasing subsequence that ends at position k. Then, if we calculate all values of $\texttt{length}(k)$ where $0 \leq k \leq n - 1$, we will find out the length of the longest increasing subsequence. The values of the function for our example array are as follows:

$$\texttt{length}(0) = 1$$
$$\texttt{length}(1) = 1$$
$$\texttt{length}(2) = 2$$
$$\texttt{length}(3) = 1$$
$$\texttt{length}(4) = 3$$
$$\texttt{length}(5) = 2$$
$$\texttt{length}(6) = 4$$
$$\texttt{length}(7) = 2$$

For example, $\texttt{length}(6) = 4$, because the longest increasing subsequence that ends at position 6 consists of 4 elements.

To calculate a value of $\texttt{length}(k)$, we should find a position $i < k$ for which $\texttt{array}[i] < \texttt{array}[k]$ and $\texttt{length}(i)$ is as large as possible. Then we know that $\texttt{length}(k) = \texttt{length}(i) + 1$, because this is an optimal way to append $\texttt{array}[k]$ to a subsequence. However, if there is no such position i, then $\texttt{length}(k) = 1$, which means that the subsequence only contains $\texttt{array}[k]$.

Since all values of the function can be calculated from its smaller values, we can use dynamic programming to calculate the values. In the following code, the values of the function will be stored in an array $\texttt{length}$.

Fig. 6.1 Longest increasing subsequence of this array is [2, 5, 7, 8]

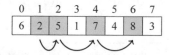

Fig. 6.2 Optimal path from
the upper-left corner to the
lower-right corner

3	7	9	2	7
9	8	3	5	5
1	7	9	8	5
3	8	6	4	10
6	3	9	7	8

```
for (int k = 0; k < n; k++) {
    length[k] = 1;
    for (int i = 0; i < k; i++) {
        if (array[i] < array[k]) {
            length[k] = max(length[k],length[i]+1);
        }
    }
}
```

The resulting algorithm clearly works in $O(n^2)$ time.[2]

6.2.2 Paths in a Grid

Our next problem is to find a path from the upper-left corner to the lower-right corner
of an $n \times n$ grid, with the restriction that we may only move down and right. Each
square contains an integer, and the path should be constructed so that the sum of the
values along the path is as large as possible.

As an example, Fig. 6.2 shows an optimal path in a 5×5 grid. The sum of the
values on the path is 67, and this is the largest possible sum on a path from the
upper-left corner to the lower-right corner.

Assume that the rows and columns of the grid are numbered from 1 to n, and
value[y][x] equals the value of square (y, x). Let sum(y, x) denote the maximum
sum on a path from the upper-left corner to square (y, x). Then, sum(n, n) tells us
the maximum sum from the upper-left corner to the lower-right corner. For example,
in the above grid, sum$(5, 5) = 67$. Now we can use the formula

$$\text{sum}(y, x) = \max(\text{sum}(y, x - 1), \text{sum}(y - 1, x)) + \text{value}[y][x],$$

which is based on the observation that a path that ends at square (y, x) can come
either from square $(y, x - 1)$ or from square $(y - 1, x)$ (Fig. 6.3). Thus, we select
the direction that maximizes the sum. We assume that sum$(y, x) = 0$ if $y = 0$ or
$x = 0$, so the recursive formula also works for leftmost and topmost squares.

---

[2]In this problem, it is also possible to calculate the dynamic programming values more efficiently
in $O(n \log n)$ time. Can you find a way to do this?.

Fig. 6.3 Two possible ways
to reach a square on a path

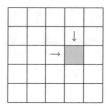

Since the function sum has two parameters, the dynamic programming array also
has two dimensions. For example, we can use an array

```
int sum[N][N];
```

and calculate the sums as follows:

```
for (int y = 1; y <= n; y++) {
    for (int x = 1; x <= n; x++) {
        sum[y][x] = max(sum[y][x-1],sum[y-1][x])+value[y][x];
    }
}
```

The time complexity of the algorithm is $O(n^2)$.

6.2.3 Knapsack Problems

The term *knapsack* refers to problems where a set of objects is given, and subsets
with some properties have to be found. Knapsack problems can often be solved using
dynamic programming.

In this section, we focus on the following problem: Given a list of weights
$[w_1, w_2, \ldots, w_n]$, determine all sums that can be constructed using the weights.
For example, Fig. 6.4 shows the possible sums for weights $[1, 3, 3, 5]$. In this case,
all sums between $0 \ldots 12$ are possible, except 2 and 10. For example, the sum 7 is
possible because we can choose the weights $[1, 3, 3]$.

To solve the problem, we focus on subproblems where we only use the first k
weights to construct sums. Let possible$(x, k) = $ true if we can construct a sum
x using the first k weights, and otherwise possible$(x, k) = $ false. The values
of the function can be recursively calculated using the formula

$$\text{possible}(x, k) = \text{possible}(x - w_k, k - 1) \text{ or possible}(x, k - 1),$$

Fig. 6.4 Constructing sums
using the weights $[1, 3, 3, 5]$

0	1	2	3	4	5	6	7	8	9	10	11	12
✓	✓		✓	✓	✓	✓	✓	✓	✓		✓	✓

Fig. 6.5 Solving the knapsack problem for the weights [1, 3, 3, 5] using dynamic programming

	0	1	2	3	4	5	6	7	8	9	10	11	12
$k=0$	✓												
$k=1$	✓	✓											
$k=2$	✓	✓		✓	✓								
$k=3$	✓	✓		✓	✓		✓	✓					
$k=4$	✓	✓		✓	✓	✓	✓	✓	✓	✓		✓	✓

which is based on the fact that we can either use or not use the weight w_k in the sum. If we use w_k, the remaining task is to form the sum $x - w_k$ using the first $k - 1$ weights, and if we do not use w_k, the remaining task is to form the sum x using the first $k - 1$ weights. The base cases are

$$\texttt{possible}(x, 0) = \begin{cases} \texttt{true} & x = 0 \\ \texttt{false} & x \neq 0, \end{cases}$$

because if no weights are used, we can only form the sum 0. Finally, $\texttt{possible}(x, n)$ tells us whether we can construct a sum x using *all* weights.

Figure 6.5 shows all values of the function for the weights [1, 3, 3, 5] (the symbol "✓" indicates the $\texttt{true}$ values). For example, the row $k = 2$ tells us that we can construct the sums [0, 1, 3, 4] using the weights [1, 3].

Let m denote the total sum of the weights. The following $O(nm)$ time dynamic programming solution corresponds to the recursive function:

```
possible[0][0] = true;
for (int k = 1; k <= n; k++) {
    for (int x = 0; x <= m; x++) {
        if (x-w[k] >= 0) {
            possible[x][k] |= possible[x-w[k]][k-1];
        }
        possible[x][k] |= possible[x][k-1];
    }
}
```

It turns out that there is also a more compact way to implement the dynamic programming calculation, using only a one-dimensional array $\texttt{possible}[x]$ that indicates whether we can construct a subset with sum x. The trick is to update the array from right to left for each new weight:

```
possible[0] = true;
for (int k = 1; k <= n; k++) {
    for (int x = m-w[k]; x >= 0; x--) {
        possible[x+w[k]] |= possible[x];
    }
}
```

Note that the general dynamic programming idea presented in this section can also be used in other knapsack problems, such as in a situation where objects have weights and values and we have to find a maximum value subset whose weight does not exceed a given limit.

6.2.4 From Permutations to Subsets

Using dynamic programming, it is often possible to change an iteration over permutations into an iteration over subsets. The benefit of this is that $n!$, the number of permutations, is much larger than 2^n, the number of subsets. For example, if $n = 20$, $n! \approx 2.4 \cdot 10^{18}$ and $2^n \approx 10^6$. Thus, for certain values of n, we can efficiently go through the subsets but not through the permutations.

As an example, consider the following problem: There is an elevator with maximum weight x and n people who want to get from the ground floor to the top floor. The people are numbered $0, 1, \ldots, n - 1$, and the weight of person i is weight[i]. What is the minimum number of rides needed to get everybody to the top floor?

For example, suppose that $x = 12$, $n = 5$, and the weights are as follows:

- weight[0] = 2
- weight[1] = 3
- weight[2] = 4
- weight[3] = 5
- weight[4] = 9

In this scenario, the minimum number of rides is two. One optimal solution is as follows: first, people 0, 2, and 3 take the elevator (total weight 11), and then, people 1 and 4 take the elevator (total weight 12).

The problem can be easily solved in $O(n!n)$ time by testing all possible permutations of n people. However, we can use dynamic programming to create a more efficient $O(2^n n)$ time algorithm. The idea is to calculate for each subset of people two values: the minimum number of rides needed and the minimum weight of people who ride in the last group.

Let rides(S) denote the minimum number of rides for a subset S, and let last(S) denote the minimum weight of the last ride in a solution where the number of rides is minimum. For example, in the above scenario

$$\text{rides}(\{3, 4\}) = 2 \text{ and } \text{last}(\{3, 4\}) = 5,$$

because the optimal way for people 3 and 4 to get to the top floor is that they take two separate rides and person 4 goes first, which minimizes the weight of the second ride. Of course, our final goal is to calculate the value of $\texttt{rides}(\{0 \ldots n - 1\})$.

We can calculate the values of the functions recursively and then apply dynamic programming. To calculate the values for a subset S, we go through all people who belong to S and optimally choose the last person p who enters the elevator. Each such choice yields a subproblem for a smaller subset of people. If $\texttt{last}(S \setminus p) + \texttt{weight}[p] \leq x$, we can add p to the last ride. Otherwise, we have to reserve a new ride that only contains p.

A convenient way to implement the dynamic programming calculation is to use bit operations. First, we declare an array

```
pair<int,int> best[1<<N];
```

that contains for each subset S a pair $(\texttt{rides}(S), \texttt{last}(S))$. For the empty subset, we create a single empty ride:

```
best[0] = {1,0};
```

Then, we can fill the array as follows:

```
for (int s = 1; s < (1<<n); s++) {
    // initial value: n+1 rides are needed
    best[s] = {n+1,0};
    for (int p = 0; p < n; p++) {
        if (s&(1<<p)) {
            auto option = best[s^(1<<p)];
            if (option.second+weight[p] <= x) {
                // add p to an existing ride
                option.second += weight[p];
            } else {
                // reserve a new ride for p
                option.first++;
                option.second = weight[p];
            }
            best[s] = min(best[s], option);
        }
    }
}
```

Note that the above loop guarantees that for any two subsets S_1 and S_2 such that $S_1 \subset S_2$, we process S_1 before S_2. Thus, the dynamic programming values are calculated in the correct order.

Fig. 6.6 One way to fill the 4×7 grid using 1×2 and 2×1 tiles

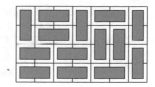

6.2.5   Counting Tilings

Sometimes the states of a dynamic programming solution are more complex than fixed combinations of values. As an example, consider the problem of calculating the number of distinct ways to fill an $n \times m$ grid using 1×2 and 2×1 size tiles. For example, there are a total of 781 ways to fill the 4×7 grid, one of them being the solution shown in Fig. 6.6.

The problem can be solved using dynamic programming by going through the grid row by row. Each row in a solution can be represented as a string that contains m characters from the set {⊓, ⊔, ⊏, ⊐}. For example, the solution in Fig. 6.6 consists of four rows that correspond to the following strings:

- ⊓⊏⊐⊓⊏⊐⊓
- ⊔⊏⊐⊔⊓⊓⊔
- ⊏⊐⊏⊐⊔⊔⊓
- ⊏⊐⊏⊐⊏⊐⊔

Suppose that the rows of the grid are indexed from 1 to n. Let $\text{count}(k, x)$ denote the number of ways to construct a solution for rows $1 \ldots k$ such that string x corresponds to row k. It is possible to use dynamic programming here, because the state of a row is constrained only by the state of the previous row.

A solution is valid if row 1 does not contain the character ⊔, row n does not contain the character ⊓, and all consecutive rows are compatible. For example, the rows ⊔⊏⊐⊔⊓⊓⊔ and ⊏⊐⊏⊐⊔⊔⊓ are compatible, while the rows ⊓⊏⊐⊓⊏⊐⊓ and ⊏⊐⊏⊐⊏⊐⊔ are not compatible.

Since a row consists of m characters and there are four choices for each character, the number of distinct rows is at most 4^m. We can go through the $O(4^m)$ possible states for each row, and for each state, there are $O(4^m)$ possible states for the previous row, so the time complexity of the solution is $O(n4^{2m})$. In practice, it is a good idea to rotate the grid so that the shorter side has length m, because the factor 4^{2m} dominates the time complexity.

It is possible to make the solution more efficient by using a more compact representation for the rows. It turns out that it suffices to know which columns of the previous row contain the upper square of a vertical tile. Thus, we can represent a row using only the characters ⊓ and □, where □ is a combination of the characters ⊔, ⊏, and ⊐. Using this representation, there are only 2^m distinct rows and the time complexity is $O(n2^{2m})$.

As a final note, there is also a direct formula for calculating the number of tilings:

$$\prod_{a=1}^{\lceil n/2 \rceil} \prod_{b=1}^{\lceil m/2 \rceil} 4 \cdot \left(\cos^2 \frac{\pi a}{n+1} + \cos^2 \frac{\pi b}{m+1} \right)$$

This formula is very efficient, because it calculates the number of tilings in $O(nm)$ time, but since the answer is a product of real numbers, a problem when using the formula is how to store the intermediate results accurately.

Graph Algorithms

7

Many programming problems can be solved by considering the situation as a graph and using an appropriate graph algorithm. In this chapter, we will learn the basics of graphs and a selection of important graph algorithms.

Section 7.1 discusses graph terminology and data structures that can be used to represent graphs in algorithms.

Section 7.2 introduces two fundamental graph traversal algorithms. Depth-first search is a simple way to visit all nodes that can be reached from a starting node, and breadth-first search visits the nodes in increasing order of their distance from the starting node.

Section 7.3 presents algorithms for finding shortest paths in weighted graphs. The Bellman–Ford algorithm is a simple algorithm that finds shortest paths from a starting node to all other nodes. Dijkstra's algorithm is a more efficient algorithm which requires that all edge weights are nonnegative. The Floyd–Warshall algorithm determines shortest paths between all node pairs of a graph.

Section 7.4 explores special properties of directed acyclic graphs. We will learn how to construct a topological sort and how to use dynamic programming to efficiently process such graphs.

Section 7.5 focuses on successor graphs where each node has a unique successor. We will discuss an efficient way to find successors of nodes and Floyd's algorithm for cycle detection.

Section 7.6 presents Kruskal's and Prim's algorithms for constructing minimum spanning trees. Kruskal's algorithm is based on an efficient union-find structure which has also other uses in algorithm design.

© Springer Nature Switzerland AG 2020

A. Laaksonen, *Guide to Competitive Programming*, Undergraduate Topics in Computer Science, https://doi.org/10.1007/978-3-030-39357-1_7

7.1 Basics of Graphs

In this section, we first go through terminology which is used when discussing graphs and their properties. After this, we focus on data structures that can be used to represent graphs in algorithm programming.

7.1.1 Graph Terminology

A *graph* consists of *nodes* (also called *vertices*) that are connected with *edges*. In this book, the variable n denotes the number of nodes in a graph, and the variable m denotes the number of edges. The nodes are numbered using integers $1, 2, \ldots, n$. For example, Fig. 7.1 shows a graph with 5 nodes and 7 edges.

A *path* leads from a node to another node through the edges of the graph. The *length* of a path is the number of edges in it. For example, Fig. 7.2 shows a path $1 \rightarrow 3 \rightarrow 4 \rightarrow 5$ of length 3 from node 1 to node 5. A *cycle* is a path where the first and last node is the same. For example, Fig. 7.3 shows a cycle $1 \rightarrow 3 \rightarrow 4 \rightarrow 1$.

A graph is *connected* if there is a path between any two nodes. In Fig. 7.4, the left graph is connected, but the right graph is not connected, because it is not possible to get from node 4 to any other node.

The connected parts of a graph are called its *components*. For example, the graph in Fig. 7.5 has three components: $\{1, 2, 3\}$, $\{4, 5, 6, 7\}$, and $\{8\}$.

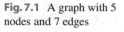

Fig. 7.1 A graph with 5 nodes and 7 edges

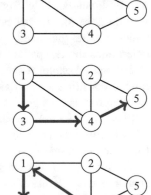

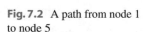

Fig. 7.2 A path from node 1 to node 5

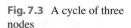

Fig. 7.3 A cycle of three nodes

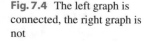

Fig. 7.4 The left graph is connected, the right graph is not

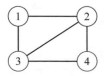
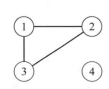

Fig. 7.5 Graph with three components

Fig. 7.6 A tree

Fig. 7.7 Directed graph

Fig. 7.8 Weighted graph

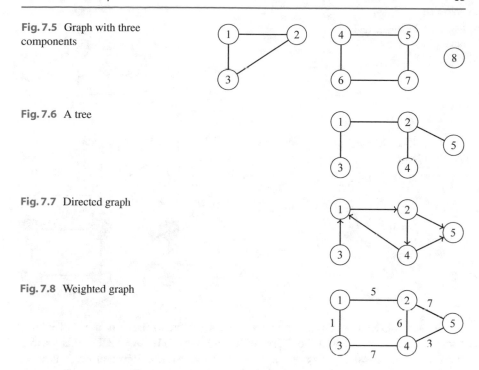

A *tree* is a connected graph that does not contain cycles. Figure 7.6 shows an example of a graph that is a tree.

In a *directed* graph, the edges can be traversed in one direction only. Figure 7.7 shows an example of a directed graph. This graph contains a path $3 \rightarrow 1 \rightarrow 2 \rightarrow 5$ from node 3 to node 5, but there is no path from node 5 to node 3.

In a *weighted* graph, each edge is assigned a *weight*. The weights are often interpreted as edge lengths, and the length of a path is the sum of its edge weights. For example, the graph in Fig. 7.8 is weighted, and the length of the path $1 \rightarrow 3 \rightarrow 4 \rightarrow 5$ is $1 + 7 + 3 = 11$. This is the *shortest* path from node 1 to node 5.

Two nodes are *neighbors* or *adjacent* if there is an edge between them. The *degree* of a node is the number of its neighbors. Figure 7.9 shows the degree of each node of a graph. For example, the degree of node 2 is 3, because its neighbors are 1, 4, and 5.

Fig. 7.9 Degrees of nodes

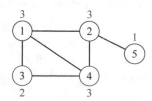

Fig. 7.10 Indegrees and outdegrees

Fig. 7.11 Bipartite graph and its coloring

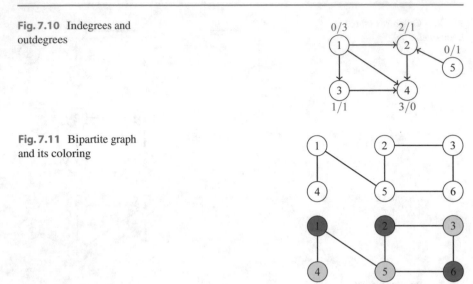

The sum of degrees in a graph is always $2m$, where m is the number of edges, because each edge increases the degree of exactly two nodes by one. For this reason, the sum of degrees is always even. A graph is *regular* if the degree of every node is a constant d. A graph is *complete* if the degree of every node is $n - 1$; i.e., the graph contains all possible edges between the nodes.

In a directed graph, the *indegree* of a node is the number of edges that end at the node, and the *outdegree* of a node is the number of edges that start at the node. Figure 7.10 shows the indegree and outdegree of each node of a graph. For example, node 2 has indegree 2 and outdegree 1.

A graph is *bipartite* if it is possible to color its nodes using two colors in such a way that no adjacent nodes have the same color. It turns out that a graph is bipartite exactly when it does not have a cycle with an odd number of edges. For example, Fig. 7.11 shows a bipartite graph and its coloring.

7.1.2   Graph Representation

There are several ways to represent graphs in algorithms. The choice of a data structure depends on the size of the graph and the way the algorithm processes it. Next we will go through three popular representations.

Adjacency Lists In the adjacency list representation, each node x of the graph is assigned an *adjacency list* that consists of nodes to which there is an edge from x. Adjacency lists are the most popular way to represent graphs, and most algorithms can be efficiently implemented using them.

Fig. 7.12 Example graphs

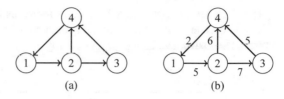

A convenient way to store the adjacency lists is to declare an array of vectors as follows:

```
vector<int> adj[N];
```

The constant N is chosen so that all adjacency lists can be stored. For example, the graph in Fig. 7.12a can be stored as follows:

```
adj[1].push_back(2);
adj[2].push_back(3);
adj[2].push_back(4);
adj[3].push_back(4);
adj[4].push_back(1);
```

If the graph is undirected, it can be stored in a similar way, but each edge is added in both directions.

For a weighted graph, the structure can be extended as follows:

```
vector<pair<int,int>> adj[N];
```

In this case, the adjacency list of node a contains the pair (b, w) always when there is an edge from node a to node b with weight w. For example, the graph in Fig. 7.12b can be stored as follows:

```
adj[1].push_back({2,5});
adj[2].push_back({3,7});
adj[2].push_back({4,6});
adj[3].push_back({4,5});
adj[4].push_back({1,2});
```

Using adjacency lists, we can efficiently find the nodes to which we can move from a given node through an edge. For example, the following loop goes through all nodes to which we can move from node s:

```
for (auto u : adj[s]) {
    // process node u
}
```

Adjacency Matrix An *adjacency matrix* indicates the edges that a graph contains. We can efficiently check from an adjacency matrix if there is an edge between two nodes. The matrix can be stored as an array

```
int adj[N][N];
```

where each value $adj[a][b]$ indicates whether the graph contains an edge from node a to node b. If the edge is included in the graph, then $adj[a][b] = 1$, and otherwise, $adj[a][b] = 0$. For example, the adjacency matrix for the graph in Fig. 7.12a is

$$\begin{bmatrix} 0 & 1 & 0 & 0 \\ 0 & 0 & 1 & 1 \\ 0 & 0 & 0 & 1 \\ 1 & 0 & 0 & 0 \end{bmatrix}.$$

If the graph is weighted, the adjacency matrix representation can be extended so that the matrix contains the weight of the edge if the edge exists. Using this representation, the graph in Fig. 7.12b corresponds to the following matrix:

$$\begin{bmatrix} 0 & 5 & 0 & 0 \\ 0 & 0 & 7 & 6 \\ 0 & 0 & 0 & 5 \\ 2 & 0 & 0 & 0 \end{bmatrix}$$

The drawback of the adjacency matrix representation is that an adjacency matrix contains n^2 elements, and usually most of them are zero. For this reason, the representation cannot be used if the graph is large.

Edge List An *edge list* contains all edges of a graph in some order. This is a convenient way to represent a graph if the algorithm processes all its edges, and it is not needed to find edges that start at a given node.

The edge list can be stored in a vector

```
vector<pair<int,int>> edges;
```

where each pair (a, b) denotes that there is an edge from node a to node b. Thus, the graph in Fig. 7.12a can be represented as follows:

```
edges.push_back({1,2});
edges.push_back({2,3});
edges.push_back({2,4});
edges.push_back({3,4});
edges.push_back({4,1});
```

If the graph is weighted, the structure can be extended as follows:

```
vector<tuple<int,int,int>> edges;
```

Each element in this list is of the form (a, b, w), which means that there is an edge from node a to node b with weight w. For example, the graph in Fig. 7.12b can be represented as follows[1]:

```
edges.push_back({1,2,5});
edges.push_back({2,3,7});
edges.push_back({2,4,6});
edges.push_back({3,4,5});
edges.push_back({4,1,2});
```

7.2 Graph Traversal

This section discusses two fundamental graph algorithms: depth-first search and breadth-first search. Both algorithms are given a starting node in the graph, and they visit all nodes that can be reached from the starting node. The difference in the algorithms is the order in which they visit the nodes.

7.2.1 Depth-First Search

Depth-first search (DFS) is a straightforward graph traversal technique. The algorithm begins at a starting node, and proceeds to all other nodes that are reachable from the starting node using the edges of the graph.

Depth-first search always follows a single path in the graph as long as it finds new nodes. After this, it returns to previous nodes and begins to explore other parts of the graph. The algorithm keeps track of visited nodes, so that it processes each node only once.

Figure 7.13 shows how depth-first search processes a graph. The search can begin at any node of the graph; in this example, we begin the search at node 1. First, the search explores the path $1 \rightarrow 2 \rightarrow 3 \rightarrow 5$, then returns back to node 1 and visits the remaining node 4.

Implementation Depth-first search can be conveniently implemented using recursion. The following function dfs begins a depth-first search at a given node. The function assumes that the graph is stored as adjacency lists in an array

---

[1] In some older compilers, the function make_tuple must be used instead of the braces (for example, make_tuple(1,2,5) instead of {1,2,5}).

Fig. 7.13 Depth-first search

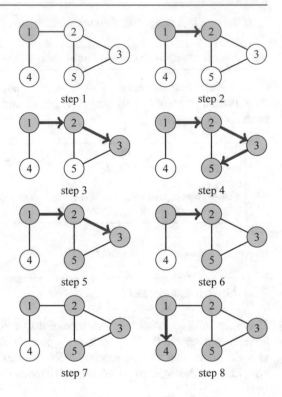

step 1   step 2

step 3   step 4

step 5   step 6

step 7   step 8

```
vector<int> adj[N];
```

and also maintains an array

```
bool visited[N];
```

that keeps track of the visited nodes. Initially, each array value is `false`, and when
the search arrives at node *s*, the value of visited[*s*] becomes `true`. The function
can be implemented as follows:

```
void dfs(int s) {
    if (visited[s]) return;
    visited[s] = true;
    // process node s
    for (auto u: adj[s]) {
        dfs(u);
    }
}
```

The time complexity of depth-first search is $O(n + m)$ where n is the number of nodes and m is the number of edges, because the algorithm processes each node and edge once.

7.2.2   Breadth-First Search

Breadth-first search (BFS) visits the nodes of a graph in increasing order of their distance from the starting node. Thus, we can calculate the distance from the starting node to all other nodes using breadth-first search. However, breadth-first search is more difficult to implement than depth-first search.

Breadth-first search goes through the nodes one level after another. First, the search explores the nodes whose distance from the starting node is 1, then the nodes whose distance is 2, and so on. This process continues until all nodes have been visited.

Figure 7.14 shows how breadth-first search processes a graph. Suppose that the search begins at node 1. First the search visits nodes 2 and 4 with distance 1, then nodes 3 and 5 with distance 2, and finally node 6 with distance 3.

Implementation Breadth-first search is more difficult to implement than depth-first search, because the algorithm visits nodes in different parts of the graph. A typical implementation is based on a queue that contains nodes. At each step, the next node in the queue will be processed.

The following code assumes that the graph is stored as adjacency lists and maintains the following data structures:

```
queue<int> q;
bool visited[N];
int distance[N];
```

The queue q contains nodes to be processed in increasing order of their distance. New nodes are always added to the end of the queue, and the node at the beginning of the queue is the next node to be processed. The array visited indicates which

Fig. 7.14 Breadth-first search

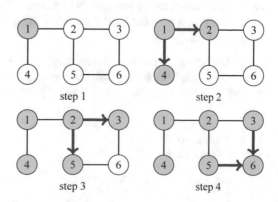

nodes the search has already visited, and the array `distance` will contain the distances from the starting node to all nodes of the graph.

The search can be implemented as follows, starting at node x:

```
visited[x] = true;
distance[x] = 0;
q.push(x);
while (!q.empty()) {
    int s = q.front(); q.pop();
    // process node s
    for (auto u : adj[s]) {
        if (visited[u]) continue;
        visited[u] = true;
        distance[u] = distance[s]+1;
        q.push(u);
    }
}
```

Like in depth-first search, the time complexity of breadth-first search is $O(n + m)$, where n is the number of nodes and m is the number of edges.

7.2.3   Applications

Using the graph traversal algorithms, we can check many properties of graphs. Usually, both depth-first search and breadth-first search may be used, but in practice, depth-first search is a better choice, because it is easier to implement. In the applications described below, we will assume that the graph is undirected.

Connectivity Check A graph is connected if there is a path between any two nodes of the graph. Thus, we can check if a graph is connected by starting at an arbitrary node and finding out if we can reach all other nodes.

For example, in Fig. 7.15, since a depth-first search from node 1 does not visit all the nodes, we can conclude that the graph is not connected. In a similar way, we can also find all connected components of a graph by iterating through the nodes and always starting a new depth-first search if the current node does not belong to any component yet.

Cycle Detection A graph contains a cycle if during a graph traversal, we find a node whose neighbor (other than the previous node in the current path) has already been visited. For example, in Fig. 7.16, a depth-first search from node 1 reveals that

Fig. 7.15 Checking the connectivity of a graph

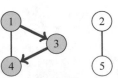

Fig. 7.16 Finding a cycle in
a graph

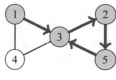

Fig. 7.17 Conflict when
checking bipartiteness

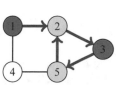

the graph contains a cycle. After moving from node 2 to node 5, we notice that the
neighbor 3 of node 5 has already been visited. Thus, the graph contains a cycle that
goes through node 3, for example, $3 \rightarrow 2 \rightarrow 5 \rightarrow 3$.

Another way to determine if a graph contains a cycle is to simply calculate the
number of nodes and edges in every component. If a component contains c nodes
and no cycle, it must contain exactly $c - 1$ edges (so it has to be a tree). If there are
c or more edges, the component surely contains a cycle.

Bipartiteness Check A graph is bipartite if its nodes can be colored using two colors
so that there are no adjacent nodes with the same color. It is surprisingly easy to check
if a graph is bipartite using graph traversal algorithms.

The idea is to pick two colors X and Y, color the starting node X, all its neighbors
Y, all their neighbors X, and so on. If at some point of the search we notice that
two adjacent nodes have the same color, this means that the graph is not bipartite.
Otherwise, the graph is bipartite and one coloring has been found.

For example, in Fig. 7.17, a depth-first search from node 1 shows that the graph is
not bipartite, because we notice that both nodes 2 and 5 should have the same color,
while they are adjacent nodes in the graph.

This algorithm always works, because when there are only two colors available,
the color of the starting node in a component determines the colors of all other nodes
in the component. It does not make any difference what the colors are.

Note that in the general case it is difficult to find out if the nodes in a graph can be
colored using k colors so that no adjacent nodes have the same color. The problem
is NP-hard already for $k = 3$.

7.3   Shortest Paths

Finding a shortest path between two nodes of a graph is an important problem that
has many practical applications. For example, a natural problem related to a road
network is to calculate the shortest possible length of a route between two cities,
given the lengths of the roads.

In an unweighted graph, the length of a path equals the number of its edges, and we can simply use breadth-first search to find a shortest path. However, in this section, we focus on weighted graphs where more sophisticated algorithms are needed for finding shortest paths.

7.3.1   Bellman–Ford Algorithm

The *Bellman–Ford algorithm* finds shortest paths from a starting node to all nodes of the graph. The algorithm can process all kinds of graphs, provided that the graph does not contain a cycle with negative length. If the graph contains a negative cycle, the algorithm can detect this.

The algorithm keeps track of distances from the starting node to all nodes of the graph. Initially, the distance to the starting node is 0 and the distance to any other node in infinite. The algorithm then reduces the distances by finding edges that shorten the paths until it is not possible to reduce any distance.

Figure 7.18 shows how the Bellman–Ford algorithm processes a graph. First, the algorithm reduces distances using the edges $1 \rightarrow 2$, $1 \rightarrow 3$ and $1 \rightarrow 4$, then using the edges $2 \rightarrow 5$ and $3 \rightarrow 4$, and finally using the edge $4 \rightarrow 5$. After this, no edge can be used to reduce distances, which means that the distances are final.

Implementation The implementation of the Bellman–Ford algorithm below determines the shortest distances from a node x to all nodes of the graph. The code assumes that the graph is stored as an edge list `edges` that consists of tuples of the form (a, b, w), meaning that there is an edge from node a to node b with weight w.

The algorithm consists of $n - 1$ rounds, and on each round, the algorithm goes through all edges of the graph and attempts to reduce the distances. The algorithm

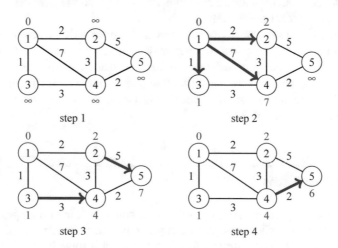

Fig. 7.18 The Bellman–Ford algorithm

constructs an array `distance` that will contain the distances from node x to all nodes. The constant `INF` denotes an infinite distance.

```
for (int i = 1; i <= n; i++) {
    distance[i] = INF;
}
distance[x] = 0;
for (int i = 1; i <= n-1; i++) {
    for (auto e : edges) {
        int a, b, w;
        tie(a, b, w) = e;
        distance[b] = min(distance[b], distance[a]+w);
    }
}
```

The time complexity of the algorithm is $O(nm)$, because the algorithm consists of $n-1$ rounds and iterates through all m edges during a round. If there are no negative cycles in the graph, all distances are final after $n-1$ rounds, because each shortest path can contain at most $n-1$ edges.

There are several ways to optimize the algorithm in practice. First, the final distances can usually be found earlier than after $n-1$ rounds, so we can simply stop the algorithm if no distance can be reduced during a round. A more advanced variant is the *SPFA algorithm* ("Shortest Path Faster Algorithm" [10]) which maintains a queue of nodes that might be used for reducing the distances. Only the nodes in the queue will be processed, which often yields a more efficient search.

Negative Cycles The Bellman–Ford algorithm can also be used to check if the graph contains a cycle with negative length. In this case, any path that contains the cycle can be shortened infinitely many times, so the concept of a shortest path is not meaningful. For example, the graph in Fig. 7.19 contains a negative cycle $2 \rightarrow 3 \rightarrow 4 \rightarrow 2$ with length -4.

A negative cycle can be detected using the Bellman–Ford algorithm by running the algorithm for n rounds. If the last round reduces any distance, the graph contains a negative cycle. Note that this algorithm can be used to search for a negative cycle in the entire graph regardless of the starting node.

Fig. 7.19 A graph with a negative cycle

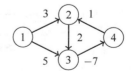

7.3.2 Dijkstra's Algorithm

Dijkstra's algorithm finds shortest paths from the starting node to all nodes of the graph, like the Bellman–Ford algorithm. The benefit of Dijkstra's algorithm is that it is more efficient and can be used for processing large graphs. However, the algorithm requires that there are no negative weight edges in the graph.

Like the Bellman–Ford algorithm, Dijkstra's algorithm maintains distances to the nodes and reduces them during the search. At each step, Dijkstra's algorithm selects a node that has not been processed yet and whose distance is as small as possible. Then, the algorithm goes through all edges that start at the node and reduces the distances using them. Dijkstra's algorithm is efficient, because it only processes each edge in the graph once, using the fact that there are no negative edges.

Figure 7.20 shows how Dijkstra's algorithm processes a graph. Like in the Bellman–Ford algorithm, the initial distance to all nodes, except for the starting node, is infinite. The algorithm processes the nodes in the order 1, 5, 4, 2, 3, and at each node reduces distances using edges that start at the node. Note that the distance to a node never changes after processing the node.

Implementation An efficient implementation of Dijkstra's algorithm requires that we can efficiently find the minimum distance node that has not been processed. An appropriate data structure for this is a priority queue that contains the remaining nodes ordered by their distances. Using a priority queue, the next node to be processed can be retrieved in logarithmic time.

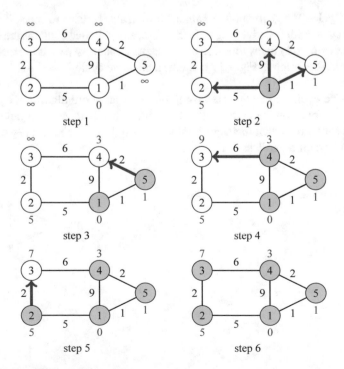

Fig. 7.20 Dijkstra's algorithm

A typical textbook implementation of Dijkstra's algorithm uses a priority queue that has an operation for modifying a value in the queue. This allows us to have a single instance of each node in the queue and update its distance when needed. However, standard library priority queues do not provide such an operation, and a somewhat different implementation is usually used in competitive programming. The idea is to add a new instance of a node to the priority queue always when its distance changes.

Our implementation of Dijkstra's algorithm calculates the minimum distances from a node x to all other nodes of the graph. The graph is stored as adjacency lists so that $\texttt{adj}[a]$ contains a pair (b, w) always when there is an edge from node a to node b with weight w. The priority queue

```
priority_queue<pair<int,int>> q;
```

contains pairs of the form $(-d, x)$, meaning that the current distance to node x is d. The array $\texttt{distance}$ contains the distance to each node, and the array $\texttt{processed}$ indicates whether a node has been processed.

Note that the priority queue contains *negative* distances to nodes. The reason for this is that the default version of the C++ priority queue finds maximum elements, while we want to find minimum elements. By exploiting negative distances, we can directly use the default priority queue.[2] Also note that while there may be several instances of a node in the priority queue, only the instance with the minimum distance will be processed.

The implementation is as follows:

```
for (int i = 1; i <= n; i++) {
    distance[i] = INF;
}
distance[x] = 0;
q.push({0,x});
while (!q.empty()) {
    int a = q.top().second; q.pop();
    if (processed[a]) continue;
    processed[a] = true;
    for (auto u : adj[a]) {
        int b = u.first, w = u.second;
        if (distance[a]+w < distance[b]) {
            distance[b] = distance[a]+w;
            q.push({-distance[b],b});
        }
    }
}
```

---

[2] Of course, we could also declare the priority queue as in Sect. 5.2.3 and use positive distances, but the implementation would be longer.

Fig. 7.21 Graph where
Dijkstra's algorithm fails

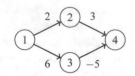

Fig. 7.22 Input for the
Floyd–Warshall algorithm

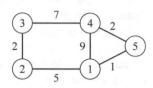

The time complexity of the above implementation is $O(n + m \log m)$, because the algorithm goes through all nodes of the graph and adds for each edge at most one distance to the priority queue.

Negative Edges The efficiency of Dijkstra's algorithm is based on the fact that the graph does not have negative edges. However, if the graph has a negative edge, the algorithm may give incorrect results. As an example, consider the graph in Fig. 7.21. The shortest path from node 1 to node 4 is $1 \rightarrow 3 \rightarrow 4$, and its length is 1. However, Dijkstra's algorithm incorrectly finds the path $1 \rightarrow 2 \rightarrow 4$ by greedily following minimum weight edges.

7.3.3 Floyd–Warshall Algorithm

The *Floyd–Warshall algorithm* provides an alternative way to approach the problem of finding shortest paths. Unlike the other algorithms in this chapter, it finds shortest paths between all node pairs of the graph in a single run.

The algorithm maintains a matrix that contains distances between the nodes. The initial matrix is directly constructed based on the adjacency matrix of the graph. Then, the algorithm consists of consecutive rounds, and on each round, it selects a new node that can act as an intermediate node in paths from now on, and reduces distances using this node.

Let us simulate the Floyd–Warshall algorithm for the graph in Fig. 7.22. In this case, the initial matrix is as follows:

$$
\begin{bmatrix}
0 & 5 & \infty & 9 & 1 \\
5 & 0 & 2 & \infty & \infty \\
\infty & 2 & 0 & 7 & \infty \\
9 & \infty & 7 & 0 & 2 \\
1 & \infty & \infty & 2 & 0
\end{bmatrix}
$$

Fig. 7.23 Shortest path from
node 2 to node 4

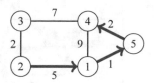

On the first round, node 1 is the new intermediate node. There is a new path
between nodes 2 and 4 with length 14, because node 1 connects them. There is also
a new path between nodes 2 and 5 with length 6.

$$
\begin{bmatrix}
0 & 5 & \infty & 9 & 1 \\
5 & 0 & 2 & \mathbf{14} & \mathbf{6} \\
\infty & 2 & 0 & 7 & \infty \\
9 & \mathbf{14} & 7 & 0 & 2 \\
1 & \mathbf{6} & \infty & 2 & 0
\end{bmatrix}
$$

On the second round, node 2 is the new intermediate node. This creates new paths
between nodes 1 and 3 and between nodes 3 and 5:

$$
\begin{bmatrix}
0 & 5 & \mathbf{7} & 9 & 1 \\
5 & 0 & 2 & 14 & 6 \\
\mathbf{7} & 2 & 0 & 7 & \mathbf{8} \\
9 & 14 & 7 & 0 & 2 \\
1 & 6 & \mathbf{8} & 2 & 0
\end{bmatrix}
$$

The algorithm continues like this, until all nodes have been appointed intermediate
nodes. After the algorithm has finished, the matrix contains the minimum distances
between any two nodes:

$$
\begin{bmatrix}
0 & 5 & 7 & 3 & 1 \\
5 & 0 & 2 & 8 & 6 \\
7 & 2 & 0 & 7 & 8 \\
3 & 8 & 7 & 0 & 2 \\
1 & 6 & 8 & 2 & 0
\end{bmatrix}
$$

For example, the matrix tells us that the shortest distance between nodes 2 and 4
is 8. This corresponds to the path in Fig. 7.23.

Implementation The Floyd–Warshall algorithm is particularly easy to implement.
The implementation below constructs a distance matrix where `dist[a][b]` denotes
the shortest distance between nodes a and b. First, the algorithm initializes `dist`
using the adjacency matrix `adj` of the graph:

```
for (int i = 1; i <= n; i++) {
    for (int j = 1; j <= n; j++) {
        if (i == j) dist[i][j] = 0;
        else if (adj[i][j]) dist[i][j] = adj[i][j];
        else dist[i][j] = INF;
    }
}
```

After this, the shortest distances can be found as follows:

```
for (int k = 1; k <= n; k++) {
    for (int i = 1; i <= n; i++) {
        for (int j = 1; j <= n; j++) {
            dist[i][j] = min(dist[i][j],dist[i][k]+dist[k][j]);
        }
    }
}
```

The time complexity of the algorithm is $O(n^3)$, because it contains three nested loops that go through the nodes of the graph.

Since the implementation of the Floyd–Warshall algorithm is simple, the algorithm can be a good choice even if it is only needed to find a *single* shortest path in the graph. However, the algorithm can only be used when the graph is so small that a cubic time complexity is fast enough.

7.4 Directed Acyclic Graphs

An important class of graphs is *directed acyclic graphs*, also called *DAGs*. Such graphs do not contain cycles, and many problems are easier to solve if we may assume that this is the case. In particular, we can always construct a topological sort for the graph and then apply dynamic programming.

7.4.1 Topological Sorting

A *topological sort* is an ordering of the nodes of a directed graph such that if there is a path from node a to node b, then node a appears before node b in the ordering. For example, in Fig. 7.24, one possible topological sort is [4, 1, 5, 2, 3, 6].

A directed graph has a topological sort exactly when it is acyclic. If the graph contains a cycle, it is not possible to form a topological sort, because no node of the cycle can appear before the other nodes of the cycle in the ordering. It turns out that depth-first search can be used to both check if a directed graph contains a cycle and, if it does not, to construct a topological sort.

Fig. 7.24 Graph and a
topological sort

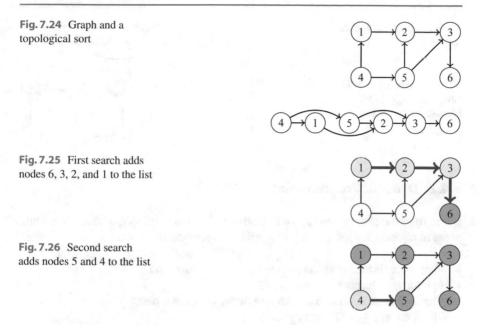

Fig. 7.25 First search adds
nodes 6, 3, 2, and 1 to the list

Fig. 7.26 Second search
adds nodes 5 and 4 to the list

The idea is to go through the nodes of the graph and always begin a depth-first search at the current node if it has not been processed yet. During the searches, the nodes have three possible states:

- state 0: the node has not been processed (white)
- state 1: the node is under processing (light gray)
- state 2: the node has been processed (dark gray)

Initially, the state of each node is 0. When a search reaches a node for the first time, its state becomes 1. Finally, after all edges from the node have been processed, its state becomes 2.

If the graph contains a cycle, we will discover this during the search, because sooner or later we will arrive at a node whose state is 1. In this case, it is not possible to construct a topological sort. If the graph does not contain a cycle, we can construct a topological sort by adding each node to a list when its state becomes 2. Finally, we reverse the list and get a topological sort for the graph.

Now we are ready to construct a topological sort for our example graph. The first search (Fig. 7.25) proceeds from node 1 to node 6, and adds nodes 6, 3, 2, and 1 to the list. Then, the second search (Fig. 7.26) proceeds from node 4 to node 5 and adds nodes 5 and 4 to the list. The final reversed list is [4, 5, 1, 2, 3, 6], which corresponds to a topological sort (Fig. 7.27). Note that a topological sort is not unique; there can be several topological sorts for a graph.

Figure 7.28 shows a graph that does not have a topological sort. During the search, we reach node 2 whose state is 1, which means that the graph contains a cycle. Indeed, there is a cycle $2 \rightarrow 3 \rightarrow 5 \rightarrow 2$.

Fig. 7.27 Final topological sort

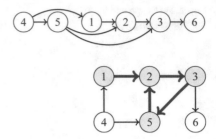

Fig. 7.28 Graph does not have a topological sort, because it contains a cycle

7.4.2 Dynamic Programming

Using dynamic programming, we can efficiently answer many questions regarding paths in directed acyclic graphs. Examples of such questions are:

- What is the shortest/longest path from node a to node b?
- How many different paths are there?
- What is the minimum/maximum number of edges in a path?
- Which nodes appear in every possible path?

Note that many of the above problems are difficult to solve or not well-defined for general graphs.

As an example, consider the problem of calculating the number of paths from node a to node b. Let $\texttt{paths}(x)$ denote the number of paths from node a to node x. As a base case, $\texttt{paths}(a) = 1$. Then, to calculate other values of $\texttt{paths}(x)$, we can use the recursive formula

$$\texttt{paths}(x) = \texttt{paths}(s_1) + \texttt{paths}(s_2) + \cdots + \texttt{paths}(s_k),$$

where $s_1, s_2, \ldots, s_k$ are the nodes from which there is an edge to x. Since the graph is acyclic, the values of $\texttt{paths}$ can be calculated in the order of a topological sort.

Figure 7.29 shows the values of $\texttt{paths}$ in an example scenario where we want to calculate the number of paths from node 1 to node 6. For example,

$$\texttt{paths}(6) = \texttt{paths}(2) + \texttt{paths}(3),$$

because the edges that end at node 6 are $2 \to 6$ and $3 \to 6$. Since $\texttt{paths}(2) = 2$ and $\texttt{paths}(3) = 2$, we conclude that $\texttt{paths}(6) = 4$. The paths are as follows:

- $1 \to 2 \to 3 \to 6$
- $1 \to 2 \to 6$
- $1 \to 4 \to 5 \to 2 \to 3 \to 6$
- $1 \to 4 \to 5 \to 2 \to 6$

Fig. 7.29 Calculating the number of paths from node 1 to node 6

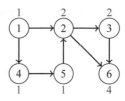

Fig. 7.30 Graph and its shortest paths graph

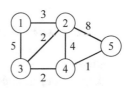

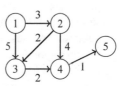

Fig. 7.31 Coin problem as a directed acyclic graph

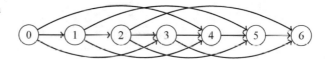

Processing Shortest Paths Dynamic programming can also be used to answer questions regarding *shortest* paths in general (not necessarily acyclic) graphs. Namely, if we know minimum distances from a starting node to other nodes (for example, after using Dijkstra's algorithm), we can easily create a directed acyclic *shortest paths graph* that indicates for each node the possible ways to reach the node using a shortest path from the starting node. For example, Fig. 7.30 shows a graph and the corresponding shortest paths graph.

Coin Problem Revisited In fact, *any* dynamic programming problem can be represented as directed acyclic graph where each node corresponds to a dynamic programming state and the edges indicate how the states depend on each other.

For example, consider the problem of forming a sum of money n using coins $\{c_1, c_2, \ldots, c_k\}$ (Sect. 6.1.1). In this scenario, we can construct a graph where each node corresponds to a sum of money, and the edges show how the coins can be chosen. For example, Fig. 7.31 shows the graph for the coins $\{1, 3, 4\}$ and $n = 6$. Using this representation, the shortest path from node 0 to node n corresponds to a solution with the minimum number of coins, and the total number of paths from node 0 to node n equals the total number of solutions.

Fig. 7.32 Successor graph

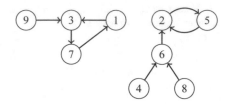

7.5 Successor Graphs

Another special class of directed graphs are *successor graphs*. In those graphs, the outdegree of each node is 1; i.e., each node has a unique *successor*. A successor graph consists of one or more components, each of which contains one cycle and some paths that lead to it.

Successor graphs are sometimes called *functional graphs*, because any successor graph corresponds to a function $\text{succ}(x)$ that defines the edges of the graph. The parameter x is a node of the graph, and the function gives the successor of the node. For example, the function

$$
\begin{array}{c|ccccccccc}
x & 1 & 2 & 3 & 4 & 5 & 6 & 7 & 8 & 9 \\
\hline
\text{succ}(x) & 3 & 5 & 7 & 6 & 2 & 2 & 1 & 6 & 3
\end{array}
$$

defines the graph in Fig. 7.32.

7.5.1 Finding Successors

Since each node of a successor graph has a unique successor, we can also define a function $\text{succ}(x, k)$ that gives the node that we will reach if we begin at node x and walk k steps forward. For example, in our example graph $\text{succ}(4, 6) = 2$, because we will reach node 2 by walking 6 steps from node 4 (Fig. 7.33).

A straightforward way to calculate a value of $\text{succ}(x, k)$ is to start at node x and walk k steps forward, which takes $O(k)$ time. However, using preprocessing, any value of $\text{succ}(x, k)$ can be calculated in only $O(\log k)$ time.

Let u denote the maximum number of steps we will ever walk. The idea is to precalculate all values of $\text{succ}(x, k)$ where k is a power of two and at most u. This can be efficiently done, because we can use the following recurrence:

$$
\text{succ}(x, k) =
\begin{cases}
\text{succ}(x) & k = 1 \\
\text{succ}(\text{succ}(x, k/2), k/2) & k > 1
\end{cases}
$$

Fig. 7.33 Walking in a successor graph

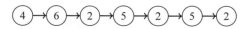

The idea is that a path of length k that begins at node x can be divided into two paths of length $k/2$. Precalculating all values of $\mathtt{succ}(x, k)$ where k is a power of two and at most u takes $O(n \log u)$ time, because $O(\log u)$ values are calculated for each node. In our example graph, the first values are as follows:

x	1 2 3 4 5 6 7 8 9
$\mathtt{succ}(x, 1)$	3 5 7 6 2 2 1 6 3
$\mathtt{succ}(x, 2)$	7 2 1 2 5 5 3 2 7
$\mathtt{succ}(x, 4)$	3 2 7 2 5 5 1 2 3
$\mathtt{succ}(x, 8)$	7 2 1 2 5 5 3 2 7
$\cdots$	

After the precalculation, any value of $\mathtt{succ}(x, k)$ can be calculated by presenting k as a sum of powers of two. Such a representation always consists of $O(\log k)$ parts, so calculating a value of $\mathtt{succ}(x, k)$ takes $O(\log k)$ time. For example, if we want to calculate the value of $\mathtt{succ}(x, 11)$, we use the formula

$$\mathtt{succ}(x, 11) = \mathtt{succ}(\mathtt{succ}(\mathtt{succ}(x, 8), 2), 1).$$

In our example graph,

$$\mathtt{succ}(4, 11) = \mathtt{succ}(\mathtt{succ}(\mathtt{succ}(4, 8), 2), 1) = 5.$$

7.5.2 Cycle Detection

Consider a successor graph that only contains a path that ends in a cycle. We may ask the following questions: if we begin our walk at the starting node, what is the first node in the cycle and how many nodes does the cycle contain? For example, in Fig. 7.34, we begin our walk at node 1, the first node that belongs to the cycle is node 4, and the cycle consists of three nodes (4, 5, and 6).

A simple way to detect the cycle is to walk in the graph and keep track of all nodes that have been visited. Once a node is visited for the second time, we can conclude that the node is the first node in the cycle. This method works in $O(n)$ time and also uses $O(n)$ memory. However, there are better algorithms for cycle detection. The time complexity of such algorithms is still $O(n)$, but they only use $O(1)$ memory, which may be an important improvement if n is large.

One such algorithm is *Floyd's algorithm*, which walks in the graph using two pointers a and b. Both pointers begin at the starting node x. Then, on each turn, the

Fig. 7.34 Cycle in a successor graph

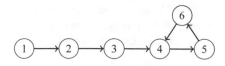

pointer a walks one step forward and the pointer b walks two steps forward. The
process continues until the pointers meet each other:

```
a = succ(x);
b = succ(succ(x));
while (a != b) {
    a = succ(a);
    b = succ(succ(b));
}
```

At this point, the pointer a has walked k steps and the pointer b has walked $2k$
steps, so the length of the cycle divides k. Thus, the first node that belongs to the
cycle can be found by moving the pointer a to node x and advancing the pointers
step by step until they meet again.

```
a = x;
while (a != b) {
    a = succ(a);
    b = succ(b);
}
first = a;
```

After this, the length of the cycle can be calculated as follows:

```
b = succ(a);
length = 1;
while (a != b) {
    b = succ(b);
    length++;
}
```

7.6 Minimum Spanning Trees

A *spanning tree* contains all nodes of a graph and some of its edges so that there is a
path between any two nodes. Like trees in general, spanning trees are connected and
acyclic. The *weight* of a spanning tree is the sum of its edge weights. For example,
Fig. 7.35 shows a graph and one of its spanning tree. The weight of this spanning
tree is $3 + 5 + 9 + 3 + 2 = 22$.

A *minimum spanning tree* is a spanning tree whose weight is as small as possible.
Figure 7.36 shows a minimum spanning tree for our example graph with weight 20.
In a similar way, a *maximum spanning tree* is a spanning tree whose weight is as large
as possible. Figure 7.37 shows a maximum spanning tree for our example graph with

Fig. 7.35 Graph and a
spanning tree

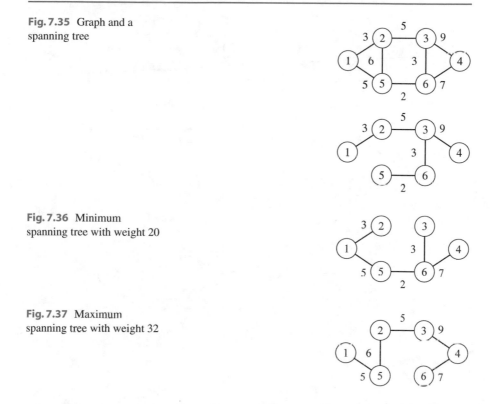

Fig. 7.36 Minimum
spanning tree with weight 20

Fig. 7.37 Maximum
spanning tree with weight 32

weight 32. Note that a graph may have several minimum and maximum spanning
trees, so the trees are not unique.

It turns out that several greedy methods can be used to construct minimum and
maximum spanning trees. This section discusses two algorithms that process the
edges of the graph ordered by their weights. We focus on finding minimum spanning
trees, but the same algorithms can also find maximum spanning trees by processing
the edges in reverse order.

7.6.1   Kruskal's Algorithm

Kruskal's algorithm builds a minimum spanning tree by greedily adding edges to a
graph that initially only contains the nodes of the original graph and no edges. The
algorithm goes through the edges of the original graph ordered by their weights and
always adds an edge to the new graph if the edge does not create a cycle.

The algorithm maintains the components of the new graph. Initially, each node
of the graph belongs to a separate component. Always when an edge is added to the
graph, two components are joined. Finally, all nodes belong to the same component,
and a minimum spanning tree has been found.

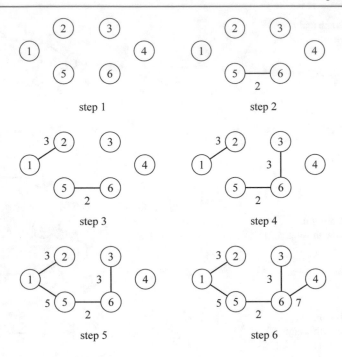

Fig. 7.38 Kruskal's algorithm

As an example, let us construct a minimum spanning tree for our example graph (Fig. 7.35). The first step is to sort the edges in increasing order of their weights:

Edge	Weight
5–6	2
1–2	3
3–6	3
1–5	5
2–3	5
2–5	6
4–6	7
3–4	9

Then, we go through the list and add each edge to the graph if it joins two separate components. Figure 7.38 shows the steps of the algorithm. Initially, each node belongs to its own component. Then, the first edges on the list (5–6, 1–2, 3–6, and 1–5) are added to the graph. After this, the next edge would be 2–3, but this edge is not added, because it would create a cycle. The same applies to edge 2–5. Finally, the edge 4–6 is added, and the minimum spanning tree is ready.

Fig. 7.39 Hypothetical
minimum spanning tree

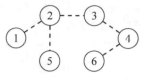

Fig. 7.40 Including the edge
5–6 reduces the weight of the
spanning tree

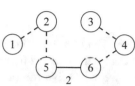

Why Does This Work? It is a good question *why* Kruskal's algorithm works. Why does the greedy strategy guarantee that we will find a minimum spanning tree?

Let us see what happens if the minimum weight edge of the graph is *not* included in the spanning tree. For example, suppose that a minimum spanning tree of our example graph would not contain the minimum weight edge 5–6. We do not know the exact structure of such a spanning tree, but in any case, it has to contain some edges. Assume that the tree would look like the tree in Fig. 7.39.

However, it is not possible that the tree in Fig. 7.39 would be a minimum spanning tree, because we can remove an edge from the tree and replace it with the minimum weight edge 5–6. This produces a spanning tree whose weight is *smaller*, shown in Fig. 7.40.

For this reason, it is always optimal to include the minimum weight edge in the tree to produce a minimum spanning tree. Using a similar argument, we can show that it is also optimal to add the next edge in weight order to the tree, and so on. Hence, Kruskal's algorithm always produces a minimum spanning tree.

Implementation When implementing Kruskal's algorithm, it is convenient to use the edge list representation of the graph. The first phase of the algorithm sorts the edges in the list in $O(m \log m)$ time. After this, the second phase of the algorithm builds the minimum spanning tree as follows:

```
for (...) {
  if (!same(a,b)) unite(a,b);
}
```

The loop goes through the edges in the list and always processes an edge (a, b) where a and b are two nodes. Two functions are needed: the function same determines if a and b are in the same component, and the function unite joins the components that contain a and b.

The problem is how to efficiently implement the functions same and unite. One possibility is to implement the function same as a graph traversal and check if we can get from node a to node b. However, the time complexity of such a function

Fig. 7.41 Union-find
structure with three sets

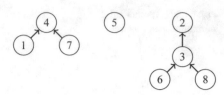

would be $O(n + m)$ and the resulting algorithm would be slow, because the function `same` will be called for each edge in the graph.

We will solve the problem using a union-find structure that implements both functions in $O(\log n)$ time. Thus, the time complexity of Kruskal's algorithm will be $O(m \log n)$ after sorting the edge list.

7.6.2 Union-Find Structure

A *union-find structure* maintains a collection of sets. The sets are disjoint, so no element belongs to more than one set. Two $O(\log n)$ time operations are supported: the `unite` operation joins two sets, and the `find` operation finds the representative of the set that contains a given element.

In a union-find structure, one element in each set is the representative of the set, and there is a path from any other element of the set to the representative. For example, assume that the sets are $\{1, 4, 7\}$, $\{5\}$, and $\{2, 3, 6, 8\}$. Figure 7.41 shows one way to represent these sets.

In this case, the representatives of the sets are 4, 5, and 2. We can find the representative of any element by following the path that begins at the element. For example, the element 2 is the representative for the element 6, because we follow the path $6 \rightarrow 3 \rightarrow 2$. Two elements belong to the same set exactly when their representatives are the same.

To join two sets, the representative of one set is connected to the representative of the other set. For example, Fig. 7.42 shows a possible way to join the sets $\{1, 4, 7\}$ and $\{2, 3, 6, 8\}$. From this on, the element 2 is the representative for the entire set and the old representative 4 points to the element 2.

The efficiency of the union-find structure depends on how the sets are joined. It turns out that we can follow a simple strategy: always connect the representative of the *smaller* set to the representative of the *larger* set (or if the sets are of equal size, we can make an arbitrary choice). Using this strategy, the length of any path will be $O(\log n)$, so we can find the representative of any element efficiently by following the corresponding path.

Fig. 7.42 Joining two sets
into a single set

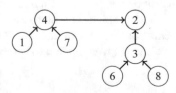

Implementation The union-find structure can be conveniently implemented using arrays. In the following implementation, the array `link` indicates for each element the next element in the path, or the element itself if it is a representative, and the array `size` indicates for each representative the size of the corresponding set.

Initially, each element belongs to a separate set:

```
for (int i = 1; i <= n; i++) link[i] = i;
for (int i = 1; i <= n; i++) size[i] = 1;
```

The function `find` returns the representative for an element x. The representative can be found by following the path that begins at x.

```
int find(int x) {
    while (x != link[x]) x = link[x];
    return x;
}
```

The function `same` checks whether elements a and b belong to the same set. This can easily be done by using the function `find`:

```
bool same(int a, int b) {
    return find(a) == find(b);
}
```

The function `unite` joins the sets that contain elements a and b (the elements have to be in different sets). The function first finds the representatives of the sets and then connects the smaller set to the larger set.

```
void unite(int a, int b) {
    a = find(a);
    b = find(b);
    if (size[a] < size[b]) swap(a,b);
    size[a] += size[b];
    link[b] = a;
}
```

The time complexity of the function `find` is $O(\log n)$ assuming that the length of each path is $O(\log n)$. In this case, the functions `same` and `unite` also work in $O(\log n)$ time. The function `unite` makes sure that the length of each path is $O(\log n)$ by connecting the smaller set to the larger set.

Path Compression Here is an alternative way to implement the `find` operation:

```
int find(int x) {
    if (x == link[x]) return x;
    return link[x] = find(link[x]);
}
```

This function uses *path compression*: each element in the path will directly point to its representative after the operation. It can be shown that using this function, the union-find operations work in amortized $O(\alpha(n))$ time, where $\alpha(n)$ is the inverse Ackermann function which grows very slowly (it is almost a constant). However, path compression cannot be used in some applications of the union-find structure, such as in the dynamic connectivity algorithm (Sect. 15.6.4).

7.6.3 Prim's Algorithm

Prim's algorithm is an alternative method for constructing minimum spanning trees. The algorithm first adds an arbitrary node to the tree, and then always chooses a minimum weight edge that adds a new node to the tree. Finally, all nodes have been added and a minimum spanning tree has been found.

Prim's algorithm resembles Dijkstra's algorithm. The difference is that Dijkstra's algorithm always selects a node whose distance from the starting node is minimum, but Prim's algorithm simply selects a node that can be added to the tree using a minimum weight edge.

As an example, Fig. 7.43 shows how Prim's algorithm constructs a minimum spanning tree for our example graph, assuming that the starting node is node 1.

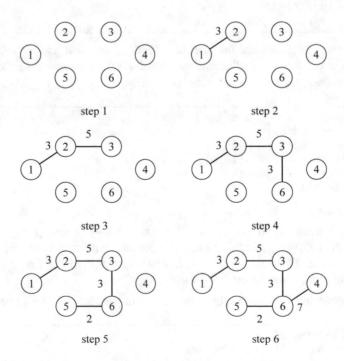

Fig. 7.43 Prim's algorithm

Like Dijkstra's algorithm, Prim's algorithm can be efficiently implemented using a priority queue. The priority queue should contain all nodes that can be connected to the current component using a single edge, in increasing order of the weights of the corresponding edges.

The time complexity of Prim's algorithm is $O(n + m \log m)$ that equals the time complexity of Dijkstra's algorithm. In practice, Prim's and Kruskal's algorithms are both efficient, and the choice of the algorithm is a matter of taste. Still, most competitive programmers use Kruskal's algorithm.

Algorithm Design Topics

8

This chapter discusses a selection of algorithm design topics.

Section 8.1 focuses on bit-parallel algorithms that use bit operations to efficiently process data. Typically, we can replace a for loop with bit operations, which may remarkably improve the running time of the algorithm.

Section 8.2 presents the amortized analysis technique, which can be used to estimate the time needed for a sequence of operations in an algorithm. Using the technique, we can analyze algorithms for determining nearest smaller elements and sliding window minima.

Section 8.3 discusses ternary search and other techniques for efficiently calculating minimum values of certain functions.

8.1 Bit-Parallel Algorithms

Bit-parallel algorithms are based on the fact that individual bits of numbers can be manipulated in parallel using bit operations. Thus, a way to design an efficient algorithm is to represent the steps of the algorithm so that they can be efficiently implemented using bit operations.

8.1.1 Hamming Distances

The *Hamming distance* hamming(a, b) between two strings a and b of equal length is the number of positions where the strings differ. For example,

$$\text{hamming}(01101, 11001) = 2.$$

© Springer Nature Switzerland AG 2020

A. Laaksonen, *Guide to Competitive Programming*, Undergraduate Topics in Computer Science, https://doi.org/10.1007/978-3-030-39357-1_8

Consider the following problem: Given n bit strings, each of length k, calculate the minimum Hamming distance between two strings. For example, the answer for [00111, 01101, 11110] is 2, because

- hamming(00111, 01101) = 2,
- hamming(00111, 11110) = 3, and
- hamming(01101, 11110) = 3.

A straightforward way to solve the problem is to go through all pairs of strings and calculate their Hamming distances, which yields an $O(n^2 k)$ time algorithm. The following function calculates the distance between strings a and b:

```
int hamming(string a, string b) {
    int d = 0;
    for (int i = 0; i < k; i++) {
        if (a[i] != b[i]) d++;
    }
    return d;
}
```

However, since the strings consist of bits, we can optimize the solution by storing the strings as integers and calculating distances using bit operations. In particular, if $k \le 32$, we can just store the strings as int values and use the following function to calculate distances:

```
int hamming(int a, int b) {
    return __builtin_popcount(a^b);
}
```

In the above function, the XOR operation constructs a string that has one bits in positions where a and b differ. Then, the number of one bits is calculated using the __builtin_popcount function.

Table 8.1 shows a comparison of running times of the original algorithm and the bit-parallel algorithm on a modern computer. In this problem, the bit-parallel algorithm is about 20 times faster than the original algorithm.

8.1.2   Counting Subgrids

As another example, consider the following problem: Given an $n \times n$ grid whose each square is either black (1) or white (0), calculate the number of subgrids whose all corners are black. For example, Fig. 8.1 shows two such subgrids in a grid.

There is an $O(n^3)$ time algorithm for solving the problem: Go through all $O(n^2)$ pairs of rows, and for each pair (a, b) calculate, in $O(n)$ time, the number of columns that contain a black square in both rows a and b. The following code assumes that color[y][x] denotes the color in row y and column x:

Table 8.1 Running times of the algorithms when calculating minimum hamming distances of n bit strings of length $k = 30$

Size n	Original algorithm (s)	Bit-parallel algorithm (s)
5000	0.84	0.06
10000	3.24	0.18
15000	7.23	0.37
20000	12.79	0.63
25000	19.99	0.97

Fig. 8.1 This grid contains two subgrids with black corners

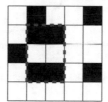 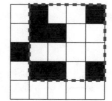

```
int count = 0;
for (int i = 0; i < n; i++) {
  if (color[a][i] == 1 && color[b][i] == 1) {
    count++;
  }
}
```

Then, after finding out that there are `count` columns where both squares are black, we can use the formula count(count − 1)/2 to calculate the number of subgrids whose first row is a and last row is b.

To create a bit-parallel algorithm, we represent each row k as an n-bit bitset `row[k]` where one bits denote black squares. Then, we can calculate the number of columns where rows a and b both have black squares using an *and* operation and counting the number of one bits. This can be conveniently done as follows using `bitset` structures:

```
int count = (row[a]&row[b]).count();
```

Table 8.2 shows a comparison of the original algorithm and the bit-parallel algorithm for different grid sizes. The comparison shows that the bit-parallel algorithm can be up to 30 times faster than the original algorithm.

Table 8.2 Running times of the algorithms for counting the subgrids

Grid size n	Original algorithm (s)	Bit-parallel algorithm (s)
1000	0.65	0.05
1500	2.17	0.14
2000	5.51	0.30
2500	12.67	0.52
3000	26.36	0.87

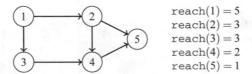

$$\text{reach}(1) = 5$$
$$\text{reach}(2) = 3$$
$$\text{reach}(3) = 3$$
$$\text{reach}(4) = 2$$
$$\text{reach}(5) = 1$$

Fig. 8.2 Graph and its `reach` values. For example, reach(2) = 3, because nodes 2, 4, and 5 can be reached from node 2

8.1.3 Reachability in Graphs

Given a directed acyclic graph of n nodes, consider the problem of calculating for each node x a value `reach(x)`: The number of nodes that can be reached from node x. For example, Fig. 8.2 shows a graph and its `reach` values.

The problem can be solved using dynamic programming in $O(n^2)$ time by constructing for each node a list of nodes that can be reached from it. Then, to create a bit-parallel algorithm, we represent each list as a bitset of n bits. This permits us to efficiently calculate the union of two such lists using an *or* operation. Assuming that `reach` is an array of `bitset` structures and the graph is stored as adjacency lists in `adj`, the calculation for node x can be done as follows:

```
reach[x][x] = 1;
for (auto u : adj[x]) {
   reach[x] |= reach[u];
}
```

Table 8.3 shows some running times for the bit-parallel algorithm. In each test, the graph has n nodes and $2n$ random edges $a \rightarrow b$ where $a < b$. Note that the algorithm uses a great amount of memory for large values of n. In many contests, the memory limit may be 512 MB or lower.

8.2 Amortized Analysis

The structure of an algorithm often directly tells us its time complexity, but sometimes a straightforward analysis does not give a true picture of the efficiency. *Amortized analysis* can be used to analyze a sequence of operations whose time complexity

Table 8.3 Running times of the algorithms when counting reachable nodes in a graph

Graph size n	Running time (s)	Memory usage (MB)
$2 \cdot 10^4$	0.06	50
$4 \cdot 10^4$	0.17	200
$6 \cdot 10^4$	0.32	450
$8 \cdot 10^4$	0.51	800
10^5	0.78	1250

varies. The idea is to estimate the total time used to all such operations during the algorithm, instead of focusing on individual operations.

8.2.1   Two Pointers Method

In the *two pointers method*, two pointers walk through an array. Both pointers move to one direction only, which ensures that the algorithm works efficiently. As a first example of how to apply the technique, consider a problem where we are given an array of n positive integers and a target sum x, and we want to find a subarray whose sum is x or report that there is no such subarray.

The problem can be solved in $O(n)$ time by using the two pointers method. The idea is to maintain pointers that point to the first and last value of a subarray. On each turn, the left pointer moves one step to the right, and the right pointer moves to the right as long as the resulting subarray sum is at most x. If the sum becomes exactly x, a solution has been found.

For example, Fig. 8.3 shows how the algorithm processes an array when the target sum is $x = 8$. The initial subarray contains the values 1, 3, and 2, whose sum is 6. Then, the left pointer moves one step right, and the right pointer does not move, because otherwise the sum would exceed x. Finally, the left pointer moves one step right, and the right pointer moves two steps right. The sum of the subarray is $2 + 5 + 1 = 8$, so the desired subarray has been found.

The running time of the algorithm depends on the number of steps the right pointer moves. While there is no useful upper bound on how many steps the pointer can move

Fig. 8.3 Finding a subarray with sum 8 using the two pointers method

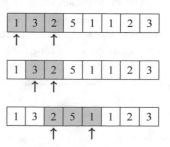

Fig. 8.4 Solving the 2SUM
problem using the two
pointers method

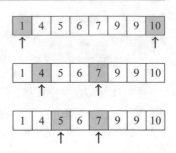

on a *single* turn, we know that the pointer moves *a total of* $O(n)$ steps during the algorithm, because it only moves to the right. Since both the left and right pointer move $O(n)$ steps, the algorithm works in $O(n)$ time.

2SUM Problem Another problem that can be solved using the two pointers method is the *2SUM problem*: Given an array of n numbers and a target sum x, find two array values such that their sum is x, or report that no such values exist.

To solve the problem, we first sort the array values in increasing order. After that, we iterate through the array using two pointers. The left pointer starts at the first value and moves one step to the right on each turn. The right pointer starts at the last value and always moves to the left until the sum of the left and right value is at most x. If the sum is exactly x, a solution has been found.

For example, Fig. 8.4 shows how the algorithm processes an array when the target sum is $x = 12$. In the initial position, the sum of the values is $1 + 10 = 11$ which is smaller than x. Then the left pointer moves one step right, and the right pointer moves three steps left, and the sum becomes $4 + 7 = 11$. After this, the left pointer moves one step right again. The right pointer does not move, and a solution $5 + 7 = 12$ has been found.

The running time of the algorithm is $O(n \log n)$, because it first sorts the array in $O(n \log n)$ time, and then both pointers move $O(n)$ steps.

Note that it is also possible to solve the problem in another way in $O(n \log n)$ time using binary search. In such a solution, we first sort the array and then iterate through the array values and for each value binary search for another value that yields the sum x. In fact, many problems that can be solved using the two pointers method can also be solved using sorting or set structures, sometimes with an additional logarithmic factor.

The more general kSUM problem is also interesting. In this problem we have to find k elements such that their sum is x. It turns out that we can solve the 3SUM problem in $O(n^2)$ time by extending the above 2SUM algorithm. Can you see how we can do it? For a long time, it was actually thought that $O(n^2)$ would be the best possible time complexity for the 3SUM problem. However, in 2014, Grønlund and Pettie [14] showed that this is not the case.

8.2.2 Nearest Smaller Elements

Amortized analysis is often used to estimate the number of operations performed on a data structure. The operations may be distributed unevenly so that most operations occur during a certain phase of the algorithm, but the total number of the operations is limited.

As an example, suppose that we want to find for each array element the *nearest smaller element*, i.e., the first smaller element that precedes the element in the array. It is possible that no such element exists, in which case the algorithm should report this. Next we will efficiently solve the problem using a stack structure.

We go through the array from left to right and maintain a stack of array elements. At each array position, we remove elements from the stack until the top element is smaller than the current element, or the stack is empty. Then, we report that the top element is the nearest smaller element of the current element, or if the stack is empty, there is no such element. Finally, we add the current element to the stack.

Figure 8.5 shows how the algorithm processes an array. First, the element 1 is added to the stack. Since it is the first element in the array, it clearly does not have a nearest smaller element. After this, the elements 3 and 4 are added to the stack. The nearest smaller element of 4 is 3, and the nearest smaller element of 3 is 1. Then, the next element 2 is smaller than the two top elements in the stack, so the elements 3 and 4 are removed from the stack. Thus, the nearest smaller element of 2 is 1. After this, the element 2 is added to the stack. The algorithm continues like this, until the entire array has been processed.

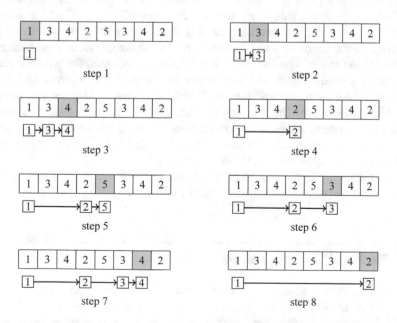

Fig. 8.5 Finding the nearest smaller elements in linear time using a stack

The efficiency of the algorithm depends on the total number of stack operations. If the current element is larger than the top element in the stack, it is directly added to the stack, which is efficient. However, sometimes the stack can contain several larger elements and it takes time to remove them. Still, each element is added *exactly once* to the stack and removed *at most once* from the stack. Thus, each element causes $O(1)$ stack operations, and the algorithm works in $O(n)$ time.

8.2.3   Sliding Window Minimum

A *sliding window* is a constant-size subarray that moves from left to right through an array. At each window position, we want to calculate some information about the elements inside the window. Next we will focus on the problem of maintaining the *sliding window minimum*, which means that we want to report the smallest value inside each window.

The sliding window minima can be calculated using a similar idea that we used to calculate the nearest smaller elements. This time we maintain a queue where each element is larger than the previous element, and the first element always corresponds to the minimum element inside the window. After each window move, we remove elements from the end of the queue until the last queue element is smaller than the new window element, or the queue becomes empty. We also remove the first queue element if it is not inside the window anymore. Finally, we add the new window element to the queue.

Figure 8.6 shows how the algorithm processes an array when the sliding window size is 4. At the first window position, the smallest value is 1. Then the window moves one step right. The new element 3 is smaller than the elements 4 and 5 in the queue, so the elements 4 and 5 are removed from the queue, and the element 3 is added to the queue. The smallest value is still 1. After this, the window moves again, and the smallest element 1 does not belong to the window anymore. Thus, it is removed from the queue, and the smallest value is now 3. Also the new element 4 is added to the queue. The next new element 1 is smaller than all elements in the queue, so all elements are removed from the queue, and it only contains the element 1. Finally, the window reaches its last position. The element 2 is added to the queue, but the smallest value inside the window is still 1.

Since each array element is added to the queue exactly once and removed from the queue at most once, the algorithm works in $O(n)$ time.

8.3   Finding Minimum Values

Suppose that there is a function $f(x)$ that first only decreases, then attains its minimum value, and then only increases. For example, Fig. 8.7 shows such a function whose minimum value is marked with an arrow. If we know that our function has this property, we can efficiently find its minimum value.

Fig. 8.6 Finding sliding
window minima in linear
time

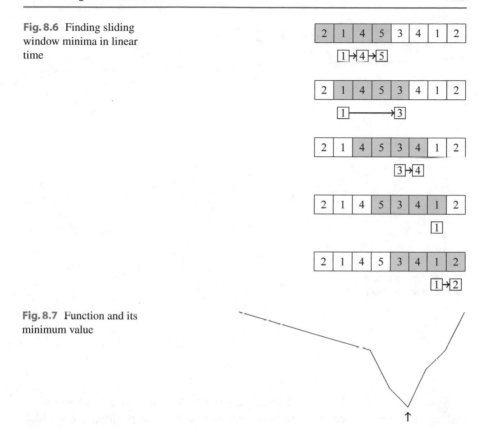

Fig. 8.7 Function and its
minimum value

8.3.1 Ternary Search

Ternary search provides an efficient way to find the minimum value of a function
that first decreases and then increases. Assume that we know that the value of x that
minimizes $f(x)$ is in a range $[x_L, x_R]$. The idea is to divide the range into three
equal-sized parts $[x_L, a]$, $[a, b]$, and $[b, x_R]$ by choosing

$$a = \frac{2x_L + x_R}{3} \quad \text{and} \quad b = \frac{x_L + 2x_R}{3}.$$

Then, if $f(a) < f(b)$, we conclude that the minimum must be in range $[x_L, b]$, and
otherwise it must be in range $[a, x_R]$. After this, we recursively continue the search,
until the size of the active range is small enough.

As an example, Fig. 8.8 shows the first step of ternary search in our example
scenario. Since $f(a) > f(b)$, the new range becomes $[a, x_R]$.

In practice, we often consider functions whose parameters are integers, and the
search is terminated when the range only contains one element. Since the size of
the new range is always $2/3$ of the previous range, the algorithm works in $O(\log n)$
time, where n is the number of elements in the original range.

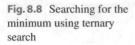

Fig. 8.8 Searching for the minimum using ternary search

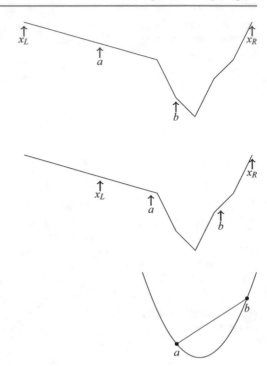

Fig. 8.9 Example of a convex function: $f(x) = x^2$

Note that when working with integer parameters, we can also use *binary search* instead of ternary search, because it suffices to find the first position x for which $f(x) \leq f(x + 1)$.

8.3.2 Convex Functions

A function is *convex* if a line segment between any two points on the graph of the function always lies above or on the graph. For example, Fig. 8.9 shows the graph of $f(x) = x^2$, which is a convex function. Indeed, the line segment between points a and b lies above the graph.

If we know that the minimum value of a convex function is in range $[x_L, x_R]$, we can use ternary search to find it. However, note that several points of a convex function may have the minimum value. For example, $f(x) = 0$ is convex and its minimum value is 0.

Convex functions have some useful properties: If $f(x)$ and $g(x)$ are convex functions, then also $f(x) + g(x)$ and $\max(f(x), g(x))$ are convex functions. For example, if we have n convex functions $f_1, f_2, \ldots, f_n$, we immediately know that also the function $f_1 + f_2 + \cdots + f_n$ has to be convex and we can use ternary search to find its minimum value.

8.3.3 Minimizing Sums

Given n numbers $a_1, a_2, \ldots, a_n$, consider the problem of finding a value of x that minimizes the sum

$$|a_1 - x| + |a_2 - x| + \cdots + |a_n - x|.$$

For example, if the numbers are $[1, 2, 9, 2, 6]$, the optimal solution is to choose $x = 2$, which produces the sum

$$|1 - 2| + |2 - 2| + |9 - 2| + |2 - 2| + |6 - 2| = 12.$$

Since each function $|a_k - x|$ is convex, the sum is also convex, so we could use ternary search to find the optimal value of x. However, there is also an easier solution. It turns out that the optimal choice for x is always the *median* of the numbers, i.e., the middle element after sorting. For example, the list $[1, 2, 9, 2, 6]$ becomes $[1, 2, 2, 6, 9]$ after sorting, so the median is 2.

The median is always optimal, because if x is smaller than the median, the sum becomes smaller by increasing x, and if x is larger than the median, the sum becomes smaller by decreasing x. If n is even and there are two medians, both medians and all values between them are optimal choices.

Then, consider the problem of minimizing the function

$$(a_1 - x)^2 + (a_2 - x)^2 + \cdots + (a_n - x)^2.$$

For example, if the numbers are $[1, 2, 9, 2, 6]$, the best solution is to choose $x = 4$, which produces the sum

$$(1 - 4)^2 + (2 - 4)^2 + (9 - 4)^2 + (2 - 4)^2 + (6 - 4)^2 = 46.$$

Again, this function is convex and we could use ternary search to solve the problem, but there is also a simple solution: The optimal choice for x is the *average* of the numbers. In the example the average is $(1 + 2 + 9 + 2 + 6)/5 = 4$. This can be proved by presenting the sum as follows:

$$nx^2 - 2x(a_1 + a_2 + \cdots + a_n) + (a_1^2 + a_2^2 + \cdots + a_n^2)$$

The last part does not depend on x, so we can ignore it. The remaining parts form a function $nx^2 - 2xs$ where $s = a_1 + a_2 + \cdots + a_n$. This is a parabola opening upward with roots $x = 0$ and $x = 2s/n$, and the minimum value is the average of the roots $x = s/n$, i.e., the average of the numbers $a_1, a_2, \ldots, a_n$.

Range Queries

9

In this chapter, we discuss data structures for efficiently processing range queries on arrays. Typical queries are range sum queries (calculating the sum of values) and range minimum queries (finding the minimum value).

Section 9.1 focuses on a simple situation where the array values are not modified between sthe queries. In this case, it suffices to preprocess the array so that we can efficiently determine the answer for any possible query. We will first learn to process sum queries using a prefix sum array, and then, we will discuss the sparse table algorithm for processing minimum queries.

Section 9.2 presents two tree structures that allow us to both process queries and update array values efficiently. A binary indexed tree supports sum queries and can be seen as a dynamic version of a prefix sum array. A segment tree is a more versatile structure that supports sum queries, minimum queries, and several other queries. The operations of both the structures work in logarithmic time.

9.1 Queries on Static Arrays

In this section, we focus on a situation where the array is *static*, i.e., the array values are never updated between the queries. In this case, it suffices to preprocess the array so that we can efficiently answer range queries.

First, we will discuss a simple way to process sum queries using a prefix sum array, which can also be generalized to higher dimensions. After this, we will learn the sparse table algorithm for processing minimum queries, which is somewhat more difficult. Note that while we focus on processing minimum queries, we can always also process maximum queries using similar methods.

The original version of this chapter was revised: The example code in Page 135 has been updated. The correction to this chapter is available at https://doi.org/10.1007/978-3-030-39357-1_16

© Springer Nature Switzerland AG 2020
A. Laaksonen, *Guide to Competitive Programming*, Undergraduate Topics in Computer Science, https://doi.org/10.1007/978-3-030-39357-1_9

9.1.1 Sum Queries

Let $\text{sum}_q(a, b)$ ("range sum query") denote the sum of array values in a range $[a, b]$. We can efficiently process any sum query by first constructing a *prefix sum array*. Each value in the prefix sum array equals the sum of values in the original array up to the corresponding position, i.e., the value at position k is $\text{sum}_q(0, k)$. For example, Fig. 9.1 shows an array and its prefix sum array.

The prefix sum array can be constructed in $O(n)$ time. Then, since the prefix sum array contains all values of $\text{sum}_q(0, k)$, we can calculate any value of $\text{sum}_q(a, b)$ in $O(1)$ time using the formula

$$\text{sum}_q(a, b) = \text{sum}_q(0, b) - \text{sum}_q(0, a - 1).$$

By defining $\text{sum}_q(0, -1) = 0$, the above formula also holds when $a = 0$.

As an example, Fig. 9.2 shows how to calculate the sum of values in the range $[3, 6]$ using the prefix sum array. We can see in the original array that $\text{sum}_q(3, 6) = 8 + 6 + 1 + 4 = 19$. Using the prefix sum array, we need to examine only two values: $\text{sum}_q(3, 6) = \text{sum}_q(0, 6) - \text{sum}_q(0, 2) = 27 - 8 = 19$.

Higher Dimensions It is also possible to generalize this idea to higher dimensions. For example, Fig. 9.3 shows a two-dimensional prefix sum array that can be used to calculate the sum of any rectangular subarray in $O(1)$ time. Each sum in this array corresponds to a subarray that begins at the upper-left corner of the array. The sum of the gray subarray can be calculated using the formula

$$S(A) - S(B) - S(C) + S(D),$$

where $S(X)$ denotes the sum of values in a rectangular subarray from the upper-left corner to the position of X.

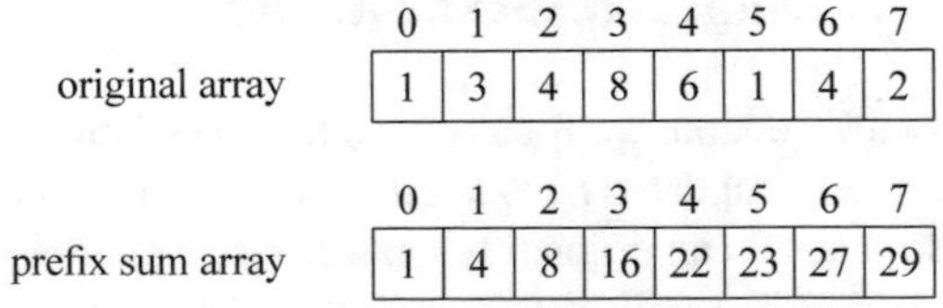

Fig. 9.1 An array and its prefix sum array

original array

0	1	2	3	4	5	6	7
1	3	4	8	6	1	4	2

prefix sum array

0	1	2	3	4	5	6	7
1	4	8	16	22	23	27	29

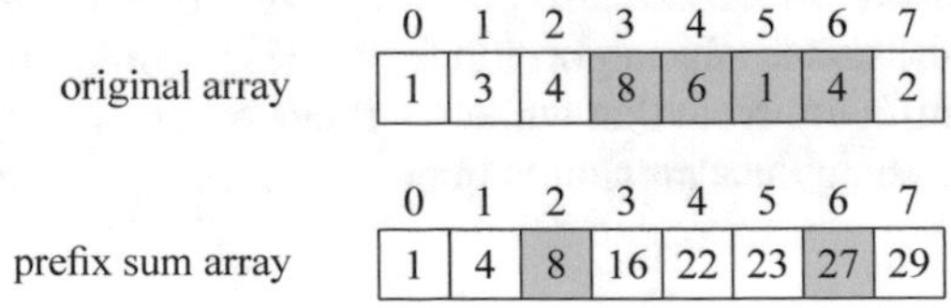

Fig. 9.2 Calculating a range sum using the prefix sum array

original array

0	1	2	3	4	5	6	7
1	3	4	8	6	1	4	2

prefix sum array

0	1	2	3	4	5	6	7
1	4	8	16	22	23	27	29

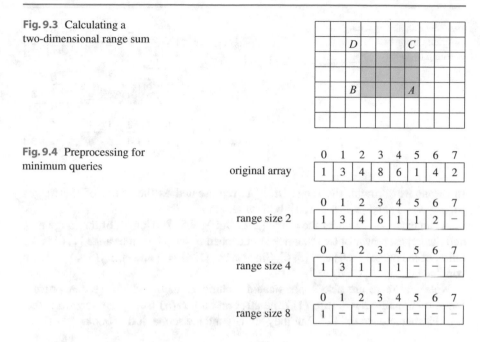

Fig. 9.3 Calculating a two-dimensional range sum

Fig. 9.4 Preprocessing for minimum queries

9.1.2   Minimum Queries

Let $\min_q(a, b)$ ("range minimum query") denote the minimum array value in a range $[a, b]$. We will next discuss a technique using which we can process any minimum query in $O(1)$ time after an $O(n \log n)$ time preprocessing. The method is due to Bender and Farach-Colton [3] and often called the *sparse table algorithm*.

The idea is to precalculate all values of $\min_q(a, b)$ where $b - a + 1$ (the length of the range) is a power of two. For example, Fig. 9.4 shows the precalculated values for an array of eight elements.

The number of precalculated values is $O(n \log n)$ because there are $O(\log n)$ range lengths that are powers of two. The values can be calculated efficiently using the recursive formula

$$\min_q(a, b) = \min(\min_q(a, a + w - 1), \min_q(a + w, b)),$$

where $b - a + 1$ is a power of two and $w = (b - a + 1)/2$. Calculating all those values takes $O(n \log n)$ time.

After this, any value of $\min_q(a, b)$ can be calculated in $O(1)$ time as a minimum of two precalculated values. Let k be the largest power of two that does not exceed $b - a + 1$. We can calculate the value of $\min_q(a, b)$ using the formula

$$\min_q(a, b) = \min(\min_q(a, a + k - 1), \min_q(b - k + 1, b)).$$

Fig. 9.5 Calculating a range minimum using two overlapping ranges

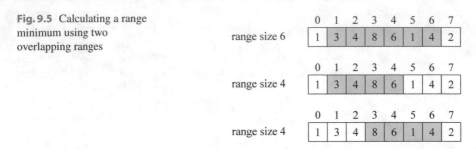

In the above formula, the range $[a, b]$ is represented as the union of the ranges $[a, a + k - 1]$ and $[b - k + 1, b]$, both of length k.

As an example, consider the range $[1, 6]$ in Fig. 9.5. The length of the range is 6, and the largest power of two that does not exceed 6 is 4. Thus, the range $[1, 6]$ is the union of the ranges $[1, 4]$ and $[3, 6]$. Since $\min_q(1, 4) = 3$ and $\min_q(3, 6) = 1$, we conclude that $\min_q(1, 6) = 1$.

Note that there are also sophisticated techniques using which we can process range minimum queries in $O(1)$ time after an only $O(n)$ time preprocessing (see, e.g., Fischer and Heun [12]), but they are beyond the scope of this book.

9.2 Tree Structures

This section presents two tree structures, using which we can both process range queries and update array values in logarithmic time. First, we discuss binary indexed trees that support sum queries, and after that, we focus on segment trees that also support several other queries.

9.2.1 Binary Indexed Trees

A *binary indexed tree* (or a *Fenwick tree*) [11] can be seen as a dynamic variant of a prefix sum array. It provides two $O(\log n)$ time operations: processing a range sum query and updating a value. Even if the name of the structure is a binary indexed *tree*, the structure is usually represented as an array. When discussing binary indexed trees, we assume that all arrays are one-indexed because it makes the implementation of the structure easier.

Let $p(k)$ denote the largest power of two that divides k. We store a binary indexed tree as an array tree such that

$$\texttt{tree}[k] = \text{sum}_q(k - p(k) + 1, k),$$

i.e., each position k contains the sum of values in a range of the original array whose length is $p(k)$ and that ends at position k. For example, since $p(6) = 2$, tree[6]

Fig. 9.6 An array and its binary indexed tree

original array

1	2	3	4	5	6	7	8
1	3	4	8	6	1	4	2

binary indexed tree

1	2	3	4	5	6	7	8
1	4	4	16	6	7	4	29

Fig. 9.7 Ranges in a binary indexed tree

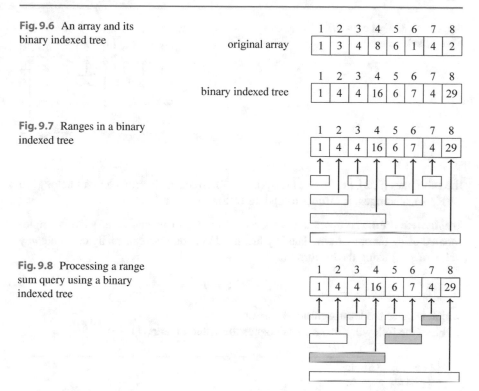

Fig. 9.8 Processing a range sum query using a binary indexed tree

contains the value of $\text{sum}_q(5, 6)$. Figure 9.6 shows an array and the corresponding binary indexed tree. Figure 9.7 shows more clearly how each value in the binary indexed tree corresponds to a range in the original array.

Using a binary indexed tree, any value of $\text{sum}_q(1, k)$ can be calculated in $O(\log n)$ time because a range $[1, k]$ can always be divided into $O(\log n)$ subranges whose sums have been stored in the tree. For example, to calculate the value of $\text{sum}_q(1, 7)$, we divide the range $[1, 7]$ into three subranges $[1, 4]$, $[5, 6]$, and $[7, 7]$ (Fig. 9.8). Since the sums of those subranges are available in the tree, we can calculate the sum of the entire range using the formula

$$\text{sum}_q(1, 7) = \text{sum}_q(1, 4) + \text{sum}_q(5, 6) + \text{sum}_q(7, 7) = 16 + 7 + 4 = 27.$$

Then, to calculate the value of $\text{sum}_q(a, b)$ where $a > 1$, we can use the same trick that we used with prefix sum arrays:

$$\text{sum}_q(a, b) = \text{sum}_q(1, b) - \text{sum}_q(1, a - 1)$$

We can calculate both $\text{sum}_q(1, b)$ and $\text{sum}_q(1, a - 1)$ in $O(\log n)$ time, so the total time complexity is $O(\log n)$.

After updating an array value, several values in the binary indexed tree should be updated. For example, when the value at position 3 changes, we should update

Fig. 9.9 Updating a value in
a binary indexed tree

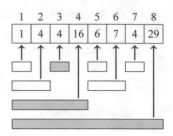

the subranges [3, 3], [1, 4], and [1, 8] (Fig. 9.9). Since each array element belongs to
$O(\log n)$ subranges, it suffices to update $O(\log n)$ tree values.

Implementation The operations of a binary indexed tree can be efficiently implemented using bit operations. The key fact needed is that we can easily calculate any
value of $p(k)$ using the bit formula

$$p(k) = k \& - k,$$

which isolates the least significant one bit of k.

First, the following function calculates the value of $\text{sum}_q(1, k)$:

```
int sum(int k) {
    int s = 0;
    while (k >= 1) {
        s += tree[k];
        k -= k&-k;
    }
    return s;
}
```

Then, the following function increases the array value at position k by x (x can
be positive or negative):

```
void add(int k, int x) {
    while (k <= n) {
        tree[k] += x;
        k += k&-k;
    }
}
```

The time complexity of both the functions is $O(\log n)$ because the functions access
$O(\log n)$ values in the binary indexed tree, and each moves to the next position takes
$O(1)$ time.

9.2.2 Segment Trees

A *segment tree* is a data structure that provides two $O(\log n)$ time operations: processing a range query and updating an array value. Segment trees support sum queries, minimum queries, and many other queries. Segment trees have their origins in geometric algorithms (see, e.g., Bentley and Wood [4]), and the elegant bottom-up implementation presented in this section follows the textbook by Stańczyk [34].

A segment tree is a binary tree whose bottom level nodes correspond to the array elements, and the other nodes contain information needed for processing range queries. When discussing segment trees, we assume that the size of the array is a power of two and zero-based indexing is used because it is convenient to build a segment tree for such an array. If the size of the array is not a power of two, we can always append extra elements to it.

We will first discuss segment trees that support sum queries. As an example, Fig. 9.10 shows an array and the corresponding segment tree for sum queries. Each internal tree node corresponds to an array range whose size is a power of two. When a segment tree supports sum queries, the value of each internal node is the sum of the corresponding array values, and it can be calculated as the sum of the values of its left and right child node.

It turns out that any range $[a, b]$ can be divided into $O(\log n)$ subranges whose values are stored in tree nodes. For example, Fig. 9.11 shows the range $[2, 7]$ in the original array and in the segment tree. In this case, two tree nodes correspond to the range, and $\text{sum}_q(2, 7) = 9 + 17 = 26$. When the sum is calculated using nodes located as high as possible in the tree, at most two nodes on each level of the tree are needed. Hence, the total number of nodes is $O(\log n)$.

After an array update, we should update all nodes whose value depends on the updated value. This can be done by traversing the path from the updated array element to the top node and updating the nodes along the path. For example, Fig. 9.12 shows the nodes that change when the value at position 5 changes. The path from bottom to top always consists of $O(\log n)$ nodes, so each update changes $O(\log n)$ nodes in the tree.

Fig. 9.10 An array and the corresponding segment tree for sum queries

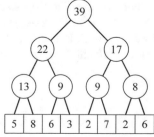

Fig. 9.11 Processing a range sum query using a segment tree

Fig. 9.12 Updating an array value in a segment tree

Fig. 9.13 Contents of a segment tree in an array

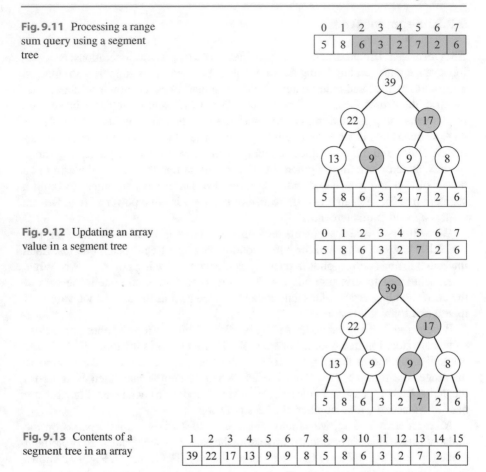

Implementation A convenient way to store the contents of a segment tree is to use an array of $2n$ elements where n is the size of the original array. The tree nodes are stored from top to bottom: tree[1] is the top node, tree[2] and tree[3] are its children, and so on. Finally, the values from tree[n] to tree[$2n - 1$] correspond to the bottom level of the tree, which contains the values of the original array. Note that the element tree[0] is not used.

For example, Fig. 9.13 shows how our example tree is stored. Note that the parent of tree[k] is tree[$\lfloor k/2 \rfloor$], its left child is tree[$2k$], and its right child is tree[$2k + 1$]. In addition, the position of a node (other than the top node) is even if it is a left child and odd if it is a right child.

The following function calculates the value of $\text{sum}_q(a, b)$:

```
int sum(int a, int b) {
    a +- n; b +- n;
    int s = 0;
    while (a <= b) {
        if (a%2 == 1) s += tree [a++];
        if (b%2 == 0) s += tree [b--];
        a /= 2; b /= 2;
    }
    return s;
}
```

The function maintains a range in the segment tree array. Initially, the range is $[a + n, b + n]$. At each step, the range is moved one level higher in the tree, and the values of the nodes that do not belong to the higher range are added to the sum.

The following function increases the array value at position k by x:

```
void add(int k, int x) {
    k += n;
    tree[k] += x;
    for (k /= 2; k >= 1; k /= 2) {
        tree[k] = tree[2*k]+tree[2*k+1];
    }
}
```

First, the value at the bottom level of the tree is updated. After this, the values of all internal tree nodes are updated, until the top node of the tree is reached.

Both the above functions work in $O(\log n)$ time because a segment tree of n elements consists of $O(\log n)$ levels and the functions move one level higher in the tree at each step.

Other Queries Segment trees can support any range queries where we can divide a range into two parts, calculate the answer separately for both parts and then efficiently combine the answers. Examples of such queries are minimum and maximum, greatest common divisor, and bit operations AND, OR, and XOR.

For example, the segment tree in Fig. 9.14 supports minimum queries. In this tree, every node contains the smallest value in the corresponding array range. The top node of the tree contains the smallest value in the whole array. The operations can be implemented like previously, but instead of sums, minima are calculated.

The structure of a segment tree also allows us to use a binary search style method for locating array elements. For example, if the tree supports minimum queries, we can find the position of an element with the smallest value in $O(\log n)$ time. For example, Fig. 9.15 shows how the element with the smallest value 1 can be found by traversing a path downwards from the top node.

Fig. 9.14 A segment tree for processing range minimum queries

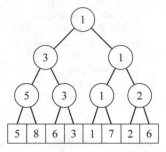

Fig. 9.15 Using binary search to find the minimum element

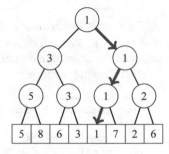

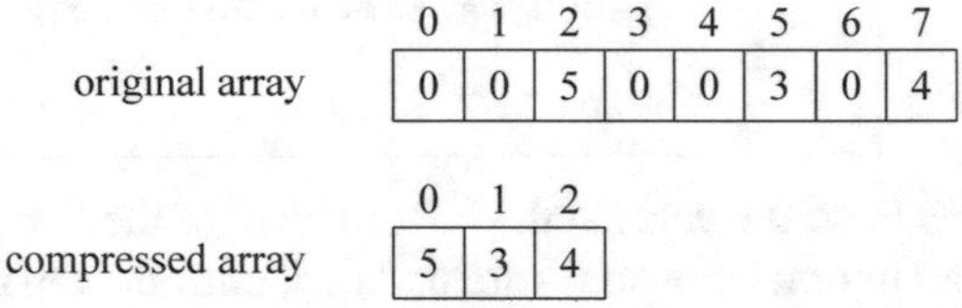

Fig. 9.16 Compressing an array using index compression

original array

compressed array

9.2.3 Additional Techniques

Index Compression A limitation in data structures that are built upon arrays is that the elements are indexed using consecutive integers. Difficulties arise when large indices are needed. For example, if we want to use the index 10^9, the array should contain 10^9 elements which would require too much memory.

However, if we know all the indices needed during the algorithm beforehand, we can bypass this limitation by using *index compression*. The idea is to replace the original indices with consecutive integers 0, 1, 2, and so on. To do this, we define a function c that compresses the indices. The function gives each original index i a compressed index $c(i)$ in such a way that if a and b are two indices and $a < b$, then $c(a) < c(b)$. After compressing the indices, we can conveniently perform queries using them.

Figure 9.16 shows a simple example of index compression. Here, only indices 2, 5, and 7 are actually used, and all other array values are zeros. The compressed indices are $c(2) = 0$, $c(5) = 1$, and $c(7) = 2$, which allow us to create a compressed array that only contains three elements.

Fig. 9.17 An array and its
difference array

original array

0	1	2	3	4	5	6	7
3	3	1	1	1	5	2	2

difference array

0	1	2	3	4	5	6	7
3	0	-2	0	0	4	-3	0

Fig. 9.18 Updating an array
range using the difference
array

original array

0	1	2	3	4	5	6	7
3	6	4	4	4	5	2	2

difference array

0	1	2	3	4	5	6	7
3	3	-2	0	0	1	-3	0

After index compression, we can, for example, build a segment tree for the compressed array and perform queries. The only modification needed is that we have to compress the indices before queries: a range $[a, b]$ in the original array corresponds to the range $[c(a), c(b)]$ in the compressed array.

Range Updates So far, we have implemented data structures that support range queries and updates of single values. Let us now consider an opposite situation, where we should update ranges and retrieve single values. We focus on an operation that increases all elements in a range $[a, b]$ by x.

It turns out that we can use the data structures presented in this chapter also in this situation. To do this, we build a *difference array* whose values indicate the differences between consecutive values in the original array. The original array is the prefix sum array of the difference array. Figure 9.17 shows an array and its difference array. For example, the value 2 at position 6 in the original array corresponds to the sum $3 - 2 + 4 - 3 = 2$ in the difference array.

The advantage of the difference array is that we can update a range in the original array by changing just two elements in the difference array. More precisely, to increase the values in range $[a, b]$ by x, we increase the value at position a by x and decrease the value at position $b + 1$ by x. For example, to increase the original array values between positions 1 and 4 by 3, we increase the difference array value at position 1 by 3 and decrease the value at position 5 by 3 (Fig. 9.18).

Thus, we only update single values and process sum queries in the difference array, so we can use a binary indexed tree or a segment tree. A more difficult task is to create a data structure that supports *both* range queries and range updates. In Sect. 15.2.1, we will see that also this is possible using a lazy segment tree.

Tree Algorithms

10

The special properties of trees allow us to create algorithms that are specialized for trees and work more efficiently than general graph algorithms. This chapter presents a selection of such algorithms.

Section 10.1 introduces basic concepts and algorithms related to trees. A central problem is finding the diameter of a tree, i.e., the maximum distance between two nodes. We will learn two linear time algorithms for solving the problem.

Section 10.2 focuses on processing queries on trees. We will learn to use a tree traversal array to process various queries related to subtrees and paths. After this, we will discuss methods for determining lowest common ancestors and an offline algorithm which is based on merging data structures.

Section 10.3 presents two advanced tree processing techniques: centroid decomposition and heavy-light decomposition.

10.1 Basic Techniques

A *tree* is a connected acyclic graph that consists of n nodes and $n - 1$ edges. Removing any edge from a tree divides it into two components, and adding any edge creates a cycle. There is always a unique path between any two nodes of a tree. The *leaves* of a tree are the nodes with only one neighbor.

As an example, consider the tree in Fig. 10.1. This tree consists of 8 nodes and 7 edges, and its leaves are nodes 3, 5, 7, and 8.

In a *rooted* tree, one of the nodes is appointed the *root* of the tree, and all other nodes are placed underneath the root. The lower neighbors of a node are called its *children*, and the upper neighbor of a node is called its *parent*. Each node has exactly one parent, except for the root that does not have a parent. The structure of a rooted tree is recursive: Each node of the tree acts as the root of a *subtree* that contains the node itself and all nodes that are in the subtrees of its children.

© Springer Nature Switzerland AG 2020

A. Laaksonen, *Guide to Competitive Programming*, Undergraduate Topics
in Computer Science, https://doi.org/10.1007/978-3-030-39357-1_10

Fig. 10.1 Tree that consists
of 8 nodes and 7 edges

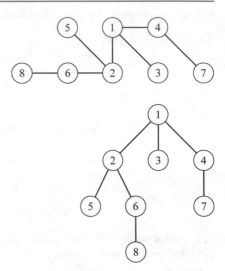

Fig. 10.2 Rooted tree where
node 1 is the root node

For example, Fig. 10.2 shows a rooted tree where node 1 is the root of the tree.
The children of node 2 are nodes 5 and 6, and the parent of node 2 is node 1. The
subtree of node 2 consists of nodes 2, 5, 6, and 8.

10.1.1 Tree Traversal

General graph traversal algorithms can be used to traverse the nodes of a tree. However, the traversal of a tree is easier to implement than that of a general graph, because
there are no cycles in the tree and it is not possible to reach a node from more than
one direction.

A typical way to traverse a tree is to start a depth-first search at an arbitrary node.
The following recursive function can be used:

```
void dfs(int s, int e) {
    // process node s
    for (auto u : adj[s]) {
        if (u != e) dfs(u, s);
    }
}
```

The function is given two parameters: the current node s and the previous node e.
The purpose of the parameter e is to make sure that the search only moves to nodes
that have not been visited yet.

The following function call starts the search at node x:

```
dfs(x, 0);
```

In the first call $e = 0$, because there is no previous node, and it is allowed to proceed to any direction in the tree.

Dynamic Programming Dynamic programming can be used to calculate some information during a tree traversal. For example, the following code calculates for each node s a value count[s]: the number of nodes in its subtree. The subtree contains the node itself and all nodes in the subtrees of its children, so we can calculate the number of nodes recursively as follows:

```
void dfs(int s, int e) {
    count[s] = 1;
    for (auto u : adj[s]) {
        if (u == e) continue;
        dfs(u, s);
        count[s] += count[u];
    }
}
```

Binary Tree Traversals In a binary tree, each node has a left and right subtree (which may be empty), and there are three popular tree traversal orderings:

- *pre-order*: first process the root node, then traverse the left subtree, then traverse the right subtree
- *in-order*: first traverse the left subtree, then process the root node, then traverse the right subtree
- *post-order*: first traverse the left subtree, then traverse the right subtree, then process the root node

For example, in Fig. 10.3, the pre-order is $[1, 2, 4, 5, 6, 3, 7]$, the in-order is $[4, 2, 6, 5, 1, 3, 7]$, and the post-order is $[4, 6, 5, 2, 7, 3, 1]$.

If we know the pre-order and in-order of a tree, we can reconstruct its exact structure. For example, the only possible tree with pre-order $[1, 2, 4, 5, 6, 3, 7]$ and

Fig. 10.3 Binary tree

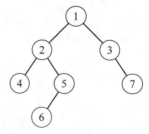

in-order [4, 2, 6, 5, 1, 3, 7] is shown in Fig. 10.3. The post-order and in-order also uniquely determine the structure of a tree. However, if we only know the pre-order and post-order, there may be more than one tree that match the orderings.

10.1.2 Calculating Diameters

The *diameter* of a tree is the maximum length of a path between two nodes. For example, Fig. 10.4 shows a tree whose diameter is 4 that corresponds to a path of length 4 between nodes 6 and 7. Note that the tree also has another path of length 4 between nodes 5 and 7.

Next we will discuss two $O(n)$ time algorithms for calculating the diameter of a tree. The first algorithm is based on dynamic programming, and the second algorithm uses depth-first searches.

First Algorithm A general way to approach tree problems is to first root the tree arbitrarily, and then solve the problem separately for each subtree. Our first algorithm for calculating diameters is based on this idea.

An important observation is that every path in a rooted tree has a *highest point*: the highest node that belongs to the path. Thus, we can calculate for each node x the length of the longest path whose highest point is x. One of those paths corresponds to the diameter of the tree. For example, in Fig. 10.5, node 1 is the highest point on the path that corresponds to the diameter.

We calculate for each node x two values:

- toLeaf(x): the maximum length of a path from x to any leaf
- maxLength(x): the maximum length of a path whose highest point is x

For example, in Fig. 10.5, toLeaf(1) = 2, because there is a path $1 \rightarrow 2 \rightarrow 6$, and maxLength($1$) = 4, because there is a path $6 \rightarrow 2 \rightarrow 1 \rightarrow 4 \rightarrow 7$. In this case, maxLength(1) equals the diameter.

Fig. 10.4 Tree whose diameter is 4

Fig. 10.5 Node 1 is the highest point on the diameter path

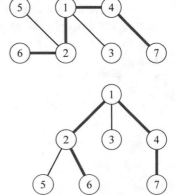

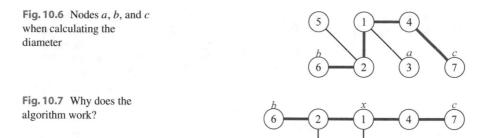

Fig. 10.6 Nodes a, b, and c when calculating the diameter

Fig. 10.7 Why does the algorithm work?

Dynamic programming can be used to calculate the above values for all nodes in $O(n)$ time. First, to calculate toLeaf(x), we go through the children of x, choose a child c with the maximum toLeaf(c) and add one to this value. Then, to calculate maxLength(x), we choose two distinct children a and b such that the sum toLeaf(a) + toLeaf(b) is maximum and add two to this sum. (The cases where x has less than two children are easy special cases.)

Second Algorithm Another efficient way to calculate the diameter of a tree is based on two depth-first searches. First, we choose an arbitrary node a in the tree and find the farthest node b from a. Then, we find the farthest node c from b. The diameter of the tree is the distance between b and c.

For example, Fig. 10.6 shows a possible way to select nodes a, b, and c when calculating the diameter for our example tree.

This is an elegant method, but why does it work? It helps to draw the tree so that the path that corresponds to the diameter is horizontal, and all other nodes hang from it (Fig. 10.7). Node x indicates the place where the path from node a joins the path that corresponds to the diameter. The farthest node from a is node b, node c, or some other node that is at least as far from node x. Thus, this node is always a valid choice for an endpoint of a path that corresponds to the diameter.

10.1.3 All Longest Paths

Our next problem is to calculate for every tree node x a value maxLength(x): the maximum length of a path that begins at node x. For example, Fig. 10.8 shows a tree and its maxLength values. This can be seen as a generalization of the tree diameter problem, because the largest of those lengths equals the diameter of the tree. Also this problem can be solved in $O(n)$ time.

Once again, a good starting point is to root the tree arbitrarily. The first part of the problem is to calculate for every node x the maximum length of a path that goes *downward* through a child of x. For example, the longest path from node 1 goes through its child 2 (Fig. 10.9). This part is easy to solve in $O(n)$ time, because we can use dynamic programming as we have done previously.

Fig. 10.8 Calculating
maximum path lengths

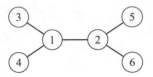

$\mathtt{maxLength}(1) = 2$
$\mathtt{maxLength}(2) = 2$
$\mathtt{maxLength}(3) = 3$
$\mathtt{maxLength}(4) = 3$
$\mathtt{maxLength}(5) = 3$
$\mathtt{maxLength}(6) = 3$

Fig. 10.9 Longest path that
starts at node 1

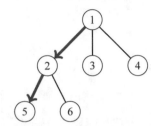

Fig. 10.10 Longest path
from node 3 goes through its
parent

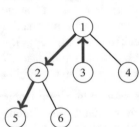

Fig. 10.11 In this case, the
second longest path from the
parent should be chosen

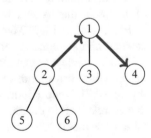

Then, the second part of the problem is to calculate for every node x the maximum length of a path *upward* through its parent p. For example, the longest path from node 3 goes through its parent 1 (Fig. 10.10). At first glance, it seems that we should first move to p and then choose the longest path (upward or downward) from p. However, this *does not* always work, because such a path may go through x (Fig. 10.11). Still, we can solve the second part in $O(n)$ time by storing the maximum lengths of *two* paths for each node x:

- $\mathtt{maxLength}_1(x)$: the maximum length of a path from x to a leaf
- $\mathtt{maxLength}_2(x)$ the maximum length of a path from x to a leaf, in another direction than the first path

For example, in Fig. 10.11, $\text{maxLength}_1(1) = 2$ using the path $1 \rightarrow 2 \rightarrow 5$, and $\text{maxLength}_2(1) = 1$ using the path $1 \rightarrow 3$.

Finally, to determine the maximum length path from node x upward through its parent p, we consider two cases: If the path that corresponds to $\text{maxLength}_1(p)$ goes through x, the maximum length is $\text{maxLength}_2(p) + 1$, and otherwise the maximum length is $\text{maxLength}_1(p) + 1$.

10.2 Tree Queries

In this section we focus on processing *queries* on rooted trees. Such queries are typically related to subtrees and paths of the tree, and they can be processed in constant or logarithmic time.

10.2.1 Finding Ancestors

The kth *ancestor* of a node x in a rooted tree is the node that we will reach if we move k levels up from x. Let $\text{ancestor}(x, k)$ denote the kth ancestor of a node x (or 0 if there is no such an ancestor). For example, in Fig. 10.12, $\text{ancestor}(2, 1) = 1$ and $\text{ancestor}(8, 2) = 4$.

An easy way to calculate any value of $\text{ancestor}(x, k)$ is to perform a sequence of k moves in the tree. However, the time complexity of this method is $O(k)$, which may be slow, because a tree of n nodes may have a path of n nodes.

Fortunately, we can efficiently calculate any value of $\text{ancestor}(x, k)$ in $O(\log k)$ time after preprocessing. As in Sect. 7.5.1, the idea is to first precalculate all values of $\text{ancestor}(x, k)$ where k is a power of two. For example, the values for the tree in Fig. 10.12 are as follows:

Fig. 10.12 Finding ancestors of nodes

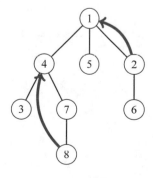

x	1 2 3 4 5 6 7 8
ancestor($x, 1$)	0 1 4 1 1 2 4 7
ancestor($x, 2$)	0 0 1 0 0 1 1 4
ancestor($x, 4$)	0 0 0 0 0 0 0 0
	$\cdots$

Since we know that a node always has less than n ancestors, it suffices to calculate $O(\log n)$ values for each node, and the preprocessing takes $O(n \log n)$ time. After this, any value of ancestor(x, k) can be calculated in $O(\log k)$ time by representing k as a sum where each term is a power of two.

10.2.2 Subtrees and Paths

A *tree traversal array* contains the nodes of a rooted tree in the order in which a depth-first search from the root node visits them. For example, Fig. 10.13 shows a tree and the corresponding tree traversal array.

An important property of tree traversal arrays is that each subtree of a tree corresponds to a subarray in the tree traversal array such that the first element of the subarray is the root node. For example, Fig. 10.14 shows the subarray that corresponds to the subtree of node 4.

Subtree Queries Suppose that each node in the tree is assigned a value, and our task is to process two types of queries: updating the value of a node and calculating the sum of values in the subtree of a node. To solve the problem, we construct a tree traversal array that contains three values for each node: the identifier of the node, the size of the subtree, and the value of the node. For example, Fig. 10.15 shows a tree and the corresponding array.

Using this array, we can calculate the sum of values in any subtree by first determining the size of the subtree and then summing up the values of the corresponding nodes. For example, Fig. 10.16 shows the values that we access when calculating the

Fig. 10.13 Tree and its tree traversal array

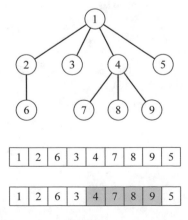

1	2	6	3	4	7	8	9	5

Fig. 10.14 Subtree of node 4 in the tree traversal array

1	2	6	3	4	7	8	9	5

Fig. 10.15 Tree traversal array for calculating subtree sums

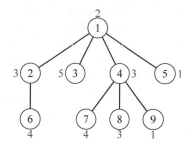

node id	1	2	6	3	4	7	8	9	5
subtree size	9	2	1	1	4	1	1	1	1
node value	2	3	4	5	3	4	3	1	1

Fig. 10.16 Calculating the sum of values in the subtree of node 4

node id	1	2	6	3	4	7	8	9	5
subtree size	9	2	1	1	4	1	1	1	1
node value	2	3	4	5	3	4	3	1	1

sum of values in the subtree of node 4. The last row of the array tells us that the sum of values is $3 + 4 + 3 + 1 = 11$.

To answer queries efficiently, it suffices to store the last row of the array in a binary indexed or segment tree. After this, we can both update a value and calculate the sum of values in $O(\log n)$ time.

Path Queries Using a tree traversal array, we can also efficiently calculate sums of values on paths from the root node to any node of the tree. As an example, consider a problem where our task is to process two types of queries: updating the value of a node and calculating the sum of values on a path from the root to a node.

To solve the problem, we construct a tree traversal array that contains for each node its identifier, the size of its subtree, and the sum of values on a path from the root to the node (Fig. 10.17). When the value of a node increases by x, the sums of all nodes in its subtree increase by x. For example, Fig. 10.18 shows the array after increasing the value of node 4 by 1.

To support both the operations, we need to be able to increase all values in a range and retrieve a single value. This can be done in $O(\log n)$ time using a binary indexed or segment tree and a difference array (see Sect. 9.2.3).

10.2.3 Lowest Common Ancestors

The *lowest common ancestor* of two nodes of a rooted tree is the lowest node whose subtree contains both the nodes. For example, in Fig. 10.19 the lowest common ancestor of nodes 5 and 8 is node 2.

Fig. 10.17 Tree traversal array for calculating path sums

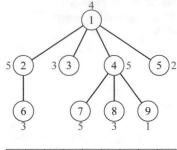

node id	1	2	6	3	4	7	8	9	5
subtree size	9	2	1	1	4	1	1	1	1
path sum	4	9	12	7	9	14	12	10	6

Fig. 10.18 Increasing the value of node 4 by 1

node id	1	2	6	3	4	7	8	9	5
subtree size	9	2	1	1	4	1	1	1	1
path sum	4	9	12	7	10	15	13	11	6

Fig. 10.19 Lowest common ancestor of nodes 5 and 8 is node 2

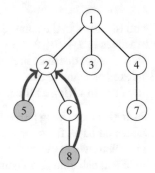

A typical problem is to efficiently process queries that require us to find the lowest common ancestor of two nodes. Next we will discuss two efficient techniques for processing such queries.

First Method Since we can efficiently find the kth ancestor of any node in the tree, we can use this fact to divide the problem into two parts. We use two pointers that initially point to the two nodes whose lowest common ancestor we should find.

First, we make sure that the pointers point to nodes at the same level in the tree. If this is not the case initially, we move one of the pointers upward. After this, we determine the minimum number of steps needed to move both pointers upward so that they will point to the same node. The node to which the pointers point after this is the lowest common ancestor. Since both parts of the algorithm can be performed in $O(\log n)$ time using precomputed information, we can find the lowest common ancestor of any two nodes in $O(\log n)$ time.

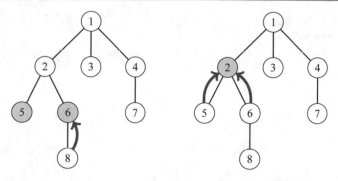

Fig. 10.20 Two steps to find the lowest common ancestor of nodes 5 and 8

	0	1	2	3	4	5	6	7	8	9	10	11	12	13	14
node id	1	2	5	2	6	8	6	2	1	3	1	4	7	4	1
depth	1	2	3	2	3	4	3	2	1	2	1	2	3	2	1

Fig. 10.21 Extended tree traversal array for processing lowest common ancestor queries

	0	1	2	3	4	5	6	7	8	9	10	11	12	13	14
node id	1	2	5	2	6	8	6	2	1	3	1	4	7	4	1
depth	1	2	3	2	3	4	3	2	1	2	1	2	3	2	1

Fig. 10.22 Finding the lowest common ancestor of nodes 5 and 8

Figure 10.20 shows how we can find the lowest common ancestor of nodes 5 and 8 in our example scenario. First, we move the second pointer one level up so that it points to node 6 which is at the same level with node 5. Then, we move both pointers one step upward to node 2, which is the lowest common ancestor.

Second Method Another way to solve the problem, proposed by Bender and Farach-Colton [3], is based on an extended tree traversal array, sometimes called an *Euler tour tree*. To construct the array, we go through the tree nodes using depth-first search and add each node to the array *always* when the depth-first search walks through the node (not only at the first visit). Hence, a node that has k children appears $k + 1$ times in the array, and there are a total of $2n - 1$ nodes in the array. We store two values in the array: the identifier of the node and the depth of the node in the tree. Figure 10.21 shows the resulting array in our example scenario.

Now we can find the lowest common ancestor of nodes a and b by finding the node with the *minimum* depth between nodes a and b in the array. For example, Fig. 10.22 shows how to find the lowest common ancestor of nodes 5 and 8. The minimum depth node between them is node 2 whose depth is 2, so the lowest common ancestor of nodes 5 and 8 is node 2.

Fig. 10.23 Calculating the
distance between nodes 5
and 8

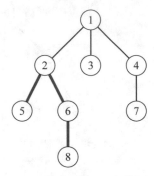

Note that since a node may appear several times in the array, there may be multiple ways to choose the positions of nodes a and b. However, any choice correctly
determines the lowest common ancestor of the nodes.

Using this technique, to find the lowest common ancestor of two nodes, it suffices
to process a range minimum query. The usual way is to use a segment tree to process
such queries in $O(\log n)$ time. However, since the array is static, we can also process
queries in $O(1)$ time after an $O(n \log n)$ time preprocessing.

Calculating Distances Finally, consider the problem of processing queries where
we need to calculate the distance between nodes a and b (i.e., the length of the path
between a and b). It turns out that this problem reduces to finding the lowest common
ancestor of the nodes. First, we root the tree arbitrarily. After this, the distance of
nodes a and b can be calculated using the formula

$$\texttt{depth}(a) + \texttt{depth}(b) - 2 \cdot \texttt{depth}(c),$$

where c is the lowest common ancestor of a and b.

For example, to calculate the distance between nodes 5 and 8 in Fig. 10.23, we
first determine that the lowest common ancestor of the nodes is node 2. Then, since
the depths of the nodes are $\texttt{depth}(5) = 3$, $\texttt{depth}(8) = 4$, and $\texttt{depth}(2) = 2$, we
conclude that the distance between nodes 5 and 8 is $3 + 4 - 2 \cdot 2 = 3$.

10.2.4   Merging Data Structures

So far, we have discussed *online* algorithms for tree queries. Those algorithms are
able to process queries one after another in such a way that each query is answered
before receiving the next query. However, in many problems, the online property
is not necessary, and we may use *offline* algorithms to solve them. Such algorithms
are given a complete set of queries which can be answered in any order. Offline
algorithms are often easier to design than online algorithms.

One method to construct an offline algorithm is to perform a depth-first tree
traversal and maintain data structures in nodes. At each node s, we create a data

Fig. 10.24 Subtree of node
4 contains two nodes whose
value is 3

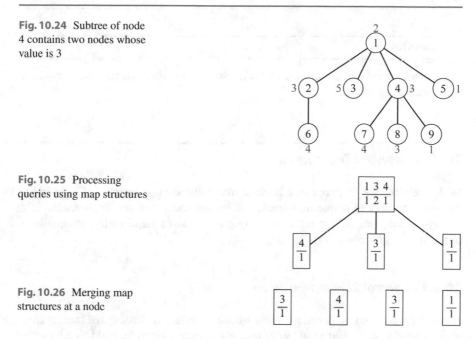

Fig. 10.25 Processing
queries using map structures

Fig. 10.26 Merging map
structures at a node

structure d[s] that is based on the data structures of the children of s. Then, using
this data structure, all queries related to s are processed.

As an example, consider the following problem: We are given a rooted tree where
each node has some value. Our task is to process queries that ask to calculate the
number of nodes with value x in the subtree of node s. For example, in Fig. 10.24,
the subtree of node 4 contains two nodes whose value is 3.

In this problem, we can use map structures to answer the queries. For example,
Fig. 10.25 shows the maps for node 4 and its children. If we create such a data
structure for each node, we can easily process all given queries, because we can
handle all queries related to a node immediately after creating its data structure.

However, it would be too slow to create all data structures from scratch. Instead,
at each node s, we create an initial data structure d[s] that only contains the value of
s. After this, we go through the children of s and *merge* d[s] and all data structures
d[u] where u is a child of s. For example, in the above tree, the map for node 4
is created by merging the maps in Fig. 10.26. Here the first map is the initial data
structure for node 4, and the other three maps correspond to nodes 7, 8, and 9.

The merging at node s can be done as follows: We go through the children of s
and at each child u merge d[s] and d[u]. We always copy the contents from d[u] to
d[s]. However, before this, we *swap* the contents of d[s] and d[u] if d[s] is smaller
than d[u]. By doing this, each value is copied only $O(\log n)$ times during the tree
traversal, which ensures that the algorithm is efficient.

To swap the contents of two data structures a and b efficiently, we can just use
the following code:

```
swap(a,b);
```

It is guaranteed that the above code works in constant time when *a* and *b* are C++ standard library data structures.

10.3 Advanced Techniques

In this section, we discuss two advanced tree processing techniques. Centroid decomposition divides a tree into smaller subtrees and processes them recursively. Heavy-light decomposition represents a tree as a set of special paths, which allows us to efficiently process path queries.

10.3.1 Centroid Decomposition

A *centroid* of a tree of n nodes is a node whose removal divides the tree into subtrees each of which contains at most $\lfloor n/2 \rfloor$ nodes. Every tree has a centroid, and it can be found by rooting the tree arbitrarily and always moving to the subtree that has the maximum number of nodes, until the current node is a centroid.

In the *centroid decomposition* technique, we first locate a centroid of the tree and process all paths that go through the centroid. After this, we remove the centroid from the tree and process the remaining subtrees recursively. Since removing the centroid always creates subtrees whose size is at most half of the size of the original tree, the time complexity of such an algorithm is $O(n \log n)$, provided that we can process each path in linear time.

For example, Fig. 10.27 shows the first step of a centroid decomposition algorithm. In this tree, node 5 is the only centroid, so we first process all paths that go through node 5. After this, node 5 is removed from the tree, and we process the three subtrees $\{1, 2\}$, $\{3, 4\}$, and $\{6, 7, 8\}$ recursively.

Using centroid decomposition, we can, for example, efficiently calculate the number of paths of length x in a tree. When processing a tree, we first find a centroid and calculate the number of paths that go through it, which can be done in linear time. After this, we remove the centroid and recursively process the smaller trees. The resulting algorithm works in $O(n \log n)$ time.

Fig. 10.27 Centroid decomposition

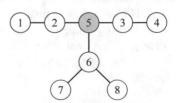

Fig. 10.28 Heavy-light
decomposition

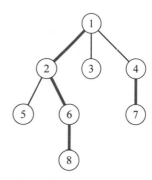

10.3.2 Heavy-Light Decomposition

Heavy-light decomposition[1] divides the nodes of a tree into a set of paths that are called *heavy* paths. The heavy paths are created so that a path between any two tree nodes can be represented as $O(\log n)$ subpaths of heavy paths. Using the technique, we can manipulate nodes on paths between tree nodes almost like elements in an array, with only an additional $O(\log n)$ factor.

To construct the heavy paths, we first root the tree arbitrarily. Then, we start the first heavy path at the root of the tree, and always move to a node that has a maximum size subtree. After this, we recursively process the remaining subtrees. For example, in Fig. 10.28, there are four heavy paths: 1–2–6–8, 3, 4–7, and 5 (note that two of the paths only have one node).

Now, consider any path between two nodes in the tree. Since we always chose the maximum size subtree when creating heavy paths, this guarantees that we can divide the path into $O(\log n)$ subpaths so that each of them is a subpath of a single heavy path. For example, in Fig. 10.28, the path between nodes 7 and 8 can be divided into two heavy subpaths: first 7–4, then 1–2–6–8.

The benefit of heavy-light decomposition is that each heavy path can be treated like an array of nodes. For example, we can assign a segment tree for each heavy path and support sophisticated path queries, such as calculating the minimum node value in a path or increasing the value of every node in a path. Such queries can be processed in $O(\log^2 n)$ time,[2] because each path consists of $O(\log n)$ heavy paths and each heavy path can be processed in $O(\log n)$ time.

While many problems can be solved using heavy-light decomposition, it is good to keep in mind that there is often another solution that is easier to implement. In particular, the techniques presented in Sect. 10.2.2 can often be used instead of heavy-light decomposition.

---

[1] Sleator and Tarjan [33] introduced the idea in the context of their link/cut tree data structure.
[2] The notation $\log^k n$ corresponds to $(\log n)^k$.

Mathematics

11

This chapter deals with mathematical topics that are recurrent in competitive programming. We will both discuss theoretical results and learn how to use them in practice in algorithms.

Section 11.1 discusses number-theoretical topics. We will learn algorithms for finding prime factors of numbers, techniques related to modular arithmetic, and efficient methods for solving integer equations.

Section 11.2 explores ways to approach combinatorial problems: how to efficiently count all valid combinations of objects. The topics of this section include binomial coefficients, Catalan numbers, and inclusion-exclusion.

Section 11.3 shows how to use matrices in algorithm programming. For example, we will learn how to make a dynamic programming algorithm more efficient by exploiting an efficient way to calculate matrix powers.

Section 11.4 first discusses basic techniques for calculating probabilities of events and the concept of Markov chains. After this, we will see examples of algorithms that are based on randomness.

Section 11.5 focuses on game theory. First we will learn to optimally play a simple stick game using nim theory, and after this, we will generalize the strategy to a wide range of other games.

Section 11.6 presents the fast Fourier transform (FFT) algorithm using which we can efficiently calculate convolutions, such as products of polynomials.

11.1 Number Theory

Number theory is a branch of mathematics that studies integers. In this section, we discuss a selection of number-theoretical topics and algorithms, such as finding prime numbers and factors, and solving integer equations.

© Springer Nature Switzerland AG 2020
A. Laaksonen, *Guide to Competitive Programming*, Undergraduate Topics
in Computer Science, https://doi.org/10.1007/978-3-030-39357-1_11

11.1.1 Primes and Factors

An integer a is called a *factor* or a *divisor* of an integer b if a divides b. If a is a factor of b, we write $a \mid b$, and otherwise we write $a \nmid b$. For example, the factors of 24 are 1, 2, 3, 4, 6, 8, 12, and 24.

An integer $n > 1$ is a *prime* if its only positive factors are 1 and n. For example, 7, 19, and 41 are primes, but 35 is not a prime, because $5 \cdot 7 = 35$. For every integer $n > 1$, there is a unique *prime factorization*

$$n = p_1^{\alpha_1} p_2^{\alpha_2} \cdots p_k^{\alpha_k},$$

where $p_1, p_2, \ldots, p_k$ are distinct primes and $\alpha_1, \alpha_2, \ldots, \alpha_k$ are positive integers. For example, the prime factorization for 84 is

$$84 = 2^2 \cdot 3^1 \cdot 7^1.$$

Let $\tau(n)$ denote the number of factors of an integer n. For example, $\tau(12) = 6$, because the factors of 12 are 1, 2, 3, 4, 6, and 12. To calculate the value of $\tau(n)$, we can use the formula

$$\tau(n) = \prod_{i=1}^{k} (\alpha_i + 1),$$

because for each prime p_i, there are $\alpha_i + 1$ ways to choose how many times it appears in the factor. For example, since $12 = 2^2 \cdot 3$, $\tau(12) = 3 \cdot 2 = 6$.

Then, let $\sigma(n)$ denote the sum of factors of an integer n. For example, $\sigma(12) = 28$, because $1 + 2 + 3 + 4 + 6 + 12 = 28$. To calculate the value of $\sigma(n)$, we can use the formula

$$\sigma(n) = \prod_{i=1}^{k} (1 + p_i + \cdots + p_i^{\alpha_i}) = \prod_{i=1}^{k} \frac{p_i^{\alpha_i+1} - 1}{p_i - 1},$$

where the latter form is based on the geometric progression formula. For example, $\sigma(12) = (2^3 - 1)/(2 - 1) \cdot (3^2 - 1)/(3 - 1) = 28$.

Basic Algorithms If an integer n is not prime, it can be represented as a product $a \cdot b$, where $a \le \sqrt{n}$ or $b \le \sqrt{n}$, so it certainly has a factor between 2 and $\lfloor \sqrt{n} \rfloor$. Using this observation, we can both test if an integer is prime and find its prime factorization in $O(\sqrt{n})$ time.

The following function `prime` checks if a given integer n is prime. The function attempts to divide n by all integers between 2 and $\lfloor \sqrt{n} \rfloor$, and if none of them divides n, then n is prime.

```
bool prime(int n) {
    if (n < 2) return false;
    for (int x = 2; x*x <= n; x++) {
        if (n%x == 0) return false;
    }
    return true;
}
```

Then, the following function `factors` constructs a vector that contains the prime factorization of n. The function divides n by its prime factors and adds them to the vector. The process ends when the remaining number n has no factors between 2 and $\lfloor \sqrt{n} \rfloor$. If $n > 1$, it is prime and the last factor.

```
vector<int> factors(int n) {
    vector<int> f;
    for (int x = 2; x*x <= n; x++) {
        while (n%x == 0) {
            f.push_back(x);
            n /= x;
        }
    }
    if (n > 1) f.push_back(n);
    return f;
}
```

Note that each prime factor appears in the vector as many times as it divides the number. For example, $12 = 2^2 \cdot 3$, so the result of the function is $[2, 2, 3]$.

Properties of Primes It is easy to show that there is an infinite number of primes. If the number of primes would be finite, we could construct a set $P = \{p_1, p_2, \ldots, p_n\}$ that would contain all the primes. For example, $p_1 = 2$, $p_2 = 3$, $p_3 = 5$, and so on. However, using such a set P, we could form a new prime

$$p_1 p_2 \cdots p_n + 1$$

that would be larger than all elements in P. This is a contradiction, and the number of primes has to be infinite.

The *prime-counting function* $\pi(n)$ gives the number of primes up to n. For example, $\pi(10) = 4$, because the primes up to 10 are 2, 3, 5, and 7. It is possible to show that

$$\pi(n) \approx \frac{n}{\ln n},$$

which means that primes are quite frequent. For example, an approximation for $\pi(10^6)$ is $10^6 / \ln 10^6 \approx 72382$, and the exact value is 78498.

11.1.2   Sieve of Eratosthenes

The *sieve of Eratosthenes* is a preprocessing algorithm that constructs an array
sieve from which we can efficiently check if any integer x between $2 \ldots n$ is
prime. If x is prime, then $sieve[x] = 0$, and otherwise $sieve[x] = 1$. For example, Fig. 11.1 shows the contents of sieve for $n = 20$.

To construct the array, the algorithm iterates through the integers $2 \ldots n$ one by
one. Always when a new prime x is found, the algorithm records that the numbers $2x, 3x, 4x$, etc., are not primes. The algorithm can be implemented as follows,
assuming that every element of sieve is initially zero:

```
for (int x = 2; x <= n; x++) {
    if (sieve[x]) continue;
    for (int u = 2*x; u <= n; u += x) {
        sieve[u] = 1;
    }
}
```

The inner loop of the algorithm is executed $\lfloor n/x \rfloor$ times for each value of x. Thus,
an upper bound for the running time of the algorithm is the harmonic sum

$$\sum_{x=2}^{n} \lfloor n/x \rfloor = \lfloor n/2 \rfloor + \lfloor n/3 \rfloor + \lfloor n/4 \rfloor + \cdots = O(n \log n).$$

In fact, the algorithm is more efficient, because the inner loop will be executed
only if the number x is prime. It can be shown that the running time of the algorithm
is only $O(n \log \log n)$, a complexity very near to $O(n)$. In practice, the sieve of
Eratosthenes is very efficient; Table 11.1 shows some real running times.

2	3	4	5	6	7	8	9	10	11	12	13	14	15	16	17	18	19	20
0	0	1	0	1	0	1	1	1	0	1	0	1	1	1	0	1	0	1

Fig. 11.1 Outcome of the sieve of Eratosthenes for $n = 20$

Table 11.1 Running times of
the sieve of Eratosthenes

Upper bound n	Running time (s)
10^6	0.01
$2 \cdot 10^6$	0.03
$4 \cdot 10^6$	0.07
$8 \cdot 10^6$	0.14
$16 \cdot 10^6$	0.28
$32 \cdot 10^6$	0.57
$64 \cdot 10^6$	1.16
$128 \cdot 10^6$	2.35

2	3	4	5	6	7	8	9	10	11	12	13	14	15	16	17	18	19	20
2	3	2	5	2	7	2	3	2	11	2	13	2	3	2	17	2	19	2

Fig. 11.2 An extended sieve of Eratosthenes that contains the smallest prime factor of each number

There are several ways to extend the sieve of Eratosthenes. For example, we can calculate for each number k its smallest prime factor (Fig. 11.2). After this, we can efficiently factorize any number between $2 \dots n$ using the sieve. (Note that a number n has $O(\log n)$ prime factors.)

11.1.3 Euclid's Algorithm

The *greatest common divisor* of integers a and b, denoted $\gcd(a, b)$, is the largest integer that divides both a and b. For example, $\gcd(30, 12) = 6$. A related concept is the *lowest common multiple*, denoted $\text{lcm}(a, b)$, which is the smallest integer that is divisible by both a and b. The formula

$$\text{lcm}(a, b) = \frac{ab}{\gcd(a, b)}$$

can be used to calculate lowest common multiples. For example, $\text{lcm}(30, 12) = 360/\gcd(30, 12) = 60$.

One way to find $\gcd(a, b)$ is to divide a and b into prime factors, and then choose for each prime the largest power that appears in both factorizations. For example, to calculate $\gcd(30, 12)$, we can construct the factorizations $30 = 2 \cdot 3 \cdot 5$ and $12 = 2^2 \cdot 3$ and conclude that $\gcd(30, 12) = 2 \cdot 3 = 6$. However, this technique is not efficient if a and b are large numbers.

Euclid's algorithm provides an efficient way to calculate the value of $\gcd(a, b)$. The algorithm is based on the formula

$$\gcd(a, b) = \begin{cases} a & b = 0 \\ \gcd(b, a \bmod b) & b \neq 0. \end{cases}$$

For example,

$$\gcd(30, 12) = \gcd(12, 6) = \gcd(6, 0) = 6.$$

The algorithm can be implemented as follows:

```
int gcd(int a, int b) {
    if (b == 0) return a;
    return gcd(b, a%b);
}
```

Fig. 11.3 Why does
Euclid's algorithm work?

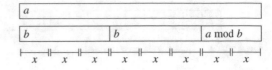

Why does the algorithm work? To understand this, consider Fig. 11.3 where $x = \gcd(a, b)$. Since x divides both a and b, it must also divide $a \bmod b$, which shows why the recursive formula holds.

It can be proved that Euclid's algorithm works in $O(\log n)$ time, where $n = \min(a, b)$.

Extended Euclid's Algorithm Euclid's algorithm can also be extended so that it gives integers x and y for which

$$ax + by = \gcd(a, b).$$

For example, when $a = 30$ and $b = 12$,

$$30 \cdot 1 + 12 \cdot (-2) = 6.$$

We can solve also this problem using the formula $\gcd(a, b) = \gcd(b, a \bmod b)$. Suppose that we have already solved the problem for $\gcd(b, a \bmod b)$, and we know values x' and y' for which

$$bx' + (a \bmod b)y' = gcd(a, b).$$

Then, since $a \bmod b = a - \lfloor a/b \rfloor \cdot b$,

$$bx' + (a - \lfloor a/b \rfloor \cdot b)y' = gcd(a, b),$$

which equals

$$ay' + b(x' - \lfloor a/b \rfloor \cdot y') = gcd(a, b).$$

Thus, we can choose $x = y'$ and $y = x' - \lfloor a/b \rfloor \cdot y'$. Using this idea, the following function returns a tuple $(x, y, \gcd(a, b))$ that satisfies the equation.

```
tuple<int,int,int> gcd(int a, int b) {
   if (b == 0) {
      return {1,0,a};
   } else {
      int x,y,g;
      tie(x,y,g) = gcd(b,a%b);
      return {y,x-(a/b)*y,g};
   }
}
```

We can use the function as follows:

```
int x,y,g;
tie(x,y,g) = gcd(30,12);
cout << x << " " << y << " " << g << "\n"; // 1 -2 6
```

11.1.4 Modular Exponentiation

There is often a need to efficiently calculate the value of x^n mod m. This can be done in $O(\log n)$ time using the following recursive formula:

$$x^n = \begin{cases} 1 & n = 0 \\ x^{n/2} \cdot x^{n/2} & n \text{ is even} \\ x^{n-1} \cdot x & n \text{ is odd} \end{cases}$$

For example, to calculate the value of x^{100}, we first calculate the value of x^{50} and then use the formula $x^{100} = x^{50} \cdot x^{50}$. Then, to calculate the value of x^{50}, we first calculate the value of x^{25}, and so on. Since n always halves when it is even, the calculation takes only $O(\log n)$ time.

The algorithm can be implemented as follows:

```
int modpow(int x, int n, int m) {
    if (n == 0) return 1%m;
    long long u = modpow(x,n/2,m);
    u = (u*u)%m;
    if (n%2 == 1) u = (u*x)%m;
    return u;
}
```

11.1.5 Euler's Theorem

Two integers a and b are called *coprime* if $\gcd(a, b) = 1$. *Euler's totient function* $\varphi(n)$ gives the number of integers between $1 \ldots n$ that are coprime to n. For example, $\varphi(10) = 4$, because 1, 3, 7, and 9 are coprime to 10.

Any value of $\varphi(n)$ can be calculated from the prime factorization of n using the formula

$$\varphi(n) = \prod_{i=1}^{k} p_i^{\alpha_i - 1}(p_i - 1).$$

For example, since $10 = 2 \cdot 5$, $\varphi(10) = 2^0 \cdot (2 - 1) \cdot 5^0 \cdot (5 - 1) = 4$.

Euler's theorem states that

$$x^{\varphi(m)} \bmod m = 1$$

for all positive coprime integers x and m. For example, Euler's theorem tells us that $7^4 \bmod 10 = 1$, because 7 and 10 are coprime and $\varphi(10) = 4$.

If m is prime, $\varphi(m) = m - 1$, so the formula becomes

$$x^{m-1} \bmod m = 1,$$

which is known as *Fermat's little theorem*. This also implies that

$$x^n \bmod m = x^{n \bmod (m-1)} \bmod m,$$

which can be used to calculate values of x^n if n is very large.

Modular Multiplicative Inverses The *modular multiplicative inverse* of x with respect to m is a value $\mathrm{inv}_m(x)$ such that

$$x \cdot \mathrm{inv}_m(x) \bmod m = 1.$$

For example, $\mathrm{inv}_{17}(6) = 3$, because $6 \cdot 3 \bmod 17 = 1$.

Using modular multiplicative inverses, we can divide numbers modulo m, because division by x corresponds to multiplication by $\mathrm{inv}_m(x)$. For example, since we know that $\mathrm{inv}_{17}(6) = 3$, we can calculate the value of $36/6 \bmod 17$ in another way using the formula $36 \cdot 3 \bmod 17$.

A modular multiplicative inverse exists exactly when x and m are coprime. In this case, it can be calculated using the formula

$$\mathrm{inv}_m(x) = x^{\varphi(m)-1},$$

which is based on Euler's theorem. In particular, if m is prime, $\varphi(m) = m - 1$ and the formula becomes

$$\mathrm{inv}_m(x) = x^{m-2}.$$

For example,

$$\mathrm{inv}_{17}(6) \bmod 17 = 6^{17-2} \bmod 17 = 3.$$

The above formula allows us to efficiently calculate modular multiplicative inverses using the modular exponentiation algorithm (Sect. 11.1.4).

11.1.6 Solving Equations

Diophantine Equations A *Diophantine equation* is an equation of the form

$$ax + by = c,$$

where a, b, and c are constants and the values of x and y should be found. Each number in the equation has to be an integer. For example, one solution to the equation

$$5x + 2y = 11$$

is $x = 3$ and $y = -2$.

We can efficiently solve a Diophantine equation by using the extended Euclid's algorithm (Sect. 11.1.3) which gives integers x and y that satisfy the equation

$$ax + by = \gcd(a, b).$$

A Diophantine equation can be solved exactly when c is divisible by $\gcd(a, b)$.

As an example, let us find integers x and y that satisfy the equation

$$39x + 15y = 12.$$

The equation can be solved, because $\gcd(39, 15) = 3$ and $3 \mid 12$. The extended Euclid's algorithm gives us

$$39 \cdot 2 + 15 \cdot (-5) = 3,$$

and by multiplying this by 4, the equation becomes

$$39 \cdot 8 + 15 \cdot (-20) = 12,$$

so a solution to the equation is $x = 8$ and $y = -20$.

A solution to a Diophantine equation is not unique, because we can form an infinite number of solutions if we know one solution. If a pair (x, y) is a solution, then also all pairs

$$\left(x + \frac{kb}{\gcd(a, b)}, y - \frac{ka}{\gcd(a, b)} \right)$$

are solutions, where k is any integer.

Chinese Remainder Theorem

The *Chinese remainder theorem* solves a group of equations of the form

$$\begin{aligned} x &= a_1 \bmod m_1 \\ x &= a_2 \bmod m_2 \\ &\cdots \\ x &= a_n \bmod m_n \end{aligned}$$

where all pairs of $m_1, m_2, \ldots, m_n$ are coprime.

It turns out that a solution to the equations is

$$x = a_1 X_1 \mathrm{inv}_{m_1}(X_1) + a_2 X_2 \mathrm{inv}_{m_2}(X_2) + \cdots + a_n X_n \mathrm{inv}_{m_n}(X_n),$$

where
$$X_k = \frac{m_1 m_2 \dots m_n}{m_k}.$$

In this solution, for each $k = 1, 2, \dots, n,$
$$a_k X_k \text{inv}_{m_k}(X_k) \bmod m_k = a_k,$$

because
$$X_k \text{inv}_{m_k}(X_k) \bmod m_k = 1.$$

Since all other terms in the sum are divisible by m_k, they have no effect on the remainder and $x \bmod m_k = a_k$.

For example, a solution for
$$x = 3 \bmod 5$$
$$x = 4 \bmod 7$$
$$x = 2 \bmod 3$$

is
$$3 \cdot 21 \cdot 1 + 4 \cdot 15 \cdot 1 + 2 \cdot 35 \cdot 2 = 263.$$

Once we have found a solution x, we can create an infinite number of other solutions, because all numbers of the form
$$x + m_1 m_2 \cdots m_n$$

are solutions.

11.2 Combinatorics

Combinatorics studies methods for counting combinations of objects. Usually, the goal is to find a way to count the combinations efficiently without generating each combination separately. In this section, we discuss a selection of combinatorial techniques that can applied to a large number of problems.

11.2.1 Binomial Coefficients

The *binomial coefficient* $\binom{n}{k}$ gives the number of ways we can choose a subset of k elements from a set of n elements. For example, $\binom{5}{3} = 10$, because the set $\{1, 2, 3, 4, 5\}$ has 10 subsets of 3 elements:

$$\{1, 2, 3\}, \{1, 2, 4\}, \{1, 2, 5\}, \{1, 3, 4\}, \{1, 3, 5\},$$

$$\{1, 4, 5\}, \{2, 3, 4\}, \{2, 3, 5\}, \{2, 4, 5\}, \{3, 4, 5\}$$

Binomial coefficients can be recursively calculated using the formula

$$\binom{n}{k} = \binom{n-1}{k-1} + \binom{n-1}{k}.$$

with the base cases

$$\binom{n}{0} = \binom{n}{n} = 1.$$

To see why this formula works, consider an arbitrary element x in the set. If we decide to include x in our subset, the remaining task is to choose $k - 1$ elements from $n - 1$ elements. Then, if we do not include x in our subset, we have to choose k elements from $n - 1$ elements.

Another way to calculate binomial coefficients is to use the formula

$$\binom{n}{k} = \frac{n!}{k!(n-k)!}$$

which is based on the following reasoning: There are $n!$ permutations of n elements. We go through all permutations and always include the first k elements of the permutation in the subset. Since the order of the elements in the subset and outside the subset does not matter, the result is divided by $k!$ and $(n - k)!$

For binomial coefficients,

$$\binom{n}{k} = \binom{n}{n-k},$$

because we actually divide a set of n elements into two subsets: The first contains k elements, and the second contains $n - k$ elements.

The sum of binomial coefficients is

$$\binom{n}{0} + \binom{n}{1} + \binom{n}{2} + \cdots + \binom{n}{n} = 2^n.$$

The reason for the name "binomial coefficient" can be seen when the binomial $(a + b)$ is raised to the nth power:

$$(a+b)^n = \binom{n}{0}a^n b^0 + \binom{n}{1}a^{n-1}b^1 + \cdots + \binom{n}{n-1}a^1 b^{n-1} + \binom{n}{n}a^0 b^n.$$

Binomial coefficients also appear in *Pascal's triangle* (Fig. 11.4) where each value equals the sum of two above values.

Multinomial Coefficients The *multinomial coefficient*

$$\binom{n}{k_1, k_2, \ldots, k_m} = \frac{n!}{k_1! k_2! \cdots k_m!},$$

Fig. 11.4 First 5 rows of
Pascal's triangle

$$
\begin{array}{ccccccccc}
& & & & 1 & & & & \\
& & & 1 & & 1 & & & \\
& & 1 & & 2 & & 1 & & \\
& 1 & & 3 & & 3 & & 1 & \\
1 & & 4 & & 6 & & 4 & & 1 \\
\cdots & & \cdots & & \cdots & & \cdots & & \cdots
\end{array}
$$

gives the number of ways a set of n elements can be divided into subsets of sizes $k_1, k_2, \ldots, k_m$, where $k_1 + k_2 + \cdots + k_m = n$. Multinomial coefficients can be seen as a generalization of binomial coefficients; if $m = 2$, the above formula corresponds to the binomial coefficient formula.

Boxes and Balls "Boxes and balls" is a useful model, where we count the ways to place k balls in n boxes. Let us consider three scenarios:

Scenario 1: Each box can contain at most one ball. For example, when $n = 5$ and $k = 2$, there are 10 combinations (Fig. 11.5). In this scenario, the number of combinations is directly the binomial coefficient $\binom{n}{k}$.

Scenario 2: A box can contain multiple balls. For example, when $n = 5$ and $k = 2$, there are 15 combinations (Fig. 11.6). In this scenario, the process of placing the balls in the boxes can be represented as a string that consists of symbols "o" and "→". Initially, assume that we are standing at the leftmost box. The symbol "o" means that we place a ball in the current box, and the symbol "→" means that we move to the next box to the right. Now each solution is a string of length $k + n - 1$ that contains k symbols "o" and $n - 1$ symbols "→". For example, the upper-right solution in Fig. 11.6 corresponds to the string "→ → o → o →". Thus, we can conclude that the number of combinations is $\binom{k+n-1}{k}$.

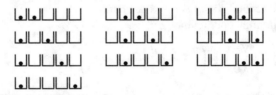

Fig. 11.5 Scenario 1: Each box contains at most one ball

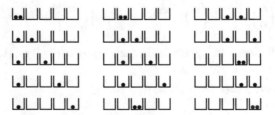

Fig. 11.6 Scenario 2: A box may contain multiple balls

Fig. 11.7 Scenario 3: Each box contains at most one ball, and no two adjacent boxes contain a ball

Scenario 3: Each box may contain at most one ball, and in addition, no two adjacent boxes may both contain a ball. For example, when $n = 5$ and $k = 2$, there are 6 combinations (Fig. 11.7). In this scenario, we can assume that k balls are initially placed in the boxes and there is an empty box between each two adjacent boxes. The remaining task is to choose the positions for the remaining empty boxes. There are $n - 2k + 1$ such boxes and $k + 1$ positions for them. Thus, using the formula of Scenario 2, the number of solutions is $\binom{n-k+1}{n-2k+1}$.

11.2.2 Catalan Numbers

The *Catalan number* C_n gives the number of valid parenthesis expressions that consist of n left parentheses and n right parentheses. For example, $C_3 = 5$, because we can construct a total of five parenthesis expressions using three left parentheses and three right parentheses:

- ( ) ( ) ( )
- (( )) ( )
- ( ) (( ))
- ((( )))
- (( ) ( ))

What is exactly a *valid parenthesis expression*? The following rules precisely define all valid parenthesis expressions:

- An empty parenthesis expression is valid.
- If an expression A is valid, then also the expression (A) is valid.
- If expressions A and B are valid, then also the expression AB is valid.

Another way to characterize valid parenthesis expressions is that if we choose any prefix of such an expression, it has to contain at least as many left parentheses as right parentheses, and the complete expression has to contain an equal number of left and right parentheses.

Catalan numbers can be calculated using the formula

$$C_n = \sum_{i=0}^{n-1} C_i C_{n-i-1}$$

where we consider the ways to divide the parenthesis expression into two parts that are both valid parenthesis expressions, and the first part is as short as possible but not empty. For each i, the first part contains $i + 1$ pairs of parentheses and the number of valid expressions is the product of the following values:

- C_i: the number of ways to construct a parenthesis expression using the parentheses of the first part, not counting the outermost parentheses.
- C_{n-i-1}: the number of ways to construct a parenthesis expression using the parentheses of the second part.

The base case is $C_0 = 1$, because we can construct an empty parenthesis expression using zero pairs of parentheses.

Catalan numbers can also be calculated using the formula

$$C_n = \frac{1}{n+1}\binom{2n}{n},$$

which can be explained as follows:

There are a total of $\binom{2n}{n}$ ways to construct a (not necessarily valid) parenthesis expression that contains n left parentheses and n right parentheses. Let us calculate the number of such expressions that are *not* valid.

If a parenthesis expression is not valid, it has to contain a prefix where the number of right parentheses exceeds the number of left parentheses. The idea is to pick the shortest such prefix and reverse each parenthesis in the prefix. For example, the expression ( )) ( ) (has the prefix ( )), and after reversing the parentheses, the expression becomes) ((( ) (. The resulting expression consists of $n + 1$ left and $n - 1$ right parentheses. In fact, there is a unique way to produce any expression of $n + 1$ left and $n - 1$ right parentheses in the above manner. The number of such expressions is $\binom{2n}{n+1}$, which equals the number of non-valid parenthesis expressions. Thus, the number of valid parenthesis expressions can be calculated using the formula

$$\binom{2n}{n} - \binom{2n}{n+1} = \binom{2n}{n} - \frac{n}{n+1}\binom{2n}{n} = \frac{1}{n+1}\binom{2n}{n}.$$

Counting Trees We can also count certain tree structures using Catalan numbers. First, C_n equals the number of binary trees of n nodes, assuming that left and right children are distinguished. For example, since $C_3 = 5$, there are 5 binary trees of 3 nodes (Fig. 11.8). Then, C_n also equals the number of general rooted trees of $n + 1$ nodes. For example, there are 5 rooted trees of 4 nodes (Fig. 11.9).

Fig. 11.8 There are 5 binary trees of 3 nodes

Fig. 11.9 There are 5 rooted trees of 4 nodes

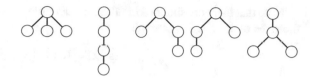

11.2.3 Inclusion-Exclusion

Inclusion-exclusion is a technique that can be used for counting the size of a union of sets when the sizes of the intersections are known, and vice versa. A simple example of the technique is the formula

$$|A \cup B| = |A| + |B| - |A \cap B|,$$

where A and B are sets and $|X|$ denotes the size of X. Figure 11.10 illustrates the formula. In this case, we want to calculate the size of the union $A \cup B$ that corresponds to the area of the region that belongs to at least one circle in Fig. 11.10. We can calculate the area of $A \cup B$ by first summing up the areas of A and B and then subtracting the area of $A \cap B$ from the result.

The same idea can be applied when the number of sets is larger. When there are three sets, the inclusion-exclusion formula is

$$|A \cup B \cup C| = |A| + |B| + |C| - |A \cap B| - |A \cap C| - |B \cap C| + |A \cap B \cap C|,$$

which corresponds to Fig. 11.11.

In the general case, the size of the union $X_1 \cup X_2 \cup \cdots \cup X_n$ can be calculated by going through all possible intersections that contain some of the sets $X_1, X_2, \ldots, X_n$. If an intersection contains an odd number of sets, its size is added to the answer, and otherwise its size is subtracted from the answer.

Fig. 11.10

Inclusion-exclusion principle for two sets

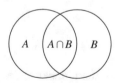

Fig. 11.11

Inclusion-exclusion principle for three sets

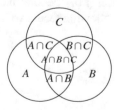

Note that there are similar formulas for calculating the size of an intersection from the sizes of unions. For example,

$$|A \cap B| = |A| + |B| - |A \cup B|$$

and

$$|A \cap B \cap C| = |A| + |B| + |C| - |A \cup B| - |A \cup C| - |B \cup C| + |A \cup B \cup C|.$$

Counting Derangements As an example, let us count the number of *derangements* of $\{1, 2, \ldots, n\}$, i.e., permutations where no element remains in its original place. For example, when $n = 3$, there are two derangements: $(2, 3, 1)$ and $(3, 1, 2)$.

One approach for solving the problem is to use inclusion-exclusion. Let X_k be the set of permutations that contain the element k at position k. For example, when $n = 3$, the sets are as follows:

$$X_1 = \{(1, 2, 3), (1, 3, 2)\}$$
$$X_2 = \{(1, 2, 3), (3, 2, 1)\}$$
$$X_3 = \{(1, 2, 3), (2, 1, 3)\}$$

The number of derangements equals

$$n! - |X_1 \cup X_2 \cup \cdots \cup X_n|,$$

so it suffices to calculate $|X_1 \cup X_2 \cup \cdots \cup X_n|$. Using inclusion-exclusion, this reduces to calculating sizes of intersections. Moreover, an intersection of c distinct sets X_k has $(n - c)!$ elements, because such an intersection consists of all permutations that contain c elements in their original places. Thus, we can efficiently calculate the sizes of the intersections. For example, when $n = 3$,

$$
\begin{aligned}
|X_1 \cup X_2 \cup X_3| &= |X_1| + |X_2| + |X_3| \\
&\quad - |X_1 \cap X_2| - |X_1 \cap X_3| - |X_2 \cap X_3| \\
&\quad + |X_1 \cap X_2 \cap X_3| \\
&= 2 + 2 + 2 - 1 - 1 - 1 + 1 \\
&= 4,
\end{aligned}
$$

so the number of derangements is $3! - 4 = 2$.

It turns out that the problem can also be solved *without* using inclusion-exclusion. Let $f(n)$ denote the number of derangements for $\{1, 2, \ldots, n\}$. We can use the following recursive formula:

$$
f(n) = \begin{cases}
0 & n = 1 \\
1 & n = 2 \\
(n - 1)(f(n - 2) + f(n - 1)) & n > 2
\end{cases}
$$

The formula can be proved by considering the possibilities how the element 1 changes in the derangement. There are $n - 1$ ways to choose an element x that replaces the element 1. In each such choice, there are two options:

Option 1: We also replace the element x with the element 1. After this, the remaining task is to construct a derangement of $n - 2$ elements.

Option 2: We replace the element x with some other element than 1. Now we have to construct a derangement of $n - 1$ element, because we cannot replace the element x with the element 1, and all other elements must be changed.

11.2.4 Burnside's Lemma

Burnside's lemma can be used to count the number of distinct combinations so that symmetric combinations are counted only once. Burnside's lemma states that the number of combinations is

$$\frac{1}{n} \sum_{k=1}^{n} c(k),$$

where there are n ways to change the position of a combination, and there are $c(k)$ combinations that remain unchanged when the kth way is applied.

As an example, let us calculate the number of necklaces of n pearls, where each pearl has m possible colors. Two necklaces are symmetric if they are similar after rotating them. For example, Fig. 11.12 shows four symmetric necklaces, which should be counted as a single combination.

There are n ways to change the position of a necklace, because it can be rotated $k = 0, 1, \ldots, n - 1$ steps clockwise. For example, if $k = 0$, all m^n necklaces remain the same, and if $k = 1$, only the m necklaces where each pearl has the same color remain the same. In the general case, a total of $m^{\gcd(k,n)}$ necklaces remain the same, because blocks of pearls of size $\gcd(k, n)$ will replace each other. Thus, according to Burnside's lemma, the number of distinct necklaces is

$$\frac{1}{n} \sum_{k=0}^{n-1} m^{\gcd(k,n)}.$$

For example, the number of distinct necklaces of 4 pearls and 3 colors is

$$\frac{3^4 + 3 + 3^2 + 3}{4} = 24.$$

Fig. 11.12 Four symmetric necklaces

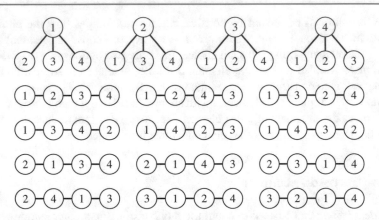

Fig. 11.13 There are 16 distinct labeled trees of 4 nodes

Fig. 11.14 Prüfer code of
this tree is [4, 4, 2]

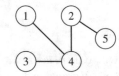

11.2.5 Cayley's Formula

Cayley's formula states that there are a total of n^{n-2} distinct labeled trees of n nodes.
The nodes are labeled $1, 2, \ldots, n$, and two trees are considered distinct if either their
structure or labeling is different. For example, when $n = 4$, there are $4^{4-2} = 16$
labeled trees, shown in Fig. 11.13.

Cayley's formula can be proved using Prüfer codes. A *Prüfer code* is a sequence
of $n - 2$ numbers that describes a labeled tree. The code is constructed by following
a process that removes $n - 2$ leaves from the tree. At each step, the leaf with the
smallest label is removed, and the label of its only neighbor is added to the code.
For example, the Prüfer code of the tree in Fig. 11.14 is [4, 4, 2], because we remove
leaves 1, 3, and 4.

We can construct a Prüfer code for any tree, and more importantly, the original
tree can be reconstructed from a Prüfer code. Hence, the number of labeled trees of
n nodes equals n^{n-2}, the number of Prüfer codes of length n.

11.3   Matrices

A *matrix* is a mathematical concept that corresponds to a two-dimensional array in
programming. For example,

$$A = \begin{bmatrix} 6 & 13 & 7 & 4 \\ 7 & 0 & 8 & 2 \\ 9 & 5 & 4 & 18 \end{bmatrix}$$

is a matrix of size 3×4, i.e., it has 3 rows and 4 columns. The notation $[i, j]$ refers to the element in row i and column j in a matrix. For example, in the above matrix, $A[2, 3] = 8$ and $A[3, 1] = 9$.

A special case of a matrix is a *vector* that is a one-dimensional matrix of size $n \times 1$. For example,

$$V = \begin{bmatrix} 4 \\ 7 \\ 5 \end{bmatrix}$$

is a vector that contains three elements.

The *transpose* A^T of a matrix A is obtained when the rows and columns of A are swapped, i.e., $A^T[i, j] = A[j, i]$:

$$A^T = \begin{bmatrix} 6 & 7 & 9 \\ 13 & 0 & 5 \\ 7 & 8 & 4 \\ 4 & 2 & 18 \end{bmatrix}$$

A matrix is a *square matrix* if it has the same number of rows and columns. For example, the following matrix is a square matrix:

$$S = \begin{bmatrix} 3 & 12 & 4 \\ 5 & 9 & 15 \\ 0 & 2 & 4 \end{bmatrix}$$

11.3.1 Matrix Operations

The sum $A + B$ of matrices A and B is defined if the matrices are of the same size. The result is a matrix where each element has the sum of the corresponding elements in A and B. For example,

$$\begin{bmatrix} 6 & 1 & 4 \\ 3 & 9 & 2 \end{bmatrix} + \begin{bmatrix} 4 & 9 & 3 \\ 8 & 1 & 3 \end{bmatrix} = \begin{bmatrix} 6+4 & 1+9 & 4+3 \\ 3+8 & 9+1 & 2+3 \end{bmatrix} = \begin{bmatrix} 10 & 10 & 7 \\ 11 & 10 & 5 \end{bmatrix}.$$

Multiplying a matrix A by a value x means that each element of A is multiplied by x. For example,

$$2 \cdot \begin{bmatrix} 6 & 1 & 4 \\ 3 & 9 & 2 \end{bmatrix} = \begin{bmatrix} 2 \cdot 6 & 2 \cdot 1 & 2 \cdot 4 \\ 2 \cdot 3 & 2 \cdot 9 & 2 \cdot 2 \end{bmatrix} = \begin{bmatrix} 12 & 2 & 8 \\ 6 & 18 & 4 \end{bmatrix}.$$

The product AB of matrices A and B is defined if A is of size $a \times n$ and B is of size $n \times b$, i.e., the width of A equals the height of B. The result is a matrix of size

Fig. 11.15 Intuition behind
the matrix multiplication
formula

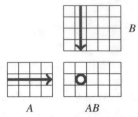

$a \times b$ whose elements are calculated using the formula

$$AB[i, j] = \sum_{k=1}^{n}(A[i, k] \cdot B[k, j]).$$

The idea is that each element of AB is a sum of products of elements of A and B according to Fig. 11.15. For example,

$$\begin{bmatrix} 1 & 4 \\ 3 & 9 \\ 8 & 6 \end{bmatrix} \cdot \begin{bmatrix} 1 & 6 \\ 2 & 9 \end{bmatrix} = \begin{bmatrix} 1 \cdot 1 + 4 \cdot 2 & 1 \cdot 6 + 4 \cdot 9 \\ 3 \cdot 1 + 9 \cdot 2 & 3 \cdot 6 + 9 \cdot 9 \\ 8 \cdot 1 + 6 \cdot 2 & 8 \cdot 6 + 6 \cdot 9 \end{bmatrix} = \begin{bmatrix} 9 & 42 \\ 21 & 99 \\ 20 & 102 \end{bmatrix}.$$

We can directly use the above formula to calculate the product C of two $n \times n$ matrices A and B in $O(n^3)$ time[1]:

```
for (int i = 1; i <= n; i++) {
    for (int j = 1; j <= n; j++) {
        for (int k = 1; k <= n; k++) {
            C[i][j] += A[i][k]*B[k][j];
        }
    }
}
```

Matrix multiplication is associative, so $A(BC) = (AB)C$ holds, but it is not commutative, so usually $AB \neq BA$.

An *identity matrix* is a square matrix where each element on the diagonal is 1 and all other elements are 0. For example, the following matrix is the 3×3 identity matrix:

$$I = \begin{bmatrix} 1 & 0 & 0 \\ 0 & 1 & 0 \\ 0 & 0 & 1 \end{bmatrix}$$

---

[1]While the straightforward $O(n^3)$ time algorithm is sufficient in competitive programming, there are *theoretically* more efficient algorithms. In 1969, Strassen [35] discovered the first such algorithm, now called *Strassen's algorithm*, whose time complexity is $O(n^{2.81})$. The best current algorithm, proposed by Le Gall [13] in 2014, works in $O(n^{2.37})$ time.

Multiplying a matrix by an identity matrix does not change it. For example,

$$\begin{bmatrix} 1 & 0 & 0 \\ 0 & 1 & 0 \\ 0 & 0 & 1 \end{bmatrix} \cdot \begin{bmatrix} 1 & 4 \\ 3 & 9 \\ 8 & 6 \end{bmatrix} = \begin{bmatrix} 1 & 4 \\ 3 & 9 \\ 8 & 6 \end{bmatrix} \quad \text{and} \quad \begin{bmatrix} 1 & 4 \\ 3 & 9 \\ 8 & 6 \end{bmatrix} \cdot \begin{bmatrix} 1 & 0 \\ 0 & 1 \end{bmatrix} = \begin{bmatrix} 1 & 4 \\ 3 & 9 \\ 8 & 6 \end{bmatrix}.$$

The power A^k of a matrix A is defined if A is a square matrix. The definition is based on matrix multiplication:

$$A^k = \underbrace{A \cdot A \cdot A \cdots A}_{k \text{ times}}$$

For example,

$$\begin{bmatrix} 2 & 5 \\ 1 & 4 \end{bmatrix}^3 = \begin{bmatrix} 2 & 5 \\ 1 & 4 \end{bmatrix} \cdot \begin{bmatrix} 2 & 5 \\ 1 & 4 \end{bmatrix} \cdot \begin{bmatrix} 2 & 5 \\ 1 & 4 \end{bmatrix} = \begin{bmatrix} 48 & 165 \\ 33 & 114 \end{bmatrix}.$$

In addition, A^0 is an identity matrix. For example,

$$\begin{bmatrix} 2 & 5 \\ 1 & 4 \end{bmatrix}^0 = \begin{bmatrix} 1 & 0 \\ 0 & 1 \end{bmatrix}.$$

The matrix A^k can be efficiently calculated in $O(n^3 \log k)$ time using the algorithm in Sec. 11.1.4. For example,

$$\begin{bmatrix} 2 & 5 \\ 1 & 4 \end{bmatrix}^8 = \begin{bmatrix} 2 & 5 \\ 1 & 4 \end{bmatrix}^4 \cdot \begin{bmatrix} 2 & 5 \\ 1 & 4 \end{bmatrix}^4.$$

11.3.2 Linear Recurrences

A *linear recurrence* is a function $f(n)$ whose initial values are $f(0), f(1), \ldots, f(k-1)$, and larger values are calculated recursively using the formula

$$f(n) = c_1 f(n-1) + c_2 f(n-2) + \cdots + c_k f(n-k),$$

where $c_1, c_2, \ldots, c_k$ are constant coefficients.

Dynamic programming can be used to calculate any value of $f(n)$ in $O(kn)$ time by calculating all values of $f(0), f(1), \ldots, f(n)$ one after another. However, as we will see next, we can also calculate the value of $f(n)$ in $O(k^3 \log n)$ time using matrix operations. This is an important improvement if k is small and n is large.

Fibonacci Numbers A simple example of a linear recurrence is the following function that defines the Fibonacci numbers:

$$f(0) = 0$$
$$f(1) = 1$$
$$f(n) = f(n-1) + f(n-2)$$

In this case, $k = 2$ and $c_1 = c_2 = 1$.

To efficiently calculate Fibonacci numbers, we represent the Fibonacci formula as a square matrix X of size 2×2, for which the following holds:

$$X \cdot \begin{bmatrix} f(i) \\ f(i+1) \end{bmatrix} = \begin{bmatrix} f(i+1) \\ f(i+2) \end{bmatrix}$$

Thus, values $f(i)$ and $f(i+1)$ are given as "input" for X, and X calculates values $f(i+1)$ and $f(i+2)$ from them. It turns out that such a matrix is

$$X = \begin{bmatrix} 0 & 1 \\ 1 & 1 \end{bmatrix}.$$

For example,

$$\begin{bmatrix} 0 & 1 \\ 1 & 1 \end{bmatrix} \cdot \begin{bmatrix} f(5) \\ f(6) \end{bmatrix} = \begin{bmatrix} 0 & 1 \\ 1 & 1 \end{bmatrix} \cdot \begin{bmatrix} 5 \\ 8 \end{bmatrix} = \begin{bmatrix} 8 \\ 13 \end{bmatrix} = \begin{bmatrix} f(6) \\ f(7) \end{bmatrix}.$$

Thus, we can calculate $f(n)$ using the formula

$$\begin{bmatrix} f(n) \\ f(n+1) \end{bmatrix} = X^n \cdot \begin{bmatrix} f(0) \\ f(1) \end{bmatrix} = \begin{bmatrix} 0 & 1 \\ 1 & 1 \end{bmatrix}^n \cdot \begin{bmatrix} 0 \\ 1 \end{bmatrix}.$$

The value of X^n can be calculated in $O(\log n)$ time, so the value of $f(n)$ can also be calculated in $O(\log n)$ time.

General Case Let us now consider the general case where $f(n)$ is any linear recurrence. Again, our goal is to construct a matrix X for which

$$X \cdot \begin{bmatrix} f(i) \\ f(i+1) \\ \vdots \\ f(i+k-1) \end{bmatrix} = \begin{bmatrix} f(i+1) \\ f(i+2) \\ \vdots \\ f(i+k) \end{bmatrix}.$$

Such a matrix is

$$X = \begin{bmatrix} 0 & 1 & 0 & \cdots & 0 \\ 0 & 0 & 1 & \cdots & 0 \\ \vdots & \vdots & \vdots & \ddots & \vdots \\ 0 & 0 & 0 & \cdots & 1 \\ c_k & c_{k-1} & c_{k-2} & \cdots & c_1 \end{bmatrix}.$$

In the first $k - 1$ rows, each element is 0 except that one element is 1. These rows replace $f(i)$ with $f(i+1)$, $f(i+1)$ with $f(i+2)$, and so on. Then, the last row contains the coefficients of the recurrence to calculate the new value $f(i+k)$.

Now, $f(n)$ can be calculated in $O(k^3 \log n)$ time using the formula

$$
\begin{bmatrix} f(n) \\ f(n+1) \\ \vdots \\ f(n+k-1) \end{bmatrix} = X^n \cdot \begin{bmatrix} f(0) \\ f(1) \\ \vdots \\ f(k-1) \end{bmatrix}.
$$

11.3.3 Graphs and Matrices

The powers of adjacency matrices of graphs have interesting properties. When M is an adjacency matrix of an unweighted graph, the matrix M^n gives for each node pair (a, b) the number of paths that begin at node a, end at node b, and contain exactly n edges. It is allowed that a node appears on a path several times.

As an example, consider the graph in Fig. 11.16a. The adjacency matrix of this graph is

$$
M = \begin{bmatrix} 0 & 0 & 0 & 1 & 0 & 0 \\ 1 & 0 & 0 & 0 & 1 & 1 \\ 0 & 1 & 0 & 0 & 0 & 0 \\ 0 & 1 & 0 & 0 & 0 & 0 \\ 0 & 0 & 0 & 0 & 0 & 0 \\ 0 & 0 & 1 & 0 & 1 & 0 \end{bmatrix}.
$$

Then, the matrix

$$
M^4 = \begin{bmatrix} 0 & 0 & 1 & 1 & 1 & 0 \\ 2 & 0 & 0 & 0 & 2 & 2 \\ 0 & 2 & 0 & 0 & 0 & 0 \\ 0 & 2 & 0 & 0 & 0 & 0 \\ 0 & 0 & 0 & 0 & 0 & 0 \\ 0 & 0 & 1 & 1 & 1 & 0 \end{bmatrix}
$$

gives the number of paths that contain exactly 4 edges. For example, $M^4[2, 5] = 2$, because there are two paths of 4 edges from node 2 to node 5: $2 \rightarrow 1 \rightarrow 4 \rightarrow 2 \rightarrow 5$ and $2 \rightarrow 6 \rightarrow 3 \rightarrow 2 \rightarrow 5$.

Using a similar idea in a weighted graph, we can calculate for each node pair (a, b) the shortest length of a path that goes from a to b and contains exactly n

Fig. 11.16 Example graphs for matrix operations

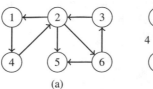

(a)

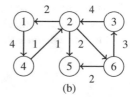

(b)

edges. To calculate this, we define matrix multiplication in a new way, so that we do not calculate numbers of paths but minimize lengths of paths.

As an example, consider the graph in Fig. 11.16b. Let us construct an adjacency matrix where ∞ means that an edge does not exist, and other values correspond to edge weights. The matrix is

$$M = \begin{bmatrix} \infty & \infty & \infty & 4 & \infty & \infty \\ 2 & \infty & \infty & \infty & 1 & 2 \\ \infty & 4 & \infty & \infty & \infty & \infty \\ \infty & 1 & \infty & \infty & \infty & \infty \\ \infty & \infty & \infty & \infty & \infty & \infty \\ \infty & \infty & 3 & \infty & 2 & \infty \end{bmatrix}.$$

Instead of the formula

$$AB[i, j] = \sum_{k=1}^{n}(A[i, k] \cdot B[k, j])$$

we now use the formula

$$AB[i, j] = \min_{k=1}^{n}(A[i, k] + B[k, j])$$

for matrix multiplication, so we calculate minima instead of sums, and sums of elements instead of products. After this modification, matrix powers minimize path lengths in the graph. For example, as

$$M^4 = \begin{bmatrix} \infty & \infty & 10 & 11 & 9 & \infty \\ 9 & \infty & \infty & \infty & 8 & 9 \\ \infty & 11 & \infty & \infty & \infty & \infty \\ \infty & 8 & \infty & \infty & \infty & \infty \\ \infty & \infty & \infty & \infty & \infty & \infty \\ \infty & \infty & 12 & 13 & 11 & \infty \end{bmatrix},$$

we can conclude that the minimum length of a path of 4 edges from node 2 to node 5 is 8. Such a path is $2 \to 1 \to 4 \to 2 \to 5$.

11.3.4   Gaussian Elimination

Gaussian elimination is a systematic way to solve a group of linear equations. The idea is to represent the equations as a matrix and then apply a sequence of simple matrix row operations that both preserve the information of the equations and determine a value for each variable.

Suppose that we are given a group of n linear equations, each of which contains n variables:

$$a_{1,1}x_1 + a_{1,2}x_2 + \cdots + a_{1,n}x_n = b_1$$
$$a_{2,1}x_1 + a_{2,2}x_2 + \cdots + a_{2,n}x_n = b_2$$
$$\cdots$$
$$a_{n,1}x_1 + a_{n,2}x_2 + \cdots + a_{n,n}x_n = b_n$$

We represent the equations as a matrix as follows:

$$\begin{bmatrix} a_{1,1} & a_{1,2} & \cdots & a_{1,n} & b_1 \\ a_{2,1} & a_{2,2} & \cdots & a_{2,n} & b_2 \\ \vdots & \vdots & \ddots & \vdots & \vdots \\ a_{n,1} & a_{n,2} & \cdots & a_{n,n} & b_n \end{bmatrix}$$

To solve the equations, we want to transform the matrix to

$$\begin{bmatrix} 1 & 0 & \cdots & 0 & c_1 \\ 0 & 1 & \cdots & 0 & c_2 \\ \vdots & \vdots & \ddots & \vdots & \vdots \\ 0 & 0 & \cdots & 1 & c_n \end{bmatrix},$$

which tells us that the solution is $x_1 = c_1, x_2 = c_2, \ldots, x_n = c_n$. To do this, we use three types of matrix row operations:

1. Swap the values of two rows.
2. Multiply each value in a row by a nonnegative constant.
3. Add a row, multiplied by a constant, to another row.

Each above operation preserves the information of the equations, which guarantees that the final solution agrees with the original equations. We can systematically process each matrix column so that the resulting algorithm works in $O(n^3)$ time.

As an example, consider the following group of equations:

$$2x_1 + 4x_2 + x_3 = 16$$
$$x_1 + 2x_2 + 5x_3 = 17$$
$$3x_1 + x_2 + x_3 = 8$$

In this case, the matrix is as follows:

$$\begin{bmatrix} 2 & 4 & 1 & 16 \\ 1 & 2 & 5 & 17 \\ 3 & 1 & 1 & 8 \end{bmatrix}$$

We process the matrix column by column. At each step, we make sure that the current column has a one in the correct position and all other values are zeros. To process the first column, we first multiply the first row by $\frac{1}{2}$:

$$\begin{bmatrix} 1 & 2 & \frac{1}{2} & 8 \\ 1 & 2 & 5 & 17 \\ 3 & 1 & 1 & 8 \end{bmatrix}$$

Then, we add the first row to the second row (multiplied by -1) and the first row to the third row (multiplied by -3):

$$\begin{bmatrix} 1 & 2 & \frac{1}{2} & 8 \\ 0 & 0 & \frac{9}{2} & 9 \\ 0 & -5 & -\frac{1}{2} & -16 \end{bmatrix}$$

After this, we process the second column. Since the second value in the second row is zero, we first swap the second and third row:

$$\begin{bmatrix} 1 & 2 & \frac{1}{2} & 8 \\ 0 & -5 & -\frac{1}{2} & -16 \\ 0 & 0 & \frac{9}{2} & 9 \end{bmatrix}$$

Then, we multiply the second row by $-\frac{1}{5}$ and add it to the first row (multiplied by -2):

$$\begin{bmatrix} 1 & 0 & \frac{3}{10} & \frac{8}{5} \\ 0 & 1 & \frac{1}{10} & \frac{16}{5} \\ 0 & 0 & \frac{9}{2} & 9 \end{bmatrix}$$

Finally, we process the third column by first multiplying it by $\frac{2}{9}$ and then adding it to the first row (multiplied by $-\frac{3}{10}$) and to the second row (multiplied by $-\frac{1}{10}$):

$$\begin{bmatrix} 1 & 0 & 0 & 1 \\ 0 & 1 & 0 & 3 \\ 0 & 0 & 1 & 2 \end{bmatrix}$$

Now the last column of the matrix tells us that the solution to the original group of equations is $x_1 = 1$, $x_2 = 3$, $x_3 = 2$.

Note that Gaussian elimination only works if the group of equations has a *unique* solution. For example, the group

$$\begin{aligned} x_1 + x_2 &= 2 \\ 2x_1 + 2x_2 &= 4 \end{aligned}$$

has an infinite number of solutions, because both the equations contain the same information. On the other hand, the group

$$\begin{aligned} x_1 + x_2 &= 5 \\ x_1 + x_2 &= 7 \end{aligned}$$

cannot be solved, because the equations are contradictory. If there is no unique solution, we will notice this during the algorithm, because at some point we will not be able to successfully process a column.

11.4 Probability

A *probability* is a real number between 0 and 1 that indicates how probable an event is. If an event is certain to happen, its probability is 1, and if an event is impossible, its probability is 0. The probability of an event is denoted $P(\cdots)$ where the three dots describe the event. For example, when throwing a dice, there are six possible outcomes $1, 2, \ldots, 6$, and $P(\text{"the outcome is even"}) = 1/2$.

To calculate the probability of an event, we can either use combinatorics or simulate the process that generates the event. As an example, consider an experiment where we draw the three top cards from a shuffled deck of cards.[2] What is the probability that each card has the same value (e.g., ♠8, ♣8, and ◇8)?

One way to calculate the probability is to use the formula

$$\frac{\text{number of desired outcomes}}{\text{total number of outcomes}}.$$

In our example, the desired outcomes are those in which the value of each card is the same. There are $13\binom{4}{3}$ such outcomes, because there are 13 possibilities for the value of the cards and $\binom{4}{3}$ ways to choose 3 suits from 4 possible suits. Then, there are a total of $\binom{52}{3}$ outcomes, because we choose 3 cards from 52 cards. Thus, the probability of the event is

$$\frac{13\binom{4}{3}}{\binom{52}{3}} = \frac{1}{425}.$$

Another way to calculate the probability is to simulate the process that generates the event. In our example, we draw three cards, so the process consists of three steps. We require that each step of the process is successful.

Drawing the first card certainly succeeds, because any card is fine. The second step succeeds with probability $3/51$, because there are 51 cards left and 3 of them have the same value as the first card. In a similar way, the third step succeeds with probability $2/50$. Thus, the probability that the entire process succeeds is

$$1 \cdot \frac{3}{51} \cdot \frac{2}{50} = \frac{1}{425}.$$

---

[2] A deck of cards consists of 52 cards. Each card has a suit (spade ♠, diamond ◇, club ♣, or heart ♡) and a value (an integer between 1–13).

11.4.1   Working with Events

A convenient way to represent events is to use sets. For example, the possible outcomes when throwing a dice are $\{1, 2, 3, 4, 5, 6\}$, and any subset of this set is an
event. The event "the outcome is even" corresponds to the set $\{2, 4, 6\}$.

Each outcome x is assigned a probability $p(x)$, and the probability $P(X)$ of an
event X can be calculated using the formula

$$P(X) = \sum_{x \in X} p(x).$$

For example, when throwing a dice, $p(x) = 1/6$ for each outcome x, so the probability of the event "the outcome is even" is

$$p(2) + p(4) + p(6) = 1/2.$$

Since the events are represented as sets, we can manipulate them using standard
set operations:

- The *complement* $\bar{A}$ means "A does not happen." For example, when throwing a
  dice, the complement of $A = \{2, 4, 6\}$ is $\bar{A} = \{1, 3, 5\}$.
- The *union* $A \cup B$ means "A or B happen." For example, the union of $A = \{2, 5\}$
  and $B = \{4, 5, 6\}$ is $A \cup B = \{2, 4, 5, 6\}$.
- The *intersection* $A \cap B$ means "A and B happen." For example, the intersection
  of $A = \{2, 5\}$ and $B = \{4, 5, 6\}$ is $A \cap B = \{5\}$.

Complement The probability of $\bar{A}$ is calculated using the formula

$$P(\bar{A}) = 1 - P(A).$$

Sometimes, we can solve a problem easily using complements by solving the
opposite problem. For example, the probability of getting at least one six when
throwing a dice ten times is

$$1 - (5/6)^{10}.$$

Here $5/6$ is the probability that the outcome of a single throw is not six, and $(5/6)^{10}$
is the probability that none of the ten throws is a six. The complement of this is the
answer to the problem.

Union The probability of $A \cup B$ is calculated using the formula

$$P(A \cup B) = P(A) + P(B) - P(A \cap B).$$

For example, consider the events $A =$ "the outcome is even" and $B =$ "the outcome is
less than 4" when throwing a dice. In this case, the event $A \cup B$ means "the outcome

is even or less than 4," and its probability is

$$P(A \cup B) = P(A) + P(B) - P(A \cap B) = 1/2 + 1/2 - 1/6 = 5/6.$$

If the events A and B are *disjoint*, i.e., $A \cap B$ is empty, the probability of the event $A \cup B$ is simply

$$P(A \cup B) = P(A) + P(B).$$

Intersection The probability of $A \cap B$ can be calculated using the formula

$$P(A \cap B) = P(A)P(B|A),$$

where $P(B|A)$ is the *conditional probability* that B happens assuming that we know that A happens. For example, using the events of our previous example, $P(B|A) = 1/3$, because we know that the outcome belongs to the set $\{2, 4, 6\}$, and one of the outcomes is less than 4. Thus,

$$P(A \cap B) = P(A)P(B|A) = 1/2 \cdot 1/3 = 1/6.$$

Events A and B are *independent* if

$$P(A|B) = P(A) \text{ and } P(B|A) = P(B),$$

which means that the fact that B happens does not change the probability of A, and vice versa. In this case, the probability of the intersection is

$$P(A \cap B) = P(A)P(B).$$

11.4.2 Random Variables

A *random variable* is a value that is generated by a random process. For example, when throwing two dice, a possible random variable is

$$X = \text{"the sum of the outcomes."}$$

For example, if the outcomes are [4, 6] (meaning that we first throw a four and then a six), then the value of X is 10.

We denote by $P(X = x)$ the probability that the value of a random variable X is x. For example, when throwing two dice, $P(X = 10) = 3/36$, because the total number of outcomes is 36 and there are three possible ways to obtain the sum 10: [4, 6], [5, 5], and [6, 4].

Expected Values The *expected value* $E[X]$ indicates the average value of a random variable X. The expected value can be calculated as a sum

$$\sum_x P(X = x)x,$$

where x goes through all possible values of X.

Fig. 11.17 Possible ways to place two balls in two boxes

For example, when throwing a dice, the expected outcome is

$$1/6 \cdot 1 + 1/6 \cdot 2 + 1/6 \cdot 3 + 1/6 \cdot 4 + 1/6 \cdot 5 + 1/6 \cdot 6 = 7/2.$$

A useful property of expected values is *linearity*. It means that the sum $E[X_1 + X_2 + \cdots + X_n]$ always equals the sum $E[X_1] + E[X_2] + \cdots + E[X_n]$. This holds even if random variables depend on each other. For example, when throwing two dice, the expected sum of their values is

$$E[X_1 + X_2] = E[X_1] + E[X_2] = 7/2 + 7/2 = 7.$$

Let us now consider a problem where n balls are randomly placed in n boxes, and our task is to calculate the expected number of empty boxes. Each ball has an equal probability to be placed in any of the boxes.

For example, Fig. 11.17 shows the possibilities when $n = 2$. In this case, the expected number of empty boxes is

$$\frac{0 + 0 + 1 + 1}{4} = \frac{1}{2}.$$

Then, in the general case, the probability that a single box is empty is

$$\left(\frac{n-1}{n}\right)^n,$$

because no ball should be placed in it. Hence, using linearity, the expected number of empty boxes is

$$n \cdot \left(\frac{n-1}{n}\right)^n.$$

Distributions The *distribution* of a random variable X shows the probability of each value that X may have. The distribution consists of values $P(X = x)$. For example, when throwing two dice, the distribution for their sum is:

x	2	3	4	5	6	7	8	9	10	11	12
$P(X = x)$	1/36	2/36	3/36	4/36	5/36	6/36	5/36	4/36	3/36	2/36	1/36

In a *uniform distribution*, the random variable X has n possible values $a, a + 1, \ldots, b$ and the probability of each value is $1/n$. For example, when throwing a dice, $a = 1, b = 6$, and $P(X = x) = 1/6$ for each value x.

The expected value of X in a uniform distribution is

$$E[X] = \frac{a+b}{2}.$$

In a *binomial distribution*, n attempts are made and the probability that a single attempt succeeds is p. The random variable X counts the number of successful attempts, and the probability of a value x is

$$P(X = x) = p^x(1-p)^{n-x}\binom{n}{x},$$

where p^x and $(1-p)^{n-x}$ correspond to successful and unsuccessful attempts, and $\binom{n}{x}$ is the number of ways we can choose the order of the attempts.

For example, when throwing a dice ten times, the probability of throwing a six exactly three times is $(1/6)^3(5/6)^7\binom{10}{3}$.

The expected value of X in a binomial distribution is

$$E[X] = pn.$$

In a *geometric distribution*, the probability that an attempt succeeds is p, and we continue until the first success happens. The random variable X counts the number of attempts needed, and the probability of a value x is

$$P(X = x) = (1-p)^{x-1}p,$$

where $(1-p)^{x-1}$ corresponds to the unsuccessful attempts and p corresponds to the first successful attempt.

For example, if we throw a dice until we get a six, the probability that the number of throws is exactly 4 is $(5/6)^3 1/6$.

The expected value of X in a geometric distribution is

$$E[X] = \frac{1}{p}.$$

11.4.3 Markov Chains

A *Markov chain* is a random process that consists of states and transitions between them. For each state, we know the probabilities of moving to other states. A Markov chain can be represented as a graph whose nodes correspond to the states and edges describe the transitions.

As an example, consider a problem where we are in floor 1 in an n floor building. At each step, we randomly walk either one floor up or one floor down, except that we always walk one floor up from floor 1 and one floor down from floor n. What is the probability of being in floor m after k steps?

In this problem, each floor of the building corresponds to a state in a Markov chain. For example, Fig. 11.18 shows the chain when $n = 5$.

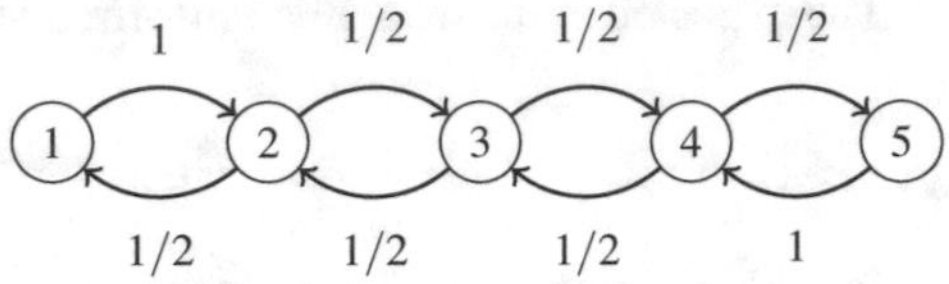

Fig. 11.18 A Markov chain for a building that consists of five floors

The probability distribution of a Markov chain is a vector $[p_1, p_2, \ldots, p_n]$, where p_k is the probability that the current state is k. The formula $p_1 + p_2 + \cdots + p_n = 1$ always holds.

In the above scenario, the initial distribution is $[1, 0, 0, 0, 0]$, because we always begin in floor 1. The next distribution is $[0, 1, 0, 0, 0]$, because we can only move from floor 1 to floor 2. After this, we can either move one floor up or one floor down, so the next distribution is $[1/2, 0, 1/2, 0, 0]$, and so on.

An efficient way to simulate the walk in a Markov chain is to use dynamic programming. The idea is to maintain the probability distribution, and at each step go through all possibilities how we can move. Using this method, we can simulate a walk of m steps in $O(n^2 m)$ time.

The transitions of a Markov chain can also be represented as a matrix that updates the probability distribution. In the above scenario, the matrix is

$$
\begin{bmatrix}
0 & 1/2 & 0 & 0 & 0 \\
1 & 0 & 1/2 & 0 & 0 \\
0 & 1/2 & 0 & 1/2 & 0 \\
0 & 0 & 1/2 & 0 & 1 \\
0 & 0 & 0 & 1/2 & 0
\end{bmatrix}.
$$

When we multiply a probability distribution by this matrix, we get the new distribution after moving one step. For example, we can move from the distribution $[1, 0, 0, 0, 0]$ to the distribution $[0, 1, 0, 0, 0]$ as follows:

$$
\begin{bmatrix}
0 & 1/2 & 0 & 0 & 0 \\
1 & 0 & 1/2 & 0 & 0 \\
0 & 1/2 & 0 & 1/2 & 0 \\
0 & 0 & 1/2 & 0 & 1 \\
0 & 0 & 0 & 1/2 & 0
\end{bmatrix}
\begin{bmatrix}
1 \\ 0 \\ 0 \\ 0 \\ 0
\end{bmatrix}
=
\begin{bmatrix}
0 \\ 1 \\ 0 \\ 0 \\ 0
\end{bmatrix}.
$$

By calculating matrix powers efficiently, we can calculate the distribution after m steps in $O(n^3 \log m)$ time.

11.4.4   Randomized Algorithms

Sometimes we can use randomness for solving a problem, even if the problem is not related to probabilities. A *randomized algorithm* is an algorithm that is based on randomness. There are two popular types of randomized algorithms:

- A *Monte Carlo algorithm* is an algorithm that may sometimes give a wrong answer. For such an algorithm to be useful, the probability of a wrong answer should be small.
- A *Las Vegas algorithm* is an algorithm that always gives the correct answer, but its running time varies randomly. The goal is to design an algorithm that is efficient with high probability.

Next we will go through three example problems that can be solved using such algorithms.

Order Statistics The kth *order statistic* of an array is the element at position k after sorting the array in increasing order. It is easy to calculate any order statistic in $O(n \log n)$ time by first sorting the array, but is it really needed to sort the entire array just to find one element?

It turns out that we can find order statistics using a Las Vegas algorithm, whose expected running time is $O(n)$. The algorithm chooses a random element x from the array, and moves elements smaller than x to the left part of the array, and all other elements to the right part of the array. This takes $O(n)$ time when there are n elements.

Assume that the left part contains a elements and the right part contains b elements. If $a = k$, element x is the kth order statistic. Otherwise, if $a > k$, we recursively find the kth order statistic for the left part, and if $a < k$, we recursively find the rth order statistic for the right part where $r = k - a - 1$. The search continues in a similar way, until the desired element has been found.

When each element x is randomly chosen, the size of the array about halves at each step, so the time complexity for finding the kth order statistic is about

$$n + n/2 + n/4 + n/8 + \cdots = O(n).$$

Note that the worst case of the algorithm requires $O(n^2)$ time, because it is possible that x is always chosen in such a way that it is one of the smallest or largest elements in the array and $O(n)$ steps are needed. However, the probability of this is so small that we may assume that this never happens in practice.

Verifying Matrix Multiplication Given matrices A, B, and C, each of size $n \times n$, our next problem is to *verify* if $AB = C$ holds. Of course, we can solve the problem by just calculating the product AB in $O(n^3)$ time, but one could hope that verifying the answer would by easier than to calculate it from scratch.

It turns out that we can solve the problem using a Monte Carlo algorithm whose time complexity is only $O(n^2)$. The idea is simple: We choose a random vector X of n elements and calculate the matrices ABX and CX. If $ABX = CX$, we report that $AB = C$, and otherwise we report that $AB \neq C$.

The time complexity of the algorithm is $O(n^2)$, because we can calculate the matrices ABX and CX in $O(n^2)$ time. We can calculate the matrix ABX efficiently by using the representation $A(BX)$, so only two multiplications of $n \times n$ and $n \times 1$ size matrices are needed.

Fig. 11.19 A valid coloring
of a graph

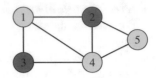

The drawback of the algorithm is that there is a small chance that the algorithm
makes a mistake when it reports that $AB = C$. For example,

$$\begin{bmatrix} 6 & 8 \\ 1 & 3 \end{bmatrix} \neq \begin{bmatrix} 8 & 7 \\ 3 & 2 \end{bmatrix},$$

but

$$\begin{bmatrix} 6 & 8 \\ 1 & 3 \end{bmatrix}\begin{bmatrix} 3 \\ 6 \end{bmatrix} = \begin{bmatrix} 8 & 7 \\ 3 & 2 \end{bmatrix}\begin{bmatrix} 3 \\ 6 \end{bmatrix}.$$

However, in practice, the probability that the algorithm makes a mistake is small,
and we can decrease the probability by verifying the result using multiple random
vectors X before reporting that $AB = C$.

Graph Coloring Given a graph that contains n nodes and m edges, our final problem
is to find a way to color the nodes using two colors so that for at least $m/2$ edges,
the endpoints have different colors. For example, Fig. 11.19 shows a valid coloring
of a graph. In this case, the graph contains seven edges, and the endpoints of five of
them have different colors in the coloring.

The problem can be solved using a Las Vegas algorithm that generates random
colorings until a valid coloring has been found. In a random coloring, the color of each
node is independently chosen so that the probability of both colors is $1/2$. Hence,
the expected number of edges whose endpoints have different colors is $m/2$. Since
it is expected that a random coloring is valid, we will quickly find a valid coloring
in practice.

11.5 Game Theory

In this section, we focus on two-player games where the players move alternately,
have the same set of moves available, and there are no random elements. Our goal
is to find a strategy that we can follow to win the game no matter what the opponent
does, if such a strategy exists.

It turns out that there is a general strategy for such games, and we can analyze the
games using *nim theory*. First, we will analyze simple games where players remove
sticks from heaps, and after this, we will generalize the strategy used in those games
to other games.

11.5.1   Game States

Let us consider a game that starts with a heap of n sticks. Two players move alternately, and on each move, the player has to remove 1, 2, or 3 sticks from the heap. Finally, the player who removes the last stick wins the game.

For example, if $n = 10$, the game may proceed as follows:

- Player A removes 2 sticks (8 sticks left).
- Player B removes 3 sticks (5 sticks left).
- Player A removes 1 stick (4 sticks left).
- Player B removes 2 sticks (2 sticks left).
- Player A removes 2 sticks and wins.

This game consists of states $0, 1, 2, \ldots, n$, where the number of the state corresponds to the number of sticks left.

A *winning state* is a state where the player will win the game if they play optimally, and a *losing state* is a state where the player will lose the game if the opponent plays optimally. It turns out that we can classify all states of a game so that each state is either a winning state or a losing state.

In the above game, state 0 is clearly a losing state, because the player cannot make any moves. States 1, 2, and 3 are winning states, because the player can remove 1, 2, or 3 sticks and win the game. State 4, in turn, is a losing state, because any move leads to a state that is a winning state for the opponent.

More generally, if there is a move that leads from the current state to a losing state, it is a winning state, and otherwise it is a losing state. Using this observation, we can classify all states of a game starting with losing states where there are no possible moves. Figure 11.20 shows the classification of states $0 \ldots 15$ (W denotes a winning state and L denotes a losing state).

It is easy to analyze this game: A state k is a losing state if k is divisible by 4, and otherwise it is a winning state. An optimal way to play the game is to always choose a move after which the number of sticks in the heap is divisible by 4. Finally, there are no sticks left, and the opponent has lost. Of course, this strategy requires that the number of sticks is *not* divisible by 4 when it is our move. If it is, there is nothing we can do, and the opponent will win the game if they play optimally.

Let us then consider another stick game, where in each state k, it is allowed to remove any number x of sticks such that x is smaller than k and divides k. For example, in state 8 we may remove 1, 2, or 4 sticks, but in state 7 the only allowed move is to remove 1 stick. Figure 11.21 shows the states $1 \ldots 9$ of the game as a *state graph*, whose nodes are the states and edges are the moves between them:

0	1	2	3	4	5	6	7	8	9	10	11	12	13	14	15
L	W	W	W	L	W	W	W	L	W	W	W	L	W	W	W

Fig. 11.20 Classification of states $0 \ldots 15$ in the stick game

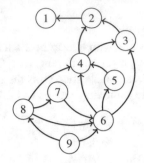

Fig. 11.21 State graph of the divisibility game

1	2	3	4	5	6	7	8	9
L	W	L	W	L	W	L	W	L

Fig. 11.22 Classification of states $1 \ldots 9$ in the divisibility game

The final state in this game is always state 1, which is a losing state, because there are no valid moves. Figure 11.22 shows the classification of states $1 \ldots 9$. It turns out that in this game, all even-numbered states are winning states, and all odd-numbered states are losing states.

11.5.2 Nim Game

The *nim game* is a simple game that has an important role in game theory, because many other games can be played using the same strategy. First, we focus on nim, and after this, we generalize the strategy to other games.

There are n heaps in nim, and each heap contains some number of sticks. The players move alternately, and on each turn, the player chooses a heap that still contains sticks and removes any number of sticks from it. The winner is the player who removes the last stick.

The states in nim are of the form $[x_1, x_2, \ldots, x_n]$, where x_i denotes the number of sticks in heap i. For example, $[10, 12, 5]$ is a state where there are three heaps with 10, 12, and 5 sticks. The state $[0, 0, \ldots, 0]$ is a losing state, because it is not possible to remove any sticks, and this is always the final state.

Analysis It turns out that we can easily classify any nim state by calculating the *nim sum* $s = x_1 \oplus x_2 \oplus \cdots \oplus x_n$, where $\oplus$ denotes the XOR operation. The states whose nim sum is 0 are losing states, and all other states are winning states. For example, the nim sum of $[10, 12, 5]$ is $10 \oplus 12 \oplus 5 = 3$, so the state is a winning state.

But how is the nim sum related to the nim game? We can explain this by looking at how the nim sum changes when the nim state changes.

Losing states: The final state $[0, 0, \ldots, 0]$ is a losing state, and its nim sum is 0, as expected. In other losing states, any move leads to a winning state, because when a single value x_i changes, the nim sum also changes, so the nim sum is different from 0 after the move.

Winning states: We can move to a losing state if there is any heap i for which $x_i \oplus s < x_i$. In this case, we can remove sticks from heap i so that it will contain $x_i \oplus s$ sticks, which will lead to a losing state. There is always such a heap, where x_i has a one bit at the position of the leftmost one bit of s.

Example As an example, consider the state [10, 12, 5]. This state is a winning state, because its nim sum is 3. Thus, there has to be a move which leads to a losing state. Next we will find out such a move.

The nim sum of the state is as follows:

$$
\begin{array}{r|l}
10 & 1010 \\
12 & 1100 \\
5 & 0101 \\
\hline
3 & 0011 \\
\end{array}
$$

In this case, the heap with 10 sticks is the only heap that has a one bit at the position of the leftmost one bit of the nim sum:

$$
\begin{array}{r|l}
10 & 10\underline{1}0 \\
12 & 1100 \\
5 & 0101 \\
\hline
3 & 00\underline{1}1 \\
\end{array}
$$

The new size of the heap has to be $10 \oplus 3 = 9$, so we will remove just one stick. After this, the state will be [9, 12, 5], which is a losing state:

$$
\begin{array}{r|l}
9 & 1001 \\
12 & 1100 \\
5 & 0101 \\
\hline
0 & 0000 \\
\end{array}
$$

Misère Game In a *misère* nim game, the goal of the game is opposite, so the player who removes the last stick loses the game. It turns out that the misère nim game can be optimally played almost like the standard nim game.

The idea is to first play the misère game like the standard game, but change the strategy at the end of the game. The new strategy will be introduced in a situation where each heap would contain at most one stick after the next move. In the standard game, we should choose a move after which there is an even number of heaps with one stick. However, in the misère game, we choose a move so that there is an odd number of heaps with one stick.

This strategy works because a state where the strategy changes always appears in the game, and this state is a winning state, because it contains exactly one heap that has more than one stick so the nim sum is not 0.

11.5.3 Sprague–Grundy Theorem

The *Sprague–Grundy theorem* generalizes the strategy used in nim to all games that
fulfill the following requirements:

- There are two players who move alternately.
- The game consists of states, and the possible moves in a state do not depend on
  whose turn it is.
- The game ends when a player cannot make a move.
- The game surely ends sooner or later.
- The players have complete information about the states and allowed moves, and
  there is no randomness in the game.

Grundy Numbers The idea is to calculate for each game state a *Grundy number*
that corresponds to the number of sticks in a nim heap. When we know the Grundy
numbers of all states, we can play the game like the nim game.

The Grundy number of a game state is calculated using the formula

$$\text{mex}(\{g_1, g_2, \ldots, g_n\}),$$

where $g_1, g_2, \ldots, g_n$ are the Grundy numbers of the states to which we can move
from the state, and the mex function gives the smallest nonnegative number that is
not in the set. For example, $\text{mex}(\{0, 1, 3\}) = 2$. If a state has no possible moves, its
Grundy number is 0, because $\text{mex}(\emptyset) = 0$.

For example, Fig. 11.23 shows a state graph of a game where each state is assigned
its Grundy number. The Grundy number of a losing state is 0, and the Grundy number
of a winning state is a positive number.

Consider a state whose Grundy number is x. We can think that it corresponds to
a nim heap that has x sticks. In particular, if $x > 0$, we can move to states whose
Grundy numbers are $0, 1, \ldots, x - 1$, which simulates removing sticks from a nim
heap. There is one difference, though: It may be possible to move to a state whose
Grundy number is larger than x and "add" sticks to a heap. However, the opponent
can always cancel any such move, so this does not change the strategy.

As an example, consider a game where the players move a figure in a maze. Each
square of the maze is either floor or wall. On each turn, the player has to move the
figure some number of steps left or up. The winner of the game is the player who
makes the last move. Figure 11.24 shows a possible initial configuration of the game,
where @ denotes the figure and * denotes a square where it can move. The states of

Fig. 11.23 Grundy numbers
of game states

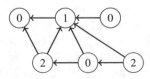

Fig. 11.24 Possible moves
on the first turn

Fig. 11.25 Grundy numbers
of game states

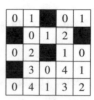

Fig. 11.26 A game that
consists of three subgames

 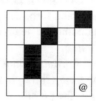 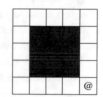

the game are all floor squares of the maze. Figure 11.25 shows the Grundy numbers of the states in this configuration.

According to the Sprague–Grundy theorem, each state of the maze game corresponds to a heap in the nim game. For example, the Grundy number of the lower-right square is 2, so it is a winning state. We can reach a losing state and win the game by moving either four steps left or two steps up.

Subgames Assume that our game consists of subgames, and on each turn, the player first chooses a subgame and then a move in the subgame. The game ends when it is not possible to make any move in any subgame. In this case, the Grundy number of a game equals the nim sum of the Grundy numbers of the subgames. The game can then be played like a nim game by calculating all Grundy numbers for subgames and then their nim sum.

As an example, consider a game that consists of three mazes. On each turn, the player chooses one of the mazes and then moves the figure in the maze. Figure 11.26 shows an initial configuration of the game, and Fig. 11.27 shows the corresponding Grundy numbers. In this configuration, the nim sum of the Grundy numbers is $2 \oplus 3 \oplus 3 = 2$, so the first player can win the game. One optimal move is to move two steps up in the first maze, which produces the nim sum $0 \oplus 3 \oplus 3 = 0$.

Grundy's Game Sometimes a move in a game divides the game into subgames that are independent of each other. In this case, the Grundy number of a game state is

$$\text{mex}(\{g_1, g_2, \ldots, g_n\}),$$

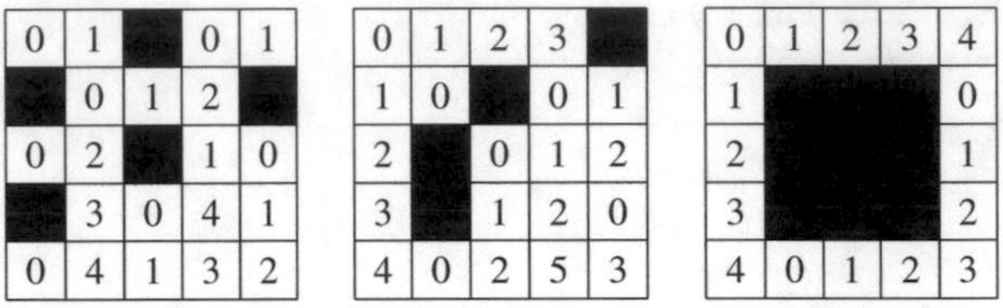

Fig. 11.27 Grundy numbers in subgames

0	1		0	1
	0	1	2	
0	2		1	0
	3	0	4	1
0	4	1	3	2

0	1	2	3	
1	0		0	1
2		0	1	2
3		1	2	0
4	0	2	5	3

0	1	2	3	4
1				0
2				1
3				2
4	0	1	2	3

where there are n possible moves and

$$g_k = a_{k,1} \oplus a_{k,2} \oplus \ldots \oplus a_{k,m},$$

meaning that move k divides the game into m subgames whose Grundy numbers are $a_{k,1}, a_{k,2}, \ldots, a_{k,m}$.

An example of such a game is *Grundy's game*. Initially, there is a single heap that has n sticks. On each turn, the player chooses a heap and divides it into two non-empty heaps such that the heaps are of different size. The player who makes the last move wins the game.

Let $g(n)$ denote the Grundy number of a heap of size n. The Grundy number can be calculated by going through all ways to divide the heap into two heaps. For example, when $n = 8$, the possibilities are $1 + 7$, $2 + 6$, and $3 + 5$, so

$$g(8) = \text{mex}(\{g(1) \oplus g(7), g(2) \oplus g(6), g(3) \oplus g(5)\}).$$

In this game, the value of $g(n)$ is based on the values of $g(1), \ldots, g(n-1)$. The base cases are $g(1) = g(2) = 0$, because it is not possible to divide the heaps of 1 and 2 sticks into smaller heaps. The first Grundy numbers are:

$$g(1) = 0$$
$$g(2) = 0$$
$$g(3) = 1$$
$$g(4) = 0$$
$$g(5) = 2$$
$$g(6) = 1$$
$$g(7) = 0$$
$$g(8) = 2$$

The Grundy number for $n = 8$ is 2, so it is possible to win the game. The winning move is to create heaps $1 + 7$, because $g(1) \oplus g(7) = 0$.

11.6 Fourier Transform

Given two polynomials $f(x)$ and $g(x)$, our goal in this section is to efficiently calculate the product $f(x)g(x)$. For example, if $f(x) = 2x + 3$ and $g(x) = 5x + 1$, the desired result is $f(x)g(x) = 10x^2 + 17x + 3$. An easy way to calculate the product would be to go through all pairs of terms from $f(x)$ and $g(x)$ and sum the products of the terms as follows:

$$f(x)g(x) = 2x \cdot 5x + 2x \cdot 1 + 3 \cdot 5x + 3 \cdot 1 = 10x^2 + 17x + 3$$

However, this simple technique is *slow*: It takes $O(n^2)$ time where n is the degree of the polynomial. Fortunately, we can calculate the product faster in $O(n \log n)$ time using the fast Fourier transform (FFT) algorithm. The idea of the algorithm is to convert the polynomials into a special point-value form where it is easier to calculate the product.

11.6.1   Working with Polynomials

Consider a polynomial

$$f(x) = c_0 + c_1 x + \cdots + c_{n-1} x^{n-1}$$

whose degree is $n - 1$. There are two standard ways to represent such a polynomial:

- *Coefficient representation*: We create a list

$$[c_0, c_1, \ldots, c_{n-1}]$$

  that contains the coefficients of the polynomial.
- *Point-value representation*: We create a list

$$[(x_0, f(x_0)), (x_1, f(x_1)), \ldots, (x_{n-1}, f(x_{n-1}))]$$

  that shows the values of the polynomial at n distinct points. This representation is based on the fact that if the degree of an polynomial is $n - 1$ and we know its values at n distinct points, this uniquely defines the polynomial.

For example, consider the polynomial $f(x) = x^3 + 2x + 5$ whose coefficient representation is $[5, 2, 0, 3]$. To create a point-value representation, we can choose any n distinct points and evaluate the polynomial at those points. One possible point-value representation is $[(0, 5), (1, 8), (2, 17), (3, 38)]$, which means that $f(0) = 5$, $f(1) = 8$, $f(2) = 17$ and $f(3) = 38$.

Both above ways to represent polynomials have some advantages. Using the coefficient representation, it is easy to calculate the value of the polynomial at any given point. However, if we have two polynomials $f(x)$ and $g(x)$ and want to calculate their product $f(x)g(x)$, the point-value representation is more convenient: If we know that $f(x_i) = a_i$ and $g(x_i) = b_i$ at some point x_i, we can easily calculate $f(x_i)g(x_i) = a_i b_i$. For example, if we know that $f(1) = 5$ and $g(1) = 6$, we directly know that $f(1)g(1) = 30$.

Still, apart from calculating products, we would usually like to use the coefficient representation. For this reason, a possible way to calculate the product of polynomials $f(x)$ and $g(x)$, given in coefficient form, is as follows:

1. Create point-value representations for $f(x)$ and $g(x)$.
2. Calculate the product $f(x)g(x)$ in point-value form.
3. Create the coefficient representation for $f(x)g(x)$.

Note that if $f(x)$ and $g(x)$ have degree $n - 1$, then $f(x)g(x)$ has degree $2n - 2$. Thus, we have to calculate $2n - 1$ values in step 1 to make sure that we can find the correct polynomial in step 3.

Step 2 is easy to do in $O(n)$ time, because we can simply calculate the products at all points. Steps 1 and 3 are more difficult, but next we will see how we can perform them in $O(n \log n)$ time using the FFT algorithm. The idea is to work with point-value representations where the polynomial is evaluated at special complex number points that allow us to efficiently switch between the representations.

11.6.2 FFT Algorithm

Given a vector $a = [c_0, c_1, \ldots, c_{n-1}]$ that represents the polynomial

$$f(x) = c_0 + c_1 x + \cdots + c_{n-1} x^{n-1},$$

the *Fourier transform* of a is a vector

$$t = [f(\omega_n^0), f(\omega_n^1), \ldots, f(\omega_n^{n-1})]$$

where

$$\omega_n = e^{2\pi i/n} = \cos(2\pi/n) + \sin(2\pi/n)i.$$

The vector t corresponds to a point-value representation of the polynomial $f(x)$, evaluated at points $\omega_n^0, \omega_n^1, \ldots, \omega_n^{n-1}$. The value ω_n is a complex number called a *principal root of unity* that satisfies $\omega_n^n = 1$. As an example, Fig. 11.28 shows the values ω_4 and ω_8 and their powers on the complex plane.

Fig. 11.28 Powers of ω_4 and ω_8 on the complex plane

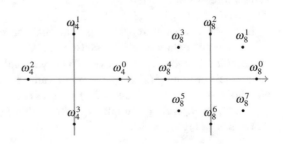

The *fast Fourier transform* (*FFT*) algorithm calculates the Fourier transform in $O(n \log n)$ time. The algorithm uses properties of the ω_n values to efficiently calculate the transform. From now on, we assume that n (the length of the input vector a) is a power of two. If it is not, we can add additional zeros to the end of the vector before the algorithm begins.

The idea of the FFT algorithm is to divide the vector $a = [c_0, c_1, \ldots, c_{n-1}]$ into two vectors $a_{EVEN} = [c_0, c_2, \ldots, c_{n-2}]$ and $a_{ODD} = [c_1, c_3, \ldots, c_{n-1}]$. The vectors consist of $n/2$ values and represent the polynomials $c_0 + c_2 x + c_4 x^2 + \cdots + c_{n-2} x^{n/2-1}$ and $c_1 + c_3 x + c_5 x^2 + \cdots + c_{n-1} x^{n/2-1}$. Then, the algorithm recursively calculates the Fourier transforms of a_{EVEN} and a_{ODD} to vectors t_{EVEN} and t_{ODD}. Finally, the algorithm calculates the Fourier transform of a using the formula

$$t[k] = t_{EVEN}[k \bmod (n/2)] + t_{ODD}[k \bmod (n/2)]\omega_n^k.$$

This formula works, because $\omega_{n/2}^k = \omega_n^{2k}$ and $\omega_n^k = \omega_n^{k \bmod n}$ (see Fig. 11.28). Since the algorithm divides the input vector of size n into two vectors of size $n/2$ and recursively processes them, the algorithm works in $O(n \log n)$ time.

The FFT algorithm can also be used to calculate the *inverse* Fourier transform, i.e., convert a point-value representation of a polynomial into a coefficient representation. Surprisingly, if we calculate the Fourier transform of the vector

$$t = [f(\omega_n^0), f(\omega_n^1), \ldots, f(\omega_n^{n-1})]$$

so that we use $1/\omega_n$ instead of ω_n and divide all output values by n, the output vector is the original coefficient vector a.

Implementation The FFT algorithm is tricky to implement well. In particular, it is not a good idea to create new vectors and process them recursively, because such an implementation would have large constant factors. Often, the algorithm is used as a *black box* to efficiently calculate Fourier transforms without focusing on the implementation details. The following implementation is based on the pseudocode given in CLRS [7]; if you want to know what the code exactly does, you can consult the book for more information.

First, we define a complex number type `cd` that uses double numbers in real and imaginary parts, and a variable `pi` that has the value of π.

```
typedef complex<double> cd;
double pi = acos(-1);
```

Then, the function `fft` performs the FFT algorithm. The function is given a vector `a` that contains the coefficients of the polynomial, and an additional parameter `d`. If `d` is 1 (default), the function calculates the ordinary Fourier transform, and if `d` is -1, it calculates the inverse transform. As mentioned above, the function assumes that n is a power of two.

The function first constructs a vector `r` that has the contents of `a` as a *bit reversal permutation* which corresponds to the order the values are accessed at the bottom level of the recursion. This trick allows us to calculate the transform without creating additional vectors and recursive calls. After this, the function calculates Fourier transforms for vectors of size 2, 4, 8, ..., n. Finally, if the inverse transform is being calculated, the function divides all output values by n.

```cpp
vector<cd> fft(vector<cd> a, int d = 1) {
    int n = a.size();
    vector<cd> r(n);
    for (int k = 0; k < n; k++) {
        int b = 0;
        for (int z = 1; z < n; z *= 2) {
            b *= 2;
            if (k&z) b++;
        }
        r[b] = a[k];
    }
    for (int m = 2; m <= n; m *= 2) {
        cd wm = exp(cd{0,d*2*pi/m});
        for (int k = 0; k < n; k += m) {
            cd w = 1;
            for (int j = 0; j < m/2; j++) {
                cd u = r[k+j];
                cd t = w*r[k+j+m/2];
                r[k+j] = u+t;
                r[k+j+m/2] = u-t;
                w = w*wm;
            }
        }
    }
    if (d == -1) {
        for (int i = 0; i < n; i++) r[i] /= n;
    }
    return r;
}
```

The following code shows how we can use the `fft` function to calculate the product of $f(x) = 2x + 3$ and $g(x) = 5x + 1$. First we convert the polynomials into point-value form, then calculate the product, and finally convert the result back into coefficient form. The result is $10x^2 + 17x + 3$ as expected.

```cpp
int n = 4;
vector<cd> f = {3,2,0,0};
vector<cd> g = {1,5,0,0};
auto tf = fft(f);
auto tg = fft(g);
vector<cd> tp(n);
for (int i = 0; i < n; i++) tp[i] = tf[i]*tg[i];
auto p = fft(tp,-1); // [3,17,10,0]
```

While the FFT algorithm operates with complex numbers, our input and output values are often integers. After calculating the product, we can use the syntax `(int)(p[i].real()+0.5)` to get the real part of the complex number `p[i]` and convert it into an integer.

11.6.3 Calculating Convolutions

In general, we can use the FFT algorithm to calculate the *convolution* of two arrays in $O(n \log n)$ time. Given arrays a and b, their convolution $c = a * b$ is an array whose each element corresponds to the formula

$$c[k] = \sum_{i+j=k} a[i]b[j].$$

If a and b consist of coefficients of polynomials, the convolution represents the product of the polynomials, but we can also calculate convolutions that are not related to polynomials. Here are some examples:

Combinations We have apples and bananas, and each of them has an integer weight between $1 \ldots n$. We want to calculate for each weight $w \le 2n$ the number of ways we can choose an apple and banana whose combined weight is w.

We can solve the problem by creating arrays a and b where $a[i]$ denotes the number of apples of weight i and $b[i]$ denotes the number of bananas of weight i. Then, the convolution of the arrays gives the desired result.

Signal Processing We can think that array a is a *signal* and array b is a *mask* that modifies the signal. The mask moves through the signal from left to right, and the sum of products is calculated at each position. We can calculate the result as a convolution if we first reverse the mask.

For example, suppose that $a = [5, 1, 3, 4, 2, 1, 2]$ and $b = [1, 3, 2]$. We first create a reverse mask $b' = [2, 3, 1]$ and then calculate the convolution

$$c = a * b' = [10, 17, 14, 18, 19, 12, 9, 7, 2].$$

Figure 11.29 shows the interpretation of the values $c[1]$ and $c[5]$.

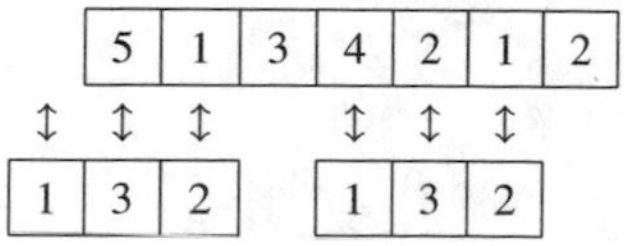

Fig. 11.29 Signal processing: $c[1] = 5 \cdot 3 + 1 \cdot 2 = 17$ and $c[5] = 4 \cdot 1 + 2 \cdot 3 + 1 \cdot 2 = 12$

Differences Given a bit string s of length n, we want to calculate for each $k = 1, 2, \ldots, n - 1$ the number of ways we can choose two positions i and j such that $s[i] = s[j] = 1$ and $j - i = k$.

We can solve the problem by calculating the convolution $c = s * s'$ where s' is the reverse of s. Then, $c[n + k - 1]$ gives the answer for each k (we can also think that s is both a signal and a mask).

Advanced Graph Algorithms

12

This chapter discusses a selection of advanced graph algorithms.

Section 12.1 presents an algorithm for finding the strongly connected components of a graph. After this, we will learn how to efficiently solve the 2SAT problem using the algorithm.

Section 12.2 focuses on Eulerian and Hamiltonian paths. An Eulerian path goes through each edge of the graph exactly once, and a Hamiltonian path visits each node exactly once. While the concepts look quite similar at first glance, the computational problems related to them are very different.

Section 12.3 first shows how we can determine the maximum flow from a source to a sink in a graph. After this, we will see how to reduce several other graph problems to the maximum flow problem.

Section 12.4 discusses properties of depth-first search and problems related to biconnected graphs.

Section 12.5 deals with another flow problem where we want to find a minimum cost flow from a source to a sink. This is quite a general problem, because we can reduce both the shortest path problem and the maximum flow problem to it.

12.1 Strong Connectivity

A directed graph is called *strongly connected* if there is a path from any node to all other nodes in the graph. For example, the left graph in Fig. 12.1 is strongly connected while the right graph is not. The right graph is not strongly connected, because, for example, there is no path from node 2 to node 1.

A directed graph can always be divided into strongly connected components. Each such component contains a maximal set of nodes such that there is a path from any node to all other nodes, and the components form an acyclic *component graph* that represents the deep structure of the original graph. For example, Fig. 12.2 shows a

© Springer Nature Switzerland AG 2020
A. Laaksonen, *Guide to Competitive Programming*, Undergraduate Topics
in Computer Science, https://doi.org/10.1007/978-3-030-39357-1_12

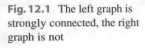

Fig. 12.1 The left graph is strongly connected, the right graph is not

Fig. 12.2 A graph, its strongly connected components and the component graph

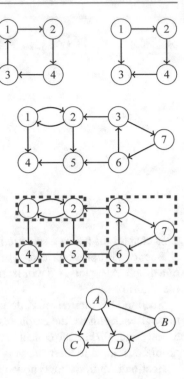

graph, its strongly connected components and the corresponding component graph. The components are $A = \{1, 2\}$, $B = \{3, 6, 7\}$, $C = \{4\}$, and $D = \{5\}$.

A component graph is a directed acyclic graph, so it is easier to process than the original graph. Since the graph does not contain cycles, we can always construct a topological sort and use dynamic programming to process it.

12.1.1 Kosaraju's Algorithm

Kosaraju's algorithm is an efficient method for finding the strongly connected components of a graph. The algorithm performs two depth-first searches: the first search constructs a list of nodes according to the structure of the graph, and the second search forms the strongly connected components.

The first phase of Kosaraju's algorithm constructs a list of nodes in the order in which depth-first search processes them. The algorithm goes through the nodes, and begins a depth-first search at each unprocessed node. Each node will be added to the list after it has been processed.

For example, Fig. 12.3 shows the processing order of the nodes in our example graph. The notation x/y means that processing the node started at time x and finished at time y. The resulting list is [4, 5, 2, 1, 6, 7, 3].

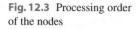

Fig. 12.3 Processing order of the nodes

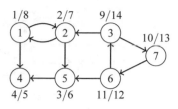

Fig. 12.4 Graph with reversed edges

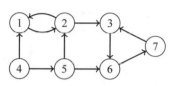

The second phase of Kosaraju's algorithm forms the strongly connected components. First, the algorithm reverses every edge of the graph. This guarantees that during the second search, we will always find valid strongly connected components. Figure 12.4 shows the graph in our example after reversing the edges.

After this, the algorithm goes through the list of nodes created by the first search, in *reverse* order. If a node does not belong to a component, the algorithm creates a new component by starting a depth-first search that adds all new nodes found during the search to the new component. Note that since all edges are reversed, the components do not "leak" to other parts of the graph.

Figure 12.5 shows how the algorithm processes our example graph. The processing order of the nodes is [3, 7, 6, 1, 2, 5, 4]. First, node 3 generates the component {3, 6, 7}. Then, nodes 7 and 6 are skipped, because they already belong to a component. After this, node 1 generates the component {1, 2}, and node 2 is skipped. Finally, nodes 5 and 4 generate the components {5} and {4}.

The time complexity of the algorithm is $O(n + m)$, because the algorithm performs two depth-first searches.

12.1.2   2SAT Problem

In the *2SAT problem*, we are given a logical formula

$$(a_1 \vee b_1) \wedge (a_2 \vee b_2) \wedge \cdots \wedge (a_m \vee b_m),$$

where each a_i and b_i is either a logical variable ($x_1, x_2, \ldots, x_n$) or a negation of a logical variable ($\neg x_1, \neg x_2, \ldots, \neg x_n$). The symbols "$\wedge$" and "$\vee$" denote logical operators "and" and "or". Our task is to assign each variable a value so that the formula is true, or state that this is not possible.

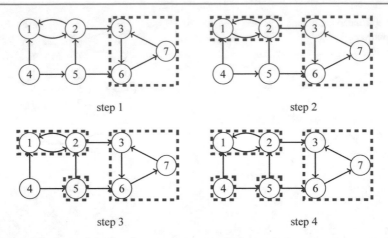

Fig. 12.5 Constructing the strongly connected components

For example, the formula

$$L_1 = (x_2 \lor \neg x_1) \land (\neg x_1 \lor \neg x_2) \land (x_1 \lor x_3) \land (\neg x_2 \lor \neg x_3) \land (x_1 \lor x_4)$$

is true when the variables are assigned as follows:

$$\begin{cases} x_1 = \text{false} \\ x_2 = \text{false} \\ x_3 = \text{true} \\ x_4 = \text{true} \end{cases}$$

However, the formula

$$L_2 = (x_1 \lor x_2) \land (x_1 \lor \neg x_2) \land (\neg x_1 \lor x_3) \land (\neg x_1 \lor \neg x_3)$$

is always false, regardless of how we assign the values. The reason for this is that we cannot choose a value for x_1 without creating a contradiction. If x_1 is false, both x_2 and $\neg x_2$ should be true which is impossible, and if x_1 is true, both x_3 and $\neg x_3$ should be true which is also impossible.

An instance of the 2SAT problem can be represented as an *implication graph* whose nodes correspond to variables x_i and negations $\neg x_i$, and edges determine the connections between the variables. Each pair $(a_i \lor b_i)$ generates two edges: $\neg a_i \rightarrow b_i$ and $\neg b_i \rightarrow a_i$. This means that if a_i does not hold, b_i must hold and vice versa. For example, Fig. 12.6 shows the implication graph of L_1, and Fig. 12.7 shows the implication graph of L_2.

The structure of the implication graph tells us whether it is possible to assign the values of the variables so that the formula is true. This can be done exactly when there are no nodes x_i and $\neg x_i$ such that both nodes belong to the same strongly

Fig. 12.6 Implication graph of L_1

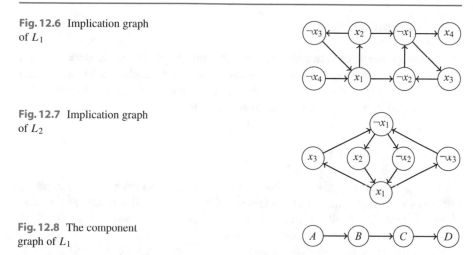

Fig. 12.7 Implication graph of L_2

Fig. 12.8 The component graph of L_1

connected component. If there are such nodes, the graph contains a path from x_i to $\neg x_i$ and also a path from $\neg x_i$ to x_i, so both x_i and $\neg x_i$ should be true which is not possible. For example, the implication graph of L_1 does not have nodes x_i and $\neg x_i$ such that both nodes belong to the same strongly connected component, so there is a solution. Then, in the implication graph of L_2 all nodes belong to the same strongly connected component, so there are no solutions.

If a solution exists, the values for the variables can be found by going through the nodes of the component graph in a reverse topological sort order. At each step, we process a component that does not contain edges that lead to an unprocessed component. If the variables in the component have not been assigned values, their values will be determined according to the values in the component, and if they already have values, the values remain unchanged. The process continues until each variable has been assigned a value.

Figure 12.8 shows the component graph of L_1. The components are $A = \{\neg x_4\}$, $B = \{x_1, x_2, \neg x_3\}$, $C = \{\neg x_1, \neg x_2, x_3\}$ and $D = \{x_4\}$. When constructing the solution, we first process the component D where x_4 becomes true. After this, we process the component C where x_1 and x_2 become false and x_3 becomes true. All variables have been assigned values, so the remaining components A and B do not change the values of the variables.

Note that this method works, because the implication graph has a special structure: if there is a path from node x_i to node x_j and from node x_j to node $\neg x_j$, then node x_i never becomes true. The reason for this is that there is also a path from node $\neg x_j$ to node $\neg x_i$, and both x_i and x_j become false.

A more difficult problem is the *3SAT problem*, where each part of the formula is of the form $(a_i \vee b_i \vee c_i)$. This problem is NP-hard, so no efficient algorithm for solving the problem is known.

12.2   Complete Paths

In this section we discuss two special types of paths in graphs: an Eulerian path is a path that goes through each edge exactly once, and a Hamiltonian path is a path that visits each node exactly once. While such paths look quite similar at first glance, the computational problems related to them are very different.

12.2.1   Eulerian Paths

An *Eulerian path* is a path that goes exactly once through each edge of a graph. Furthermore, if such a path starts and ends at the same node, it is called an *Eulerian circuit*. Figure 12.9 shows an Eulerian path from node 2 to node 5, and Fig. 12.10 shows an Eulerian circuit that starts and ends at node 1.

The existence of Eulerian paths and circuits depends on the degrees of the nodes. First, an undirected graph has an Eulerian path exactly when all the edges belong to the same connected component and

- the degree of each node is even, *or*
- the degree of exactly two nodes is odd, and the degree of all other nodes is even.

In the first case, each Eulerian path is also an Eulerian circuit. In the second case, the odd-degree nodes are the endpoints of an Eulerian path which is not an Eulerian circuit. In Fig. 12.9, nodes 1, 3, and 4 have degree 2, and nodes 2 and 5 have degree 3. Exactly two nodes have an odd degree, so there is an Eulerian path between nodes 2 and 5, but the graph does not have an Eulerian circuit. In Fig. 12.10, all nodes have an even degree, so the graph has an Eulerian circuit.

To determine whether a directed graph has Eulerian paths, we focus on indegrees and outdegrees of the nodes. A directed graph contains an Eulerian path exactly when all the edges belong to the same connected component and

Fig. 12.9 Graph and an
Eulerian path

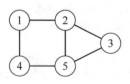   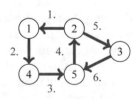

Fig. 12.10 Graph and an
Eulerian circuit

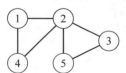   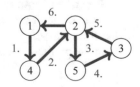

Fig. 12.11 Directed graph and an Eulerian path

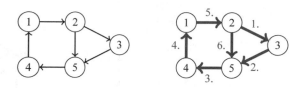

- in each node, the indegree equals the outdegree, *or*
- in one node, the indegree is one larger than the outdegree, in another node, the outdegree is one larger than the indegree, and in all other nodes, the indegree equals the outdegree.

In the first case, each Eulerian path is also an Eulerian circuit, and in the second case, the graph has an Eulerian path that begins at the node whose outdegree is larger and ends at the node whose indegree is larger. For example, in Fig. 12.11, nodes 1, 3, and 4 have both indegree 1 and outdegree 1, node 2 has indegree 1 and outdegree 2, and node 5 has indegree 2 and outdegree 1. Hence, the graph contains an Eulerian path from node 2 to node 5.

Construction *Hierholzer's algorithm* is an efficient method for constructing an Eulerian circuit for a graph. The algorithm consists of several rounds, each of which adds new edges to the circuit. Of course, we assume that the graph contains an Eulerian circuit; otherwise, Hierholzer's algorithm cannot find it.

The algorithm begins with an empty circuit that contains only a single node, and then extends the circuit step by step by adding subcircuits to it. The process continues until all edges have been added to the circuit. The circuit is extended by finding a node x that belongs to the circuit but has an outgoing edge that is not included in the circuit. Then, a new path from node x that only contains edges that are not yet in the circuit is constructed. Sooner or later, the path will return to node x, which creates a subcircuit.

If a graph does not have an Eulerian circuit but has an Eulerian path, we can still use Hierholzer's algorithm to find the path by adding an extra edge to the graph and removing the edge after the circuit has been constructed. For example, in an undirected graph, we add the extra edge between the two odd-degree nodes.

As an example, Fig. 12.12 shows how Hierholzer's algorithm constructs an Eulerian circuit in an undirected graph. First, the algorithm adds a subcircuit $1 \rightarrow 2 \rightarrow 3 \rightarrow 1$, then a subcircuit $2 \rightarrow 5 \rightarrow 6 \rightarrow 2$, and finally a subcircuit $6 \rightarrow 3 \rightarrow 4 \rightarrow 7 \rightarrow 6$. After this, since all edges have been added to the circuit, we have successfully constructed an Eulerian circuit.

12.2.2   Hamiltonian Paths

A *Hamiltonian path* is a path that visits each node of a graph exactly once. Furthermore, if a such a path begins and ends at the same node, it is called a *Hamiltonian*

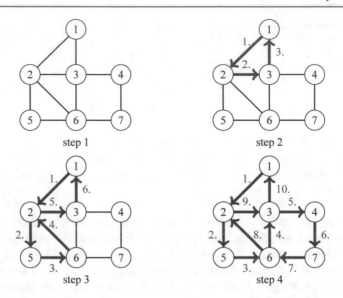

Fig. 12.12 Hierholzer's algorithm

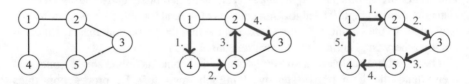

Fig. 12.13 A graph, a Hamiltonian path and a Hamiltonian circuit

circuit. For example, Fig. 12.13 shows a graph that has both a Hamiltonian path and a Hamiltonian circuit.

Problems related to Hamiltonian paths are NP-hard: nobody knows a general way to efficiently check if a graph has a Hamiltonian path or circuit. Of course, in some special cases, we can be certain that a graph contains a Hamiltonian path. For example, if the graph is complete, i.e., there is an edge between all pairs of nodes, it surely contains a Hamiltonian path.

A simple way to search for a Hamiltonian path is to use a backtracking algorithm that goes through all possible ways to construct a path. The time complexity of such an algorithm is at least $O(n!)$, because there are $n!$ different ways to choose the order of n nodes. Then, using dynamic programming, we can create a more efficient $O(2^n n^2)$ time solution, which determines for each subset of nodes S and each node $x \in S$ if there is a path that visits all nodes of S exactly once and ends at node x.

12.2.3 Applications

De Bruijn Sequences A *De Bruijn sequence* is a string that contains every string of length n exactly once as a substring, for a fixed alphabet of k characters. The length of such a string is $k^n + n - 1$ characters. For example, when $n = 3$ and $k = 2$, an example of a De Bruijn sequence is

$$0001011100.$$

The substrings of this string are all combinations of three bits: 000, 001, 010, 011, 100, 101, 110, and 111.

A De Bruijn sequence always corresponds to an Eulerian path in a graph where each node contains a string of $n - 1$ characters and each edge adds one character to the string. For example, the graph in Fig. 12.14 corresponds to the scenario where $n = 3$ and $k = 2$. To create a De Bruijn sequence, we start at an arbitrary node and follow an Eulerian path that visits each edge exactly once. When the characters in the starting node and on the edges are added together, the resulting string has $k^n + n - 1$ characters and is a valid De Bruijn sequence.

Knight's Tours A *knight's tour* is a sequence of moves of a knight on an $n \times n$ chessboard following the rules of chess such that the knight visits each square exactly once. A knight's tour is called *closed* if the knight finally returns to the starting square and otherwise it is called *open*. For example, Fig. 12.15 shows an open knight's tour on a 5×5 board.

A knight's tour corresponds to a Hamiltonian path in a graph whose nodes represent the squares of the board, and two nodes are connected with an edge if a knight can move between the squares according to the rules of chess. A natural way to construct a knight's tour is to use backtracking. Since there is a large number of possible

Fig. 12.14 Constructing a De Bruijn sequence from an Eulerian path

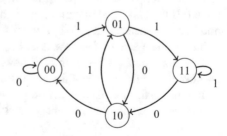

Fig. 12.15 An open knight's tour on a 5×5 board

1	4	11	16	25
12	17	2	5	10
3	20	7	24	15
18	13	22	9	6
21	8	19	14	23

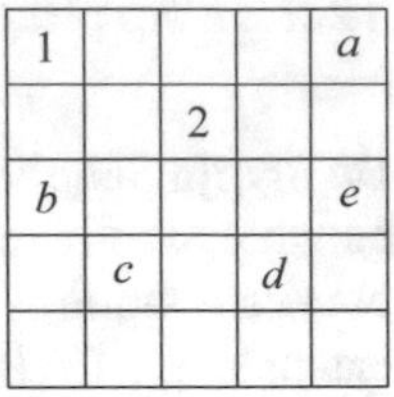

Fig. 12.16 Using
Warndorf's rule to construct
a knight's tour

1			a
		2	
b			e
	c	d	

moves, the search can be made more efficient by using *heuristics* that attempt to
guide the knight so that a complete tour will be found quickly.

   Warnsdorf's rule is a simple and effective heuristic for finding a knight's tour.
Using the rule, it is possible to efficiently construct a tour even on a large board. The
idea is to always move the knight so that it ends up in a square where the number of
possible follow-up moves is as *small* as possible. For example, in Fig. 12.16, there are
five possible squares to which the knight can move (squares $a \ldots e$). In this situation,
Warnsdorf's rule moves the knight to square a, because after this choice, there is
only a single possible move. The other choices would move the knight to squares
where there would be three moves available.

12.3   Maximum Flows

In the *maximum flow* problem, we are given a directed weighted graph that contains
two special nodes: a *source* is a node with no incoming edges, and a *sink* is a node
with no outgoing edges. Our task is to send as much flow as possible from the source
to the sink. Each edge has a capacity that restricts the flow that can go through the
edge, and in each intermediate node, the incoming and outgoing flow has to be equal.

   As an example, consider the graph in Fig. 12.17, where node 1 is the source and
node 6 is the sink. The maximum flow in this graph is 7, shown in Fig. 12.18. The
notation v/k means that a flow of v units is routed through an edge whose capacity
is k units. The size of the flow is 7, because the source sends $3 + 4$ units of flow
and the sink receives $5 + 2$ units of flow. It is easy see that this flow is maximum,
because the total capacity of the edges leading to the sink is 7.

   It turns out that the maximum flow problem is connected to another graph problem,
the *minimum cut* problem, where our task is to remove a set of edges from the graph

Fig. 12.17 Graph with
source 1 and sink 6

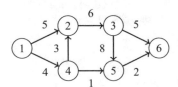

Fig. 12.18 Maximum flow of the graph is 7

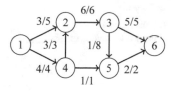

Fig. 12.19 Minimum cut of the graph is 7

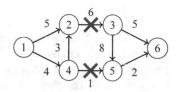

such that there will be no path from the source to the sink after the removal and the total weight of the removed edges is minimum.

For example, consider again the graph in Fig. 12.17. The minimum cut size is 7, because it suffices to remove the edges $2 \rightarrow 3$ and $4 \rightarrow 5$, as shown in Fig. 12.19. After removing the edges, there will be no path from the source to the sink. The size of the cut is $6 + 1 = 7$, and the cut is minimum, because there is no valid cut whose weight would be less than 7.

It is not a coincidence that the maximum flow and minimum cut are equal in our example graph. Rather, it turns out that they are *always* equal, so the concepts are two sides of the same coin. Next we will discuss the Ford–Fulkerson algorithm that can be used to find the maximum flow and minimum cut of a graph. The algorithm also helps us to understand *why* they are equal.

12.3.1 Ford–Fulkerson Algorithm

The *Ford–Fulkerson algorithm* finds the maximum flow in a graph. The algorithm begins with an empty flow, and at each step finds a path from the source to the sink that generates more flow. Finally, when the algorithm cannot increase the flow anymore, the maximum flow has been found.

The algorithm uses a special graph representation where each original edge has a reverse edge in another direction. The weight of each edge indicates how much more flow we could route through it. At the beginning of the algorithm, the weight of each original edge equals the capacity of the edge and the weight of each reverse edge is zero. Figure 12.20 shows the new representation for our example graph.

The Ford–Fulkerson algorithm consists of several rounds. On each round, the algorithm finds a path from the source to the sink such that each edge on the path has a positive weight. If there is more than one possible path available, any of them can be chosen. After choosing the path, the flow increases by x units, where x is the smallest edge weight on the path. In addition, the weight of each edge on the path decreases by x and the weight of each reverse edge increases by x.

Fig. 12.20 Graph
representation in the
Ford–Fulkerson algorithm

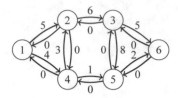

The idea is that increasing the flow decreases the amount of flow that can go through the edges in the future. On the other hand, it is possible to cancel flow later using the reverse edges if it turns out that it would be beneficial to route the flow in another way. The algorithm increases the flow as long as there is a path from the source to the sink through positive-weight edges. Then, if there are no such paths, the algorithm terminates and the maximum flow has been found.

Figure 12.21 shows how the Ford–Fulkerson algorithm finds the maximum flow for our example graph. In this case, there are four rounds. On the first round, the algorithm chooses the path $1 \rightarrow 2 \rightarrow 3 \rightarrow 5 \rightarrow 6$. The minimum edge weight on this path is 2, so the flow increases by 2 units. Then, the algorithm chooses three other paths that increase the flow by 3, 1, and 1 units. After this, there is no path with positive-weight edges, so the maximum flow is $2 + 3 + 1 + 1 = 7$.

Finding Paths The Ford–Fulkerson algorithm does not specify how we should choose the paths that increase the flow. In any case, the algorithm will terminate sooner or later and correctly find the maximum flow. However, the efficiency of the algorithm depends on how the paths are chosen. A simple way to find paths is to use depth-first search. Usually this works well, but in the worst case, each path only increases the flow by one unit and the algorithm is slow. Fortunately, we can avoid this situation by using one of the following techniques:

The *Edmonds–Karp algorithm* chooses each path so that the number of edges on the path is as small as possible. This can be done by using breadth-first search instead of depth-first search for finding paths. It can be proved that this guarantees that the flow increases quickly, and the time complexity of the algorithm is $O(m^2 n)$.

The *capacity scaling algorithm*[1] uses depth-first search to find paths where each edge weight is at least an integer threshold value. Initially, the threshold value is some large number, for example the sum of all edge weights of the graph. Always when a path cannot be found, the threshold value is divided by 2. The algorithm terminates when the threshold value becomes 0. The time complexity of the algorithm is $O(m^2 \log c)$, where c is the initial threshold value.

In practice, the capacity scaling algorithm is easier to implement, because depth-first search can be used for finding paths. Both algorithms are efficient enough for problems that typically appear in programming contests.

---

[1]This elegant algorithm is not very well known; a detailed description can be found in a textbook by Ahuja et al. [1].

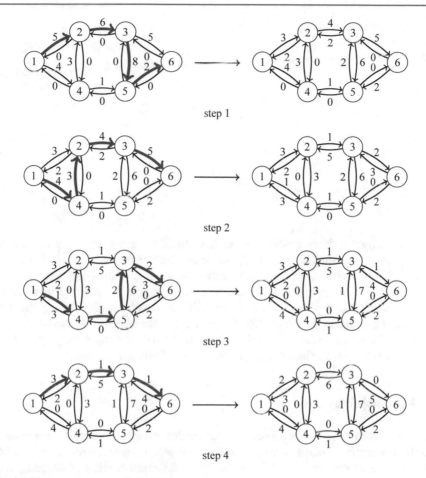

step 1

step 2

step 3

step 4

Fig. 12.21 Ford–Fulkerson algorithm

Minimum Cuts It turns out that once the Ford–Fulkerson algorithm has found a maximum flow, it has also determined a minimum cut. Consider the graph produced by the algorithm, and let A be the set of nodes that can be reached from the source using positive-weight edges. Now the minimum cut consists of the edges of the original graph that start at some node in A, end at some node outside A, and whose capacity is fully used in the maximum flow. For example, in Fig. 12.22, A consists of nodes 1, 2, and 4, and the minimum cut edges are $2 \rightarrow 3$ and $4 \rightarrow 5$, whose weight is $6 + 1 = 7$.

Why is the flow produced by the algorithm maximum and why is the cut minimum? The reason is that a graph cannot contain a flow whose size is larger than the weight of any cut of the graph. Hence, always when a flow and a cut are equal, they are a maximum flow and a minimum cut.

Fig. 12.22 Nodes 1, 2, and
4 belong to the set A

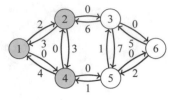

Fig. 12.23 Routing the flow
from A to B

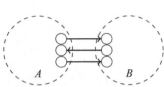

To see why the above holds, consider any cut of the graph such that the source belongs to A, the sink belongs to B and there are some edges between the sets (Fig. 12.23). The size of the cut is the sum of the weights of the edges that go from A to B. This is an upper bound for the flow in the graph, because the flow has to proceed from A to B. Thus, the size of a maximum flow is smaller than or equal to the size of any cut in the graph. On the other hand, the Ford–Fulkerson algorithm produces a flow whose size is *exactly* as large as the size of a cut in the graph. Thus, the flow has to be a maximum flow and the cut has to be a minimum cut.

12.3.2 Disjoint Paths

Many graph problems can be solved by reducing them to the maximum flow problem. Our first example of such a problem is as follows: we are given a directed graph with a source and a sink, and our task is to find the maximum number of disjoint paths from the source to the sink.

Edge-Disjoint Paths We first focus on the problem of finding the maximum number of *edge-disjoint paths* from the source to the sink. This means that each edge may appear in at most one path. For example, in Fig. 12.24, the maximum number of edge-disjoint paths is 2 ($1 \rightarrow 2 \rightarrow 4 \rightarrow 3 \rightarrow 6$ and $1 \rightarrow 4 \rightarrow 5 \rightarrow 6$).

It turns out that the maximum number of edge-disjoint paths always equals the maximum flow of the graph where the capacity of each edge is one. After the maximum flow has been constructed, the edge-disjoint paths can be found greedily by following paths from the source to the sink.

Node-Disjoint Paths Then, consider the problem of finding the maximum number of *node-disjoint paths* from the source to the sink. In this case, every node, except for the source and sink, may appear in at most one path, which may reduce the maximum number of disjoint paths. Indeed, in our example graph, the maximum number of node-disjoint paths is 1 (Fig. 12.25).

We can reduce also this problem to the maximum flow problem. Since each node can appear in at most one path, we have to limit the flow that goes through the nodes.

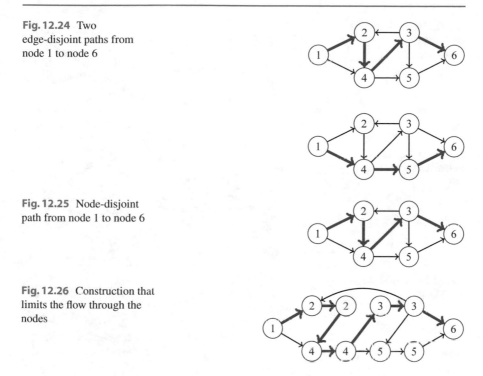

Fig. 12.24 Two edge-disjoint paths from node 1 to node 6

Fig. 12.25 Node-disjoint path from node 1 to node 6

Fig. 12.26 Construction that limits the flow through the nodes

A standard construction for this is to divide each node into two nodes such that the first node has the incoming edges of the original node, the second node has the outgoing edges of the original node, and there is a new edge from the first node to the second node. Figure 12.26 shows the resulting graph and its maximum flow in our example.

12.3.3 Maximum Matchings

A *maximum matching* of a graph is a maximum-size set of node pairs where each pair is connected with an edge and each node belongs to at most one pair. While solving the maximum matching problem in a general graph requires tricky algorithms, the problem is much easier to solve if we assume that the graph is bipartite. In this case, we can reduce the problem to the maximum flow problem.

The nodes of a bipartite graph can always be divided into two groups such that all edges of the graph go from the left group to the right group. For example, Fig. 12.27 shows a maximum matching of a bipartite graph whose left group is {1, 2, 3, 4} and right group is {5, 6, 7, 8}.

We can reduce the bipartite maximum matching problem to the maximum flow problem by adding two new nodes to the graph: a source and a sink. We also add edges from the source to each left node and from each right node to the sink. After

Fig. 12.27 Maximum matching

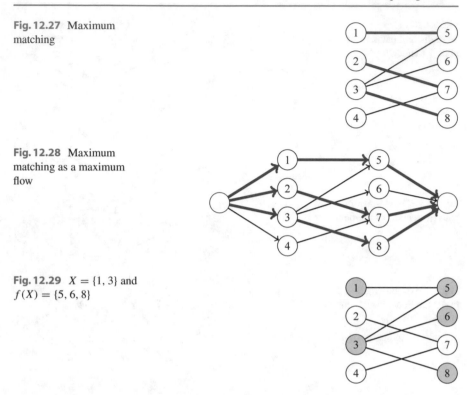

Fig. 12.28 Maximum matching as a maximum flow

Fig. 12.29 $X = \{1, 3\}$ and $f(X) = \{5, 6, 8\}$

this, the size of a maximum flow in the resulting graph equals the size of a maximum matching in the original graph. For example, Fig. 12.28 shows the reduction and the maximum flow for our example graph.

Hall's Theorem *Hall's theorem* can be used to find out whether a bipartite graph has a matching that contains all left or right nodes. If the number of left and right nodes is the same, Hall's theorem tells us if it is possible to construct a *perfect matching* that contains all nodes of the graph.

Assume that we want to find a matching that contains all left nodes. Let X be any set of left nodes and let $f(X)$ be the set of their neighbors. According to Hall's theorem, a matching that contains all left nodes exists exactly when for every possible set X, the condition $|X| \le |f(X)|$ holds.

Let us study Hall's theorem in our example graph. First, let $X = \{1, 3\}$ which yields $f(X) = \{5, 6, 8\}$ (Fig. 12.29). The condition of Hall's theorem holds, because $|X| = 2$ and $|f(X)| = 3$. Then, let $X = \{2, 4\}$ which yields $f(X) = \{7\}$ (Fig. 12.30). In this case, $|X| = 2$ and $|f(X)| = 1$, so the condition of Hall's theorem does not hold. This means that it is not possible to form a perfect matching for the graph. This result is not surprising, because we already know that the maximum matching of the graph is 3 and not 4.

If the condition of Hall's theorem does not hold, the set X explains *why* we cannot form such a matching. Since X contains more nodes than $f(X)$, there are no pairs for

Fig. 12.30 $X = \{2, 4\}$ and $f(X) = \{7\}$

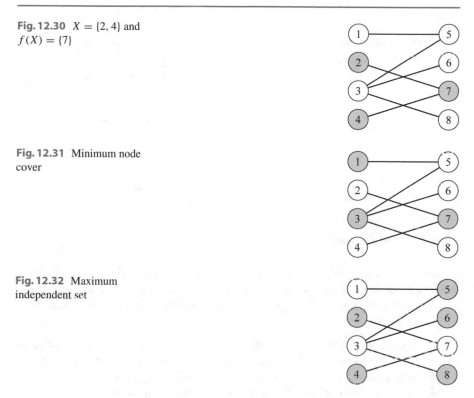

Fig. 12.31 Minimum node cover

Fig. 12.32 Maximum independent set

all nodes in X. For example, in Fig. 12.30, both nodes 2 and 4 should be connected with node 7 which is not possible.

König's Theorem A *minimum node cover* of a graph is a minimum set of nodes such that each edge of the graph has at least one endpoint in the set. In a general graph, finding a minimum node cover is a NP-hard problem. However, if the graph is bipartite, *König's theorem* tells us that the size of a minimum node cover always equals the size of a maximum matching. Thus, we can calculate the size of a minimum node cover using a maximum flow algorithm.

For example, since the maximum matching of our example graph is 3, König's theorem tells us that the size of a minimum node cover is also 3. Figure 12.31 shows how such a cover can be constructed.

The nodes that do *not* belong to a minimum node cover form a *maximum independent set*. This is the largest possible set of nodes such that no two nodes in the set are connected with an edge. Again, finding a maximum independent set in a general graph is a NP-hard problem, but in a bipartite graph we can use König's theorem to solve the problem efficiently. Figure 12.32 shows a maximum independent set for our example graph.

Fig. 12.33 Example graph
for constructing path covers

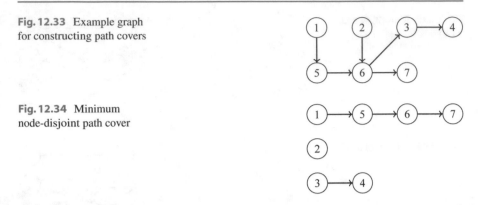

Fig. 12.34 Minimum
node-disjoint path cover

12.3.4 Path Covers

A *path cover* is a set of paths in a graph such that each node of the graph belongs
to at least one path. It turns out that in directed acyclic graphs, we can reduce the
problem of finding a minimum path cover to the problem of finding a maximum flow
in another graph.

Node-Disjoint Path Covers In a *node-disjoint* path cover, each node belongs to
exactly one path. As an example, consider the graph in Fig. 12.33. A minimum node-
disjoint path cover of this graph consists of three paths (Fig. 12.34).

We can find a minimum node-disjoint path cover by constructing a *matching graph*
where each node of the original graph is represented by two nodes: a left node and a
right node. There is an edge from a left node to a right node if there is such an edge
in the original graph. In addition, the matching graph contains a source and a sink,
and there are edges from the source to all left nodes and from all right nodes to the
sink. Each edge in the maximum matching of the matching graph corresponds to an
edge in the minimum node-disjoint path cover of the original graph. Thus, the size
of the minimum node-disjoint path cover is $n - c$, where n is the number of nodes
in the original graph and c is the size of the maximum matching.

For example, Fig. 12.35 shows the matching graph for the graph in Fig. 12.33.
The maximum matching is 4, so the minimum node-disjoint path cover consists of
$7 - 4 = 3$ paths.

General Path Covers A *general path cover* is a path cover where a node can belong to
more than one path. A minimum general path cover may be smaller than a minimum
node-disjoint path cover, because a node can be used multiple times in paths. Consider
again the graph in Fig. 12.33. The minimum general path cover of this graph consists
of two paths (Fig. 12.36).

A minimum general path cover can be found almost like a minimum node-disjoint
path cover. It suffices to add some new edges to the matching graph so that there
is an edge $a \rightarrow b$ always when there is a path from a to b in the original graph
(possibly through several nodes). Figure 12.37 shows the resulting matching graph
for our example graph.

Fig. 12.35 Matching graph
for finding a minimum
node-disjoint path cover

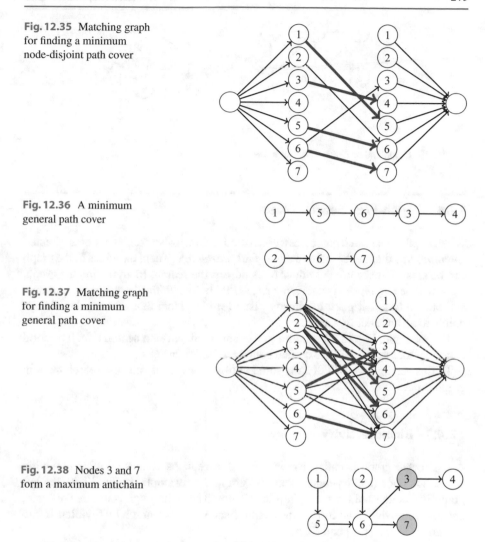

Fig. 12.36 A minimum
general path cover

Fig. 12.37 Matching graph
for finding a minimum
general path cover

Fig. 12.38 Nodes 3 and 7
form a maximum antichain

Dilworth's Theorem An *antichain* is a set of nodes in a graph such that there is no
path from any node to another node using the edges of the graph. *Dilworth's theorem*
states that in a directed acyclic graph, the size of a minimum general path cover
equals the size of a maximum antichain. For example, in Fig. 12.38, nodes 3 and 7
form an antichain of two nodes. This is a maximum antichain, because a minimum
general path cover of this graph has two paths (Fig. 12.36).

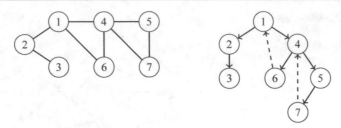

Fig. 12.39 Graph and its depth-first search tree

12.4 Depth-First Search Trees

When depth-first search processes a connected graph, it also creates a rooted directed *spanning tree* that can be called a *depth-first search tree*. Then, the edges of the graph can be classified according to their roles during the search. In an undirected graph, there will be two types of edges: *tree edges* that belong to the depth-first search tree, and *back edges* that point to already visited nodes. Note that a back edge always points to an ancestor of a node.

For example, Fig. 12.39 shows a graph and its depth-first search tree. The solid edges are tree edges, and the dashed edges are back edges.

In this section, we will discuss some applications for depth-first search trees in graph processing.

12.4.1 Biconnectivity

A connected graph is called *biconnected* if it remains connected after removing any single node (and its edges) from the graph. For example, in Fig. 12.40, the left graph is biconnected but the right graph is not. The right graph is not biconnected, because removing node 3 from the graph disconnects the graph by dividing it into two components {1, 4} and {2, 5}.

A node is called an *articulation point* if removing the node from the graph disconnects the graph. Thus, a biconnected graph does not have articulation points. In a similar way, an edge is called a *bridge* if removing the edge from the graph disconnects the graph. For example, in Fig. 12.41, nodes 4, 5, and 7 are articulation points, and edges 4–5 and 7–8 are bridges.

Fig. 12.40 Left graph is biconnected, the right graph is not

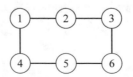
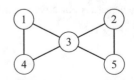

Fig. 12.41 Graph with three articulation points and two bridges

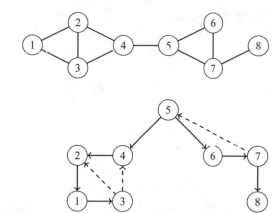

Fig. 12.42 Finding bridges and articulation points using depth-first search

We can use depth-first search to efficiently find all articulation points and bridges in a graph. First, to find bridges, we begin a depth-first search at an arbitrary node, which builds a depth-first search tree. For example, Fig. 12.42 shows a depth-first search tree for our example graph.

An edge $a \rightarrow b$ corresponds to a bridge exactly when it is a tree edge and there is no back edge from the subtree of b to a or any ancestor of a. For example, in Fig. 12.42, edge $5 \rightarrow 4$ is a bridge, because there is no back edge from nodes $\{1, 2, 3, 4\}$ to node 5. However, edge $6 \rightarrow 7$ is not a bridge, because there is a back edge $7 \rightarrow 5$ and node 5 is an ancestor of node 6.

Finding articulation points is a bit more difficult, but we can again use the depth-first search tree. First, if a node x is the root of the tree, it is an articulation point exactly when it has two or more children. Then, if x is not the root, it is an articulation point exactly when it has a child whose subtree does not contain a back edge to an ancestor of x.

For example, in Fig. 12.42, node 5 is an articulation point, because it is the root and has two children, and node 7 is an articulation point, because the subtree of its child 8 does not contain a back edge to an ancestor of 7. However, node 2 is not an articulation point, because there is a back edge $3 \rightarrow 4$, and node 8 is not an articulation point, because it does not have any children.

12.4.2 Eulerian Subgraphs

An *Eulerian subgraph* of a graph contains the nodes of the graph and a subset of the edges such that the degree of each node is *even*. For example, Fig. 12.43 shows a graph and its Eulerian subgraph.

Consider the problem of calculating the total number of Eulerian subgraphs for a connected graph. It turns out that there is a simple formula for this: there are always 2^k Eulerian subgraphs were k is the number of back edges in the depth-first search

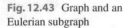

Fig. 12.43 Graph and an Eulerian subgraph

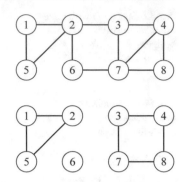

tree of the graph. Note that $k = m - (n - 1)$ where n is the number of nodes and m is the number of edges.

The depth-first search tree helps to understand why this formula holds. Consider any fixed subset of back edges in the depth-first search tree. To create an Eulerian subgraph that contains these edges, we need to choose a subset of the tree edges so that each node has an even degree. To do this, we process the tree from bottom to top and always include a tree edge in the subgraph exactly when it points to a node whose degree is even with the edge. Then, since the sum of degrees is even, also the degree of the root node will be even.

12.5   Minimum Cost Flows

In the *minimum cost flow* problem, we are given a directed graph with a source and a sink. Each edge has two values: a *capacity*, the maximum amount of flow we can send through the edge, and a *cost*, the unit price for the flow that goes through the edge. Our task is to send k units of flow from the source to the sink in such a way that the total cost of the flow is as small as possible.

The minimum cost flow problem resembles the maximum flow problem (Sect. 12.3), but there are two differences: First, we want to send exactly k units of flow even if it would be possible to send more flow. Second, edges have costs and we want to find a solution that minimizes the total cost of the flow.

For example, Fig. 12.44 shows a minimum cost flow graph where node 1 is the source and node 4 is the sink. The notation $a; b$ means that the capacity of the edge is a and the cost is b. For example, we can send at most 5 units of flow from node 2 to node 3, and the unit cost of the flow will be 3. Figure 12.45 shows an optimal way to send $k = 4$ units of flow from the source to the sink. The cost of this solution is 29, which can be calculated as follows:

- We send 2 units of flow from node 1 to node 2 (cost $2 \cdot 1 = 2$).
- We send 1 unit of flow from node 2 to node 3 (cost $1 \cdot 3 = 3$).
- We send 1 unit of flow from node 2 to node 4 (cost $1 \cdot 8 = 8$).
- We send 2 units of flow from node 1 to node 3 (cost $2 \cdot 5 = 10$).
- We send 3 units of flow from node 3 to node 4 (cost $3 \cdot 2 = 6$).

Fig. 12.44 Minimum cost
flow problem

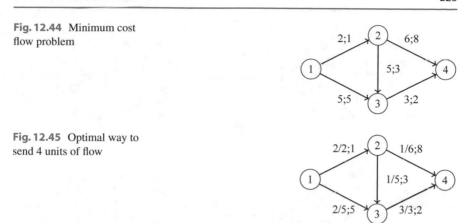

Fig. 12.45 Optimal way to
send 4 units of flow

Note that the minimum cost flow problem is quite a general problem, and some
other problems are its special cases. If we ignore the costs and want to determine
the maximum possible value of k, the problem corresponds to the maximum flow
problem. And if the capacity of each edge is infinite (or at least k), the problem
reduces to finding a minimum cost path from the source to the sink.

12.5.1 Minimum Cost Paths Algorithm

Assuming that the input graph does not have a negative cost cycle, we can solve
the minimum cost flow problem using a modified version of the Ford–Fulkerson
algorithm (Sect. 12.3). As in the maximum flow problem, we construct paths that
generate flow from the source to the sink. It turns out that if we always choose a path
whose total cost is minimum, the resulting flow will be an optimal solution for the
minimum cost flow problem [9].

To use the Ford–Fulkerson algorithm, we first add for each edge a reverse edge
with capacity 0 and cost $-c$ where c is the original cost.[2] The costs of the edges
never change during the algorithm. Then, we run the Ford–Fulkerson algorithm and
always choose a minimum cost path from the source to the sink. We increase the
flow and update the capacities like in the maximum flow problem, with the following
exception: if the current flow is f and a path would increase it by x where $f + x > k$,
we only increase it by $k - f$ and immediately terminate.

While the graph does not have a negative cost cycle, it can have edges whose costs
are negative. For this reason, we construct the minimum cost paths using the Bellman–
Ford algorithm, which supports negative edge costs. The resulting algorithm works

---

[2]If there is an edge from a to b and also an edge from b to a, we have to add a reverse edge for
both of the edges. Thus, we cannot combine edges like in the maximum flow problem, because the
edges have costs which must be taken into account.

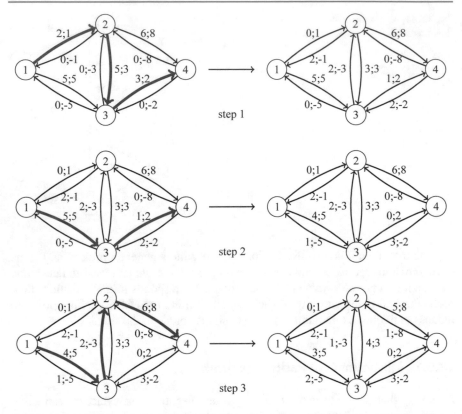

Fig. 12.46 Determining a minimum cost flow ($k = 4$) using the minimum cost paths algorithm

in $O(nmk)$ time, because each path increases the flow at least by one and it takes $O(nm)$ time to find a path using the Bellman–Ford algorithm.

Figure 12.46 shows how the algorithm works in our example graph assuming that the target flow is $k = 4$. First it constructs a path $1 \to 2 \to 3 \to 4$ whose cost is $1 + 3 + 2 = 6$. This path increases the flow by 2 and the cost by $2 \cdot 6 = 12$. Then, the algorithm constructs a path $1 \to 3 \to 4$, which increases the flow by 1 and the cost by 7. Finally, the algorithm constructs a path $1 \to 3 \to 2 \to 4$, which increases the flow by 1 and the cost by 10. Note that the last path could increase the flow by 2, but it only increases it by 1, because the target flow is 4. The total cost of the solution is $12 + 7 + 10 = 29$, as expected.

Why does the algorithm work? The algorithm is based on the following fact that we will not prove here: if the graph (with the reverse edges) has a flow of size f and there is no negative cost cycle where each edge has a positive capacity, then the flow is a minimum cost flow of size f.

We know that the initial graph does not have a negative cost cycle, and since we always construct a minimum cost path from the source to the sink, this ensures that there will never be a negative cost cycle. Thus, since we are able to establish a flow of

Fig. 12.47 Finding an
optimal assignment by
representing a minimum
weight matching as a
minimum cost flow

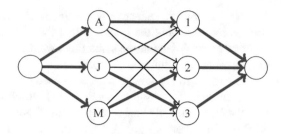

size k without creating a negative cost cycle, the resulting flow has to be a minimum
cost flow of size k.

12.5.2   Minimum Weight Matchings

One application for minimum cost flows is that we can solve the *minimum weight
bipartite matching* problem: given a bipartite weighted graph, find a matching of size
k whose total weight is minimized. This problem is a generalization of the maximum
bipartite matching problem and can be solved in a similar way using a minimum cost
flow algorithm.

For example, suppose that a company has n employees and n tasks, each employee
will be assigned exactly one task, and we know for each employee the cost of carrying
out each task. What is the minimum total cost if we act optimally? For example, for
the input

Employee	Task 1	Task 2	Task 3
Anna	150	400	200
John	400	350	200
Maria	500	100	250

the optimal solution is to assign task 1 to Anna, task 2 to Maria and task 3 to John.
The total cost of this solution is $150 + 100 + 200 = 450$.

Figure 12.47 shows how this scenario can be represented as a minimum cost flow
problem. We create a graph that has $2n + 2$ nodes: a source, a sink, and a node for
each employee and task. The capacity of each edge is 1, the cost of each edge from
the source or to the sink is 0, and the cost of each edge from an employee to a task
is the cost of giving the task to the employee. Now the minimum cost flow of size n
in the graph corresponds to the optimal solution.

12.5.3   Improving the Algorithm

If we knew that the graph used in the minimum cost paths algorithm does not have
negative cost edges with positive capacity, we could improve the algorithm by using

Dijkstra's algorithm instead of the Bellman–Ford algorithm. It turns out that we can do this by *modifying* the graph so that there will be no negative cost edges with positive capacity, and at the same time, each minimum cost path in the new graph corresponds to a minimum cost path in the original graph.

We exploit the following trick also used in Johnson's algorithm [18]: Suppose that each node x is assigned a value $p[x]$ which can be any number. Then we can modify the graph so that the cost of an edge from node a to node b becomes $c(a, b) + p[a] - p[b]$ where $c(a, b)$ is the original cost. This modification does not change any minimum cost path in the graph: if the cost of a path from node x to node y in the original graph is k, then the cost of the same path in the new graph is $k + p[x] - p[y]$ where $p[x] - p[y]$ is constant for any path from node x to node y. This happens because p values in intermediate path nodes cancel each other out.

The idea is to choose the p values so that there will be no negative cost edges after the modification. We can do this by setting $p[x]$ to be the minimum cost of a path from the source to node x. After this, for any edge from node a to node b

$$p[b] \leq p[a] + c(a, b),$$

which means that

$$c(a, b) + p[a] - p[b] \geq 0,$$

i.e., the new cost of the edge is not negative.

We can now implement the minimum cost paths algorithm as follows: We first run the Bellman–Ford algorithm once from the source and construct minimum cost paths to all nodes that can be reached using positive capacity edges. Then we modify the edge costs using the p values which ensures that each edge with positive capacity has a nonnegative cost. After this, we start the actual algorithm that generates flow and use Dijkstra's algorithm to find minimum cost paths. We always construct minimum cost paths to all nodes that can be reached using positive capacity edges, and then update the edge costs according to the p values. Then, we use the original edge costs when calculating the cost of the new path. The resulting algorithm works in $O(nm + k(m \log n))$ time, because we run the Bellman–Ford algorithm once and Dijkstra's algorithm at most k times.

Figure 12.48 shows how the improved algorithm determines the minimum cost flow in our example graph. We have already modified the initial edge costs using the Bellman–Ford algorithm, and now run Dijkstra's algorithm three times to construct minimum cost paths. Each edge with positive capacity has a nonnegative cost, so Dijkstra's algorithm works correctly. Note that each path correspond to a path in Fig. 12.46; only the edge costs are different and we have to use the original edge costs to calculate the cost of the resulting flow.

We first use the Bellman–Ford algorithm, because the initial graph may have negative cost edges with positive capacity. However, after that, we are sure that there are no such edges and we can use Dijkstra's algorithm. Note that some edge capacities change when the flow increases after constructing a path, but this never creates negative cost edges, because all such edges belong to a minimum cost path

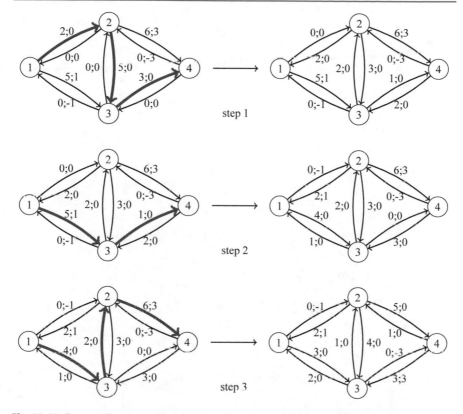

Fig. 12.48 Determining a minimum cost flow ($k = 4$) using the improved algorithm

from the source to the sink: when the path goes from node a to node b, then we know that $p[b] = p[a] + c(a, b)$, which means that both the new cost from a to b and the new cost from b to a will be 0.

In practice, when implementing the improved minimum cost paths algorithm, it is not necessary to modify the edge costs. Instead, we can just add and subtract p values when constructing paths, and then update the p values after each round.

Geometry

13

This chapter discusses algorithm techniques related to geometry. The general goal of the chapter is to find ways to *conveniently* solve geometric problems, avoiding special cases and tricky implementations.

Section 13.1 introduces the C++ complex number class which has useful tools for geometric problems. After this, we will learn to use cross products to solve various problems, such as testing whether two line segments intersect and calculating the distance from a point to a line. Finally, we discuss ways to calculate polygon areas and explore special properties of Manhattan distances.

Section 13.2 focuses on sweep line algorithms which play an important role in computational geometry. We will see how to use such algorithms for counting intersection points, finding closest points, and constructing convex hulls.

13.1 Geometric Techniques

A challenge when solving geometric problems is how to approach the problem so that the number of special cases is as small as possible and there is a convenient way to implement the solution. In this section, we will go through a set of tools that make solving geometric problems easier.

13.1.1 Complex Numbers

A *complex number* is a number of the form $x + yi$, where $i = \sqrt{-1}$ is the *imaginary unit*. A geometric interpretation of a complex number is that it represents a two-dimensional point (x, y) or a vector from the origin to a point (x, y). For example, Fig. 13.1 illustrates the complex number $4 + 2i$.

© Springer Nature Switzerland AG 2020

A. Laaksonen, *Guide to Competitive Programming*, Undergraduate Topics in Computer Science, https://doi.org/10.1007/978-3-030-39357-1_13

Fig. 13.1 Complex number
$4 + 2i$ interpreted as a point
and a vector

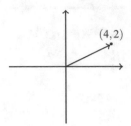

The C++ complex number class `complex` is useful when solving geometric problems. Using the class, we can represent points and vectors as complex numbers and use the features of the class to manipulate them. To do this, let us first define a coordinate type C. Depending on the situation, a suitable type is `long long` or `long double`. As a general rule, it is good to use integer coordinates whenever possible because calculations with integers are exact.

Here are possible coordinate type definitions:

```
typedef long long C;
```

```
typedef long double C;
```

After this, we can define a complex type P that represents a point or a vector:

```
typedef complex<C> P;
```

Finally, the following macros refer to x- and y-coordinates:

```
#define X real()
#define Y imag()
```

For example, the following code creates a point $p = (4, 2)$ and prints its x- and y-coordinates:

```
P p = {4,2};
cout << p.X << " " << p.Y << "\n"; // 4 2
```

Then, the following code creates vectors $v = (3, 1)$ and $u = (2, 2)$ and after that calculates the sum $s = v + u$.

```
P v = {3,1};
P u = {2,2};
P s = v+u;
cout << s.X << " " << s.Y << "\n"; // 5 3
```

Functions The `complex` class also has functions that are useful in geometric problems. The following functions should only be used when the coordinate type is `long double` (or another floating point type).

The function `abs(v)` calculates the length $|v|$ of a vector $v = (x, y)$ using the formula $\sqrt{x^2 + y^2}$. The function can also be used for calculating the distance between points (x_1, y_1) and (x_2, y_2) because that distance equals the length of the vector $(x_2 - x_1, y_2 - y_1)$. For example, the following code calculates the distance between points $(4, 2)$ and $(3, -1)$

```
P a = {4,2};
P b = {3,-1};
cout << abs(b-a) << "\n"; // 3.16228
```

The function `arg(v)` calculates the angle of a vector $v = (x, y)$ with respect to the x-axis. The function gives the angle in radians, where r radians equals $180r/\pi$ degrees. The angle of a vector that points to the right is 0, and angles decrease clockwise and increase counterclockwise.

The function `polar(s, a)` constructs a vector whose length is s and that points to an angle a, given in radians. A vector can be rotated by an angle a by multiplying it by a vector with length 1 and angle a.

The following code calculates the angle of the vector $(4, 2)$, rotates it $1/2$ radians counterclockwise, and then, calculates the angle again:

```
P v = {4,2};
cout << arg(v) << "\n"; // 0.463648
v *= polar(1.0,0.5);
cout << arg(v) << "\n"; // 0.963648
```

13.1.2   Points and Lines

The *cross product* $a \times b$ of vectors $a = (x_1, y_1)$ and $b = (x_2, y_2)$ is defined to be $x_1 y_2 - x_2 y_1$. It tells us the direction to which b turns when it is placed directly after a. There are three cases, illustrated in Fig. 13.2:

- $a \times b > 0$: b turns left
- $a \times b = 0$: b does not turn (or turns 180 degrees)
- $a \times b < 0$: b turns right

For example, the cross product of vectors $a = (4, 2)$ and $b = (1, 2)$ is $4 \cdot 2 - 2 \cdot 1 = 6$, which corresponds to the first scenario of Fig. 13.2. The cross product can be calculated using the following code:

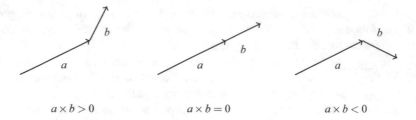

$$a \times b > 0 \qquad\qquad a \times b = 0 \qquad\qquad a \times b < 0$$

Fig. 13.2 Interpretation of cross products

Fig. 13.3 Testing the
location of a point

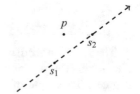

```
P a = {4,2};
P b = {1,2};
C p = (conj(a)*b).Y;  // 6
```

The above code works because the function `conj` negates the y-coordinate of a vector, and when the vectors $(x_1, -y_1)$ and (x_2, y_2) are multiplied together, the y-coordinate of the result is $x_1 y_2 - x_2 y_1$.

Next, we will go through some applications of cross products.

Testing Point Location Cross products can be used to test whether a point is located on the left or right side of a line. Assume that the line goes through points s_1 and s_2, we are looking from s_1 to s_2 and the point is p. For example, in Fig. 13.3, p is located on the left side of the line.

The cross product $(p - s_1) \times (p - s_2)$ tells us the location of the point p. If the cross product is positive, p is located on the left side, and if the cross product is negative, p is located on the right side. Finally, if the cross product is zero, the points s_1, s_2,line and they overlap and p are on the same line.

Line Segment Intersection Next, consider the problem of testing whether two line segments ab and cd intersect. It turns out that if the line segments intersect, there are three possible cases:

Case 1: The line segments are on the same line, and they overlap each other. In this case, there is an infinite number of intersection points. For example, in Fig. 13.4, all points between c and b are intersection points. To detect this case, we can use cross products to test if all points are on the same line. If they are, we can then sort them and check whether the line segments overlap each other.

Case 2: There is a single intersection point which is also a vertex. For example, in Fig. 13.5 the intersection point is c. This case is easy to check because there are

Fig. 13.4 Case 1: The line segments are on the same line and overlap each other

Fig. 13.5 Case 2: The intersection point is a vertex

Fig. 13.6 Case 3: The line segments have an intersection point that is not a vertex

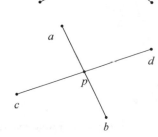

Fig. 13.7 Calculating the distance from p to the line

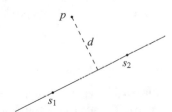

only four possible intersection points. For example, c is the intersection point exactly when it is between a and b.

Case 3: There is exactly one intersection point that is not a vertex of any line segment. In Fig. 13.6, the point p is the intersection point. In this case, the line segments intersect exactly when both points c and d are on different sides of a line through a and b, and points a and b are on different sides of a line through c and d. We can use cross products to check this.

Distance from a Point to a Line Another property of cross products is that the area of a triangle can be calculated using the formula

$$\frac{|(a - c) \times (b - c)|}{2},$$

where a, b, and c are the vertices of the triangle. Using this fact, we can derive a formula for calculating the shortest distance between a point and a line. For example, in Fig. 13.7, d is the shortest distance between the point p and the line that is defined by the points s_1 and s_2.

Fig. 13.8 Point a is inside
and point b is outside the
polygon

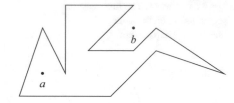

Fig. 13.9 Sending rays from
points a and b

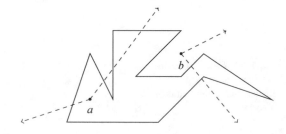

The area of a triangle whose vertices are s_1, s_2, and p can be calculated in two ways: It is both $\frac{1}{2}|s_2 - s_1|d$ (the standard formula taught in school) and $\frac{1}{2}((s_1 - p) \times (s_2 - p))$ (the cross product formula). Thus, the shortest distance is

$$d = \frac{(s_1 - p) \times (s_2 - p)}{|s_2 - s_1|}.$$

Point in a Polygon Finally, consider the problem of testing whether a point is located inside or outside a polygon. For example, in Fig. 13.8, point a is inside the polygon, and point b is outside the polygon.

A convenient way to solve the problem is to send a *ray* from the point to an arbitrary direction and calculate the number of times it touches the boundary of the polygon. If the number is odd, the point is inside the polygon, and if the number is even, the point is outside the polygon.

For example, in Fig. 13.9, the rays from a touch 1 and 3 times the boundary of the polygon, so a is inside the polygon. In a similar way, the rays from b touch 0 and 2 times the boundary of the polygon, so b is outside the polygon.

13.1.3   Polygon Area

A general formula for calculating the area of a polygon, sometimes called the *shoelace formula*, is as follows:

$$\frac{1}{2}\left|\sum_{i=1}^{n-1}(p_i \times p_{i+1})\right| = \frac{1}{2}\left|\sum_{i=1}^{n-1}(x_i y_{i+1} - x_{i+1} y_i)\right|.$$

Fig. 13.10 A polygon
whose area is 17/2

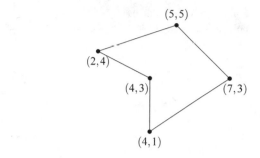

Fig. 13.11 Calculating the
area of the polygon using
trapezoids

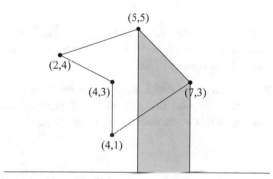

Here, the vertices are $p_1 = (x_1, y_1)$, $p_2 = (x_2, y_2), \ldots, p_n = (x_n, y_n)$ in such an order that p_i and p_{i+1} are adjacent vertices on the boundary of the polygon, and the first and last vertex are the same, i.e., $p_1 = p_n$.

For example, the area of the polygon in Fig. 13.10 is

$$\frac{|(2 \cdot 5 - 5 \cdot 4) + (5 \cdot 3 - 7 \cdot 5) + (7 \cdot 1 - 4 \cdot 3) + (4 \cdot 3 - 4 \cdot 1) + (4 \cdot 4 - 2 \cdot 3)|}{2} = 17/2.$$

The idea behind the formula is to go through trapezoids whose one side is a side of the polygon, and another side lies on the horizontal line $y = 0$. For example, Fig. 13.11 shows one such trapezoid. The area of each trapezoid is

$$(x_{i+1} - x_i) \frac{y_i + y_{i+1}}{2},$$

where the vertices of the polygon are p_i and p_{i+1}. If $x_{i+1} > x_i$, the area is positive, and if $x_{i+1} < x_i$, the area is negative. Then, the area of the polygon is the sum of areas of all such trapezoids, which yields the formula

$$\left| \sum_{i=1}^{n-1} (x_{i+1} - x_i) \frac{y_i + y_{i+1}}{2} \right| = \frac{1}{2} \left| \sum_{i=1}^{n-1} (x_i y_{i+1} - x_{i+1} y_i) \right|.$$

Fig. 13.12 Calculating the
polygon area using Pick's
theorem

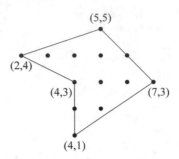

Note that the absolute value of the sum is taken because the value of the sum may be
positive or negative, depending on whether we walk clockwise or counterclockwise
along the boundary of the polygon.

Pick's Theorem *Pick's theorem* provides another way to calculate the area of a
polygon, assuming that all vertices of the polygon have integer coordinates. Pick's
theorem tells us that the area of the polygon is

$$a + b/2 - 1,$$

where a is the number of integer points inside the polygon and b is the number of
integer points on the boundary of the polygon. For example, the area of the polygon
in Fig. 13.12 is
$$6 + 7/2 - 1 = 17/2.$$

13.1.4   Distance Functions

A *distance function* defines the distance between two points. The usual distance
function is the *Euclidean distance* where the distance between points (x_1, y_1) and
(x_2, y_2) is

$$\sqrt{(x_2 - x_1)^2 + (y_2 - y_1)^2}.$$

An alternative distance function is the *Manhattan distance* where the distance
between points (x_1, y_1) and (x_2, y_2) is

$$|x_1 - x_2| + |y_1 - y_2|.$$

For example, in Fig. 13.13, the Euclidean distance between the points is

$$\sqrt{(5 - 2)^2 + (2 - 1)^2} = \sqrt{10}$$

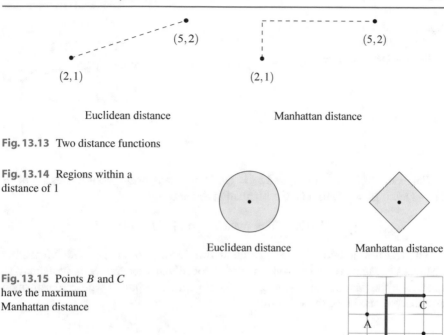

Fig. 13.13 Two distance functions

Fig. 13.14 Regions within a
distance of 1

Fig. 13.15 Points B and C
have the maximum
Manhattan distance

and the Manhattan distance is

$$|5 - 2| + |2 - 1| = 4.$$

Figure 13.14 shows regions that are within a distance of 1 from the center point, using the Euclidean and Manhattan distances.

Some problems are easier to solve if Manhattan distances are used instead of Euclidean distances. As an example, given a set of points in the two-dimensional plane, consider the problem of finding two points whose Manhattan distance is maximum. For example, in Fig. 13.15, we should select points B and C to get the maximum Manhattan distance 5.

A useful technique related to Manhattan distances is to transform the coordinates so that a point (x, y) becomes $(x + y, y - x)$. This rotates the point set 45° and scales it. For example, Fig. 13.16 shows the result of the transformation in our example scenario.

Then, consider two points $p_1 = (x_1, y_1)$ and $p_2 = (x_2, y_2)$ whose transformed coordinates are $p_1' = (x_1', y_1')$ and $p_2' = (x_2', y_2')$. Now, there are two ways to express the Manhattan distance between p_1 and p_2:

$$|x_1 - x_2| + |y_1 - y_2| = \max(|x_1' - x_2'|, |y_1' - y_2'|)$$

Fig. 13.16 Maximum
Manhattan distance after
transforming the coordinates

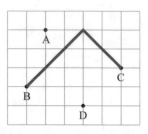

For example, if $p_1 = (1, 0)$ and $p_2 = (3, 3)$, the transformed coordinates are $p'_1 = (1, -1)$ and $p'_2 = (6, 0)$, and the Manhattan distance is

$$|1 - 3| + |0 - 3| = \max(|1 - 6|, |-1 - 0|) = 5.$$

The transformed coordinates provide a simple way to operate with Manhattan distances because we can consider x- and y-coordinates separately. In particular, to maximize the Manhattan distance, we should find two points whose transformed coordinates maximize the value of

$$\max(|x'_1 - x'_2|, |y'_1 - y'_2|).$$

This is easy because either the horizontal or vertical difference of the transformed coordinates has to be maximum.

13.2 Sweep Line Algorithms

Many geometric problems can be solved using *sweep line* algorithms. The idea in such algorithms is to represent an instance of the problem as a set of events that correspond to points in the plane. Then, the events are processed in increasing order according to their x- or y-coordinates.

13.2.1 Intersection Points

Given a set of n line segments, each of them being either horizontal or vertical, consider the problem of counting the total number of intersection points. For example, in Fig. 13.17, there are five line segments and three intersection points.

It is easy to solve the problem in $O(n^2)$ time because we can go through all possible pairs of line segments and check if they intersect. However, we can solve the problem more efficiently in $O(n \log n)$ time using a sweep line algorithm and a range query data structure. The idea is to process the endpoints of the line segments from left to right and focus on three types of events:

Fig. 13.17 Five line segments with three intersection points

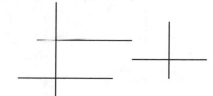

Fig. 13.18 Events that correspond to the line segments

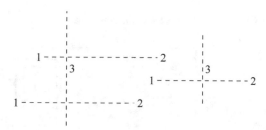

(1) horizontal segment begins
(2) horizontal segment ends
(3) vertical segment

Figure 13.18 shows the events in our example scenario.

After creating the events, we go through them from left to right and use a data structure that maintains the y-coordinates of the active horizontal segments. At event 1, we add the y-coordinate of the segment to the structure, and at event 2, we remove the y-coordinate from the structure. Intersection points are calculated at event 3: When processing a vertical segment between points y_1 and y_2, we count the number of active horizontal segments whose y-coordinate is between y_1 and y_2, and add this number to the total number of intersection points.

To store y-coordinates of horizontal segments, we can use a binary indexed or segment tree, possibly with index compression. Processing each event takes $O(\log n)$ time, so the algorithm works in $O(n \log n)$ time.

13.2.2 Closest Pair Problem

Given a set of n points, our next problem is to find two points whose Euclidean distance is minimum. For example, Fig. 13.19 shows a set of points, where the closest pair is painted black.

This is another example of a problem that can be solved in $O(n \log n)$ time using a sweep line algorithm.[1] We go through the points from left to right and maintain a value d: the minimum distance between two points seen so far. At each point, we

---

[1]Creating an efficient algorithm for the closest pair problem was once an important open problem in computational geometry. Finally, Shamos and Hoey [30] discovered a divide and conquer algorithm

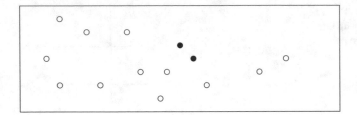

Fig. 13.19 An instance of the closest pair problem

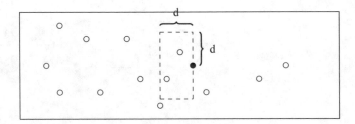

Fig. 13.20 Region where the closest point must lie

find its nearest point to the left. If the distance is less than d, it is the new minimum distance, and we update the value of d.

If the current point is (x, y) and there is a point to the left within a distance of less than d, the x-coordinate of such a point must be between $[x - d, x]$, and the y-coordinate must be between $[y - d, y + d]$. Thus, it suffices to only consider points that are located in those ranges, which makes the algorithm efficient. For example, in Fig. 13.20, the region marked with dashed lines contains the points that can be within a distance of d from the active point.

The efficiency of the algorithm is based on the fact that the region always contains only $O(1)$ points. To see why this holds, consider Fig. 13.21. Since the current minimum distance between two points is d, each $d/2 \times d/2$ square may contain at most one point. Thus, there are at most eight points in the region.

We can go through the points in the region in $O(\log n)$ time by maintaining a set of points whose x-coordinates are between $[x - d, x]$ so that the points are sorted in increasing order according to their y-coordinates. The time complexity of the algorithm is $O(n \log n)$ because we go through n points and determine for each point its nearest point to the left in $O(\log n)$ time.

---

that works in $O(n \log n)$ time. The sweep line algorithm presented here has common elements with their algorithm, but it is easier to implement.

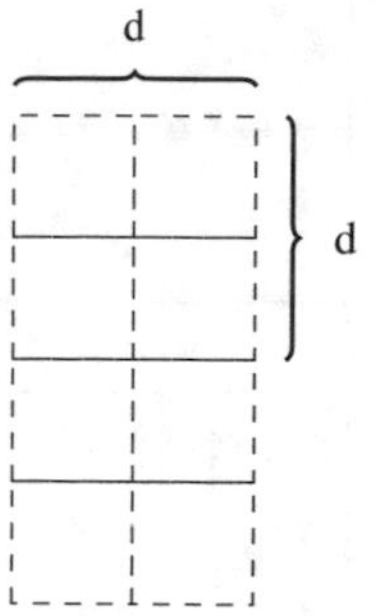

Fig. 13.21 Closest point
region contains $O(1)$ points

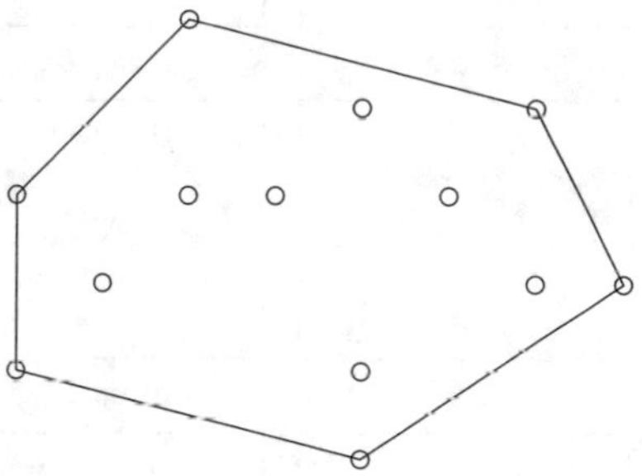

Fig. 13.22 Convex hull of a
point set

13.2.3 Convex Hull Problem

A *convex hull* is the smallest convex polygon that contains all points of a given
point set. Here, convexity means that a line segment between any two vertices of the
polygon is completely inside the polygon. For example, Fig. 13.22 shows the convex
hull of a point set.

There are many efficient algorithms for constructing convex hulls. Perhaps the
simplest among them is *Andrew's algorithm* [2], which we will describe next. The
algorithm first determines the leftmost and rightmost points in the set and then constructs the convex hull in two parts: first the upper hull and then the lower hull. Both
parts are similar, so we can focus on constructing the upper hull.

First, we sort the points primarily according to x-coordinates and secondarily
according to y-coordinates. After this, we go through the points and add each point
to the hull. Always after adding a point to the hull, we make sure that the last line
segment in the hull does not turn left. As long as it turns left, we repeatedly remove
the second last point from the hull. Fig. 13.23 shows how Andrew's algorithm creates
the upper hull for our example point set.

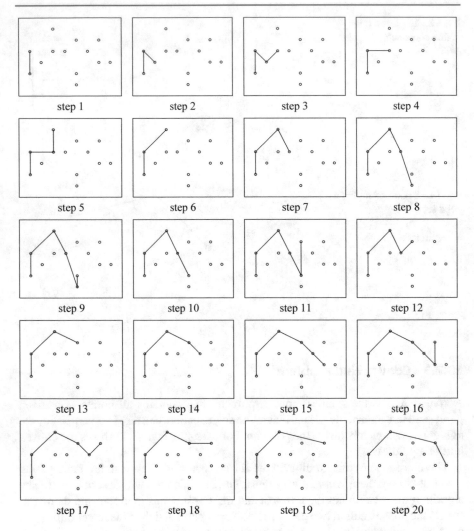

step 1 step 2 step 3 step 4

step 5 step 6 step 7 step 8

step 9 step 10 step 11 step 12

step 13 step 14 step 15 step 16

step 17 step 18 step 19 step 20

Fig. 13.23 Constructing the upper part of the convex hull using Andrew's algorithm

String Algorithms

14

This chapter deals with topics related to string processing.

Section 14.1 presents the trie structure which maintains a set of strings. After this, dynamic programming algorithms for determining the longest common subsequences and edit distances are discussed.

Section 14.2 discusses the string hashing technique which is a general tool for creating efficient string algorithms. The idea is to compare hash values of strings instead of their characters, which allows us to compare strings in constant time.

Section 14.3 introduces the Z-algorithm which determines for each string position the longest substring which is also a prefix of the string. The Z-algorithm is an alternative for many string problems that can also be solved using hashing.

Section 14.4 discusses the suffix array structure, which can be used to solve some more advanced string problems.

Section 14.5 presents an introduction to automata theory and shows how we can use pattern matching automata and suffix automata as an alternative way to solve many string problems.

14.1 Basic Topics

Throughout the chapter, we assume that all strings are zero indexed. For example, a string s of length n consists of characters $s[0], s[1], \ldots, s[n-1]$.

An *alphabet* defines the characters that can be used in strings. For example, the alphabet $\{a, b, \ldots, z\}$ consists of the lowercase Latin letters.

A *substring* is a sequence of consecutive characters in a string. We use the notation $s[a \ldots b]$ to refer to a substring of s that starts at position a and ends at position b. A *subsequence* is any sequence of characters in a string in their original order. All substrings are subsequences, but the converse is not true (Fig. 14.1). A substring or subsequence is called *proper* if it is not the entire string.

© Springer Nature Switzerland AG 2020

A. Laaksonen, *Guide to Competitive Programming*, Undergraduate Topics in Computer Science, https://doi.org/10.1007/978-3-030-39357-1_14

Fig. 14.1 NVELO is a
substring, NEP is a
subsequence

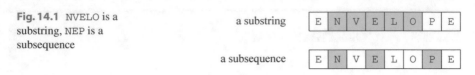

a substring

a subsequence

A *prefix* is a substring that contains the first character of a string, and a *suffix* is a substring that contains the last character of a string. For example, the string BYTE has prefixes {B, BY, BYT, BYTE} and suffixes {E, TE, YTE, BYTE}. A *border* is a substring that is both a prefix and suffix. For example, AB is a border of ABCAAB.

A *rotation* of a string can be created by repeatedly moving the first character of the string to the end of the string. For example, the rotations of ATLAS are ATLAS, TLASA, LASAT, ASATL, and SATLA.

14.1.1 Trie Structure

A *trie* is a rooted tree that maintains a set of strings. Each string in the set is stored as a character chain that starts at the root node. If two strings have a common prefix, they also have a common chain in the tree. As an example, the trie in Fig. 14.2 corresponds to the set {CANAL, CANDY, THE, THERE}. A circle in a node means that a string in the set ends at the node.

After constructing a trie, we can easily check whether it contains a given string by following the chain that starts at the root node. We can also add a new string to the trie by first following the chain and then adding new nodes if necessary. Both the operations work in $O(n)$ time where n is the length of the string.

A trie can be stored in an array

```
int trie[N][A];
```

Fig. 14.2 A trie that
contains the strings CANAL,
CANDY, THE, and THERE

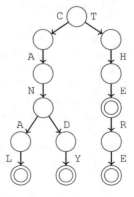

where N is the maximum number of nodes (the maximum total length of the strings in the set) and A is the size of the alphabet. The trie nodes are numbered $0, 1, 2, \ldots$ in such a way that the number of the root is 0, and $\text{trie}[s][c]$ specifies the next node in the chain when we move from node s using character c.

There are several ways how we can extend the trie structure. For example, suppose that we are given queries that require us to calculate the number of strings in the set that have a certain prefix. We can do this efficiently by storing for each trie node the number of strings whose chain goes through the node.

14.1.2 Dynamic Programming

Dynamic programming can be used to solve many string problems. Next, we will discuss two examples of such problems.

Longest Common Subsequence The *longest common subsequence* of two strings is the longest string that appears as a subsequence in both strings. For example, the longest common subsequence of TOUR and OPERA is OR.

Using dynamic programming, we can determine the longest common subsequence of two strings x and y in $O(nm)$ time, where n and m denote the lengths of the strings. To do this, we define a function $\text{lcs}(i, j)$ that gives the length of the longest common subsequence of the prefixes $x[0 \ldots i]$ and $y[0 \ldots j]$. Then, we can use the recurrence

$$\text{lcs}(i, j) = \begin{cases} \text{lcs}(i - 1, j - 1) + 1 & x[i] = y[j] \\ \max(\text{lcs}(i, j - 1), \text{lcs}(i - 1, j)) & \text{otherwise.} \end{cases}$$

The idea is that if characters $x[i]$ and $y[j]$ are equal, we match them and increase the length of the longest common subsequence by one. Otherwise, we remove the last character from either x or y, depending on which choice is optimal.

For example, Fig. 14.3 shows the values of the lcs function in our example scenario.

Edit Distances The *edit distance* (or *Levenshtein distance*) between two strings denotes the minimum number of editing operations that transform the first string into the second string. The allowed editing operations are as follows:

Fig. 14.3 Values of the lcs function for determining the longest common subsequence of TOUR and OPERA

	O	P	E	R	A
T	0	0	0	0	0
O	1	1	1	1	1
U	1	1	1	1	1
R	1	1	1	2	2

Fig. 14.4 Values of the
`edit` function for
determining the edit distance
between LOVE and MOVIE

	M	O	V	I	E
L	1	2	3	4	5
O	2	1	2	3	4
V	3	2	1	2	3
E	4	3	2	2	2

- insert a character (e.g., ABC → ABCA)
- remove a character (e.g., ABC → AC)
- modify a character (e.g., ABC → ADC)

For example, the edit distance between LOVE and MOVIE is 2 because we can first perform the operation LOVE → MOVE (modify) and then the operation MOVE → MOVIE (insert).

We can calculate the edit distance between two strings x and y in $O(nm)$ time, where n and m are the lengths of the strings. Let $\mathtt{edit}(i, j)$ denote the edit distance between the prefixes $x[0 \ldots i]$ and $y[0 \ldots j]$. The values of the function can be calculated using the recurrence

$$\begin{aligned}\mathtt{edit}(a, b) = \min(&\mathtt{edit}(a, b - 1) + 1, \\ &\mathtt{edit}(a - 1, b) + 1, \\ &\mathtt{edit}(a - 1, b - 1) + \mathtt{cost}(a, b)),\end{aligned}$$

where $\mathtt{cost}(a, b) = 0$ if $x[a] = y[b]$, and otherwise $\mathtt{cost}(a, b) = 1$. The formula considers three ways to edit the string x: insert a character at the end of x, remove the last character from x, or match/modify the last character of x. In the last case, if $x[a] = y[b]$, we can match the last characters without editing.

For example, Fig. 14.4 shows the values of the `edit` function in our example scenario.

14.2 String Hashing

Using *string hashing*, we can efficiently check whether two strings are equal by comparing their hash values. A *hash value* is an integer that is calculated from the characters of the string. If two strings are equal, their hash values are also equal, which makes it possible to compare strings based on their hash values.

14.2.1 Polynomial Hashing

A usual way to implement string hashing is *polynomial hashing*, which means that the hash value of a string s of length n is

$$(s[0]A^{n-1} + s[1]A^{n-2} + \cdots + s[n-1]A^0) \bmod B,$$

where $s[0], s[1], \ldots, s[n-1]$ are interpreted as characters codes, and A and B are prechosen constants.

For example, let us calculate the hash value of the string ABACB. The character codes of A, B, and C are 65, 66, and 67. Then, we need to fix the constants; suppose that $A = 3$ and $B = 97$. Thus, the hash value is

$$(65 \cdot 3^4 + 66 \cdot 3^3 + 65 \cdot 3^2 + 66 \cdot 3^1 + 67 \cdot 3^0) \bmod 97 = 40.$$

When polynomial hashing is used, we can calculate the hash value of any substring of a string s in $O(1)$ time after an $O(n)$ time preprocessing. The idea is to construct an array h such that h[k] contains the hash value of the prefix $s[0 \ldots k]$. The array values can be recursively calculated as follows:

$$h[0] = s[0]$$
$$h[k] = (h[k-1]A + s[k]) \bmod B$$

In addition, we construct an array p where p[k] $= A^k \bmod B$:

$$p[0] = 1$$
$$p[k] = (p[k-1]A) \bmod B.$$

Constructing the above arrays takes $O(n)$ time. After this, the hash value of any substring $s[a \ldots b]$ can be calculated in $O(1)$ time using the formula

$$(h[b] - h[a-1]p[b-a+1]) \bmod B$$

assuming that $a > 0$. If $a = 0$, the hash value is simply h[b].

14.2.2 Applications

We can efficiently solve many string problems using hashing because it allows us to compare arbitrary substrings of strings in $O(1)$ time. In fact, we can often simply take a brute force algorithm and make it efficient by using hashing.

Pattern Matching A fundamental string problem is the *pattern matching* problem: given a string s and a pattern p, find the positions where p occurs in s. For example, the pattern ABC occurs at positions 0 and 5 in the string ABCABABCA (Fig. 14.5).

Fig. 14.5 Pattern ABC
appears two times in the
string ABCABABCA

We can solve the pattern matching problem in $O(n^2)$ time using a brute force algorithm that goes through all positions where p may occur in s and compares strings character by character. Then, we can make the brute force algorithm efficient using hashing because each comparison of strings then only takes $O(1)$ time. This results in an $O(n)$ time algorithm.

Distinct Substrings Consider the problem of counting the number of *distinct* substrings of length k in a string. For example, the string ABABAB has two distinct substrings of length 3: ABA and BAB. Using hashing, we can calculate the hash value of each substring and reduce the problem to counting the number of distinct integers in a list, which can be done in $O(n \log n)$ time.

Minimal Rotation Consider the problem of finding the lexicographically *minimal* rotation of a string. For example, the minimal rotation of ATLAS is ASATL.

We can efficiently solve the problem by combining string hashing and *binary search*. The key idea is that we can find out the lexicographic order of two strings in logarithmic time. First, we calculate the length of the common prefix of the strings using binary search. Here hashing allows us to check in $O(1)$ time whether two prefixes of a certain length match. After this, we check the next character after the common prefix, which determines the order of the strings.

Then, to solve the problem, we construct a string that contains two copies of the original string (e.g., ATLASATLAS) and go through its substrings of length n maintaining the minimal substring. Since each comparison can be done in $O(\log n)$ time, the algorithm works in $O(n \log n)$ time.

14.2.3 Collisions and Parameters

An evident risk when comparing hash values is a *collision*, which means that two strings have different contents but equal hash values. In this case, an algorithm that relies on the hash values concludes that the strings are equal, but in reality, they are not, and the algorithm may give incorrect results.

Collisions are always possible because the number of different strings is larger than the number of different hash values. However, the probability of a collision is small if the constants A and B are carefully chosen. A usual way is to choose random constants near 10^9, for example, as follows:

$$A = 911382323$$
$$B = 972663749$$

Table 14.1 Collision probabilities in hashing scenarios when $n = 10^6$

Constant B	Scenario 1	Scenario 2	Scenario 3
10^3	0.00	1.00	1.00
10^6	0.00	0.63	1.00
10^9	0.00	0.00	1.00
10^{12}	0.00	0.00	0.39
10^{15}	0.00	0.00	0.00
10^{18}	0.00	0.00	0.00

Using such constants, the `long long` type can be used when calculating hash values because the products AB and BB will fit in `long long`. But is it enough to have about 10^9 different hash values?

Let us consider three scenarios where hashing can be used:

Scenario 1: Strings x and y are compared with each other. The probability of a collision is $1/B$ assuming that all hash values are equally probable.

Scenario 2: A string x is compared with strings $y_1, y_2, \ldots, y_n$. The probability of one or more collisions is

$$1 - (1 - 1/B)^n.$$

Scenario 3: All pairs of strings $x_1, x_2, \ldots, x_n$ are compared with each other. The probability of one or more collisions is

$$1 - \frac{B \cdot (B - 1) \cdot (B - 2) \ldots (B - n + 1)}{B^n}.$$

Table 14.1 shows the collision probabilities for different values of B when $n = 10^6$. The table shows that in Scenarios 1 and 2, the probability of a collision is negligible when $B \approx 10^9$. However, in Scenario 3, the situation is very different: a collision will almost always happen when $B \approx 10^9$.

The phenomenon in Scenario 3 is known as the *birthday paradox*: if there are n people in a room, the probability that *some* two people have the same birthday is large even if n is quite small. In hashing, correspondingly, when all hash values are compared with each other, the probability that some two hash values are equal is large.

We can make the probability of a collision smaller by calculating *multiple* hash values using different parameters. It is unlikely that a collision would occur in all hash values at the same time. For example, two hash values with parameter $B \approx 10^9$ correspond to one hash value with parameter $B \approx 10^{18}$, which makes the probability of a collision very small.

Fig. 14.6 Z-array of
ABCABCABAB

0	1	2	3	4	5	6	7	8	9
A	B	C	A	B	C	A	B	A	B
–	0	0	5	0	0	2	0	2	0

Some people use constants $B = 2^{32}$ and $B = 2^{64}$, which is convenient, because operations with 32 and 64 bit integers are calculated modulo 2^{32} and 2^{64}. However, this is *not* a good choice because it is possible to construct inputs that always generate collisions when constants of the form 2^x are used [27].

14.3   Z-Algorithm

The *Z-array* z of a string s of length n contains for each $k = 0, 1, \ldots, n - 1$ the length of the longest substring of s that begins at position k and is a prefix of s. Thus, $z[k] = p$ tells us that $s[0 \ldots p - 1]$ equals $s[k \ldots k + p - 1]$, but $s[p]$ and $s[k + p]$ are different characters (or the length of the string is $k + p$).

For example, Fig. 14.6 shows the Z-array of ABCABCABAB. In the array, for example, $z[3] = 5$ because the substring ABCAB of length 5 is a prefix of s, but the substring ABCABA of length 6 is not a prefix of s.

14.3.1   Constructing the Z-Array

Next, we describe an algorithm, called the *Z-algorithm* which efficiently constructs the Z-array in $O(n)$ time.[1] The algorithm calculates the Z-array values from left to right by both using information already stored in the array and by comparing substrings character by character.

To efficiently calculate the Z-array values, the algorithm maintains a range $[x, y]$ such that $s[x \ldots y]$ is a prefix of s, the value of $z[x]$ has been determined, and y is as large as possible. Since we know that $s[0 \ldots y - x]$ and $s[x \ldots y]$ are equal, we can use this information when calculating subsequent array values. Suppose that we have calculated the values of $z[0], z[1], \ldots, z[k - 1]$ and we want to calculate the value of $z[k]$. There are three possible scenarios:

Scenario 1: $y < k$. In this case, we do not have information about the position k, so we calculate the value of $z[k]$ by comparing substrings character by character. For example, in Fig. 14.7, there is no $[x, y]$ range yet, so we compare the substrings starting at positions 0 and 3 character by character. Since $z[3] = 5$, the new $[x, y]$ range becomes $[3, 7]$.

---

[1] Gusfield [15] presents the Z-algorithm as the simplest known method for linear-time pattern matching and attributes the original idea to Main and Lorentz [26].

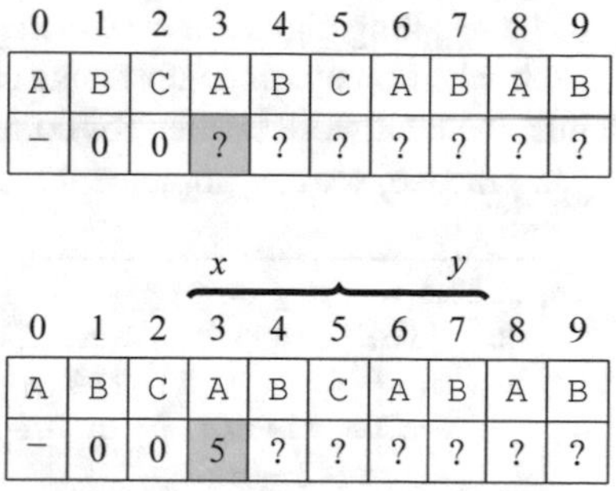

Fig. 14.7 Scenario 1:
Calculating the value of z[3]

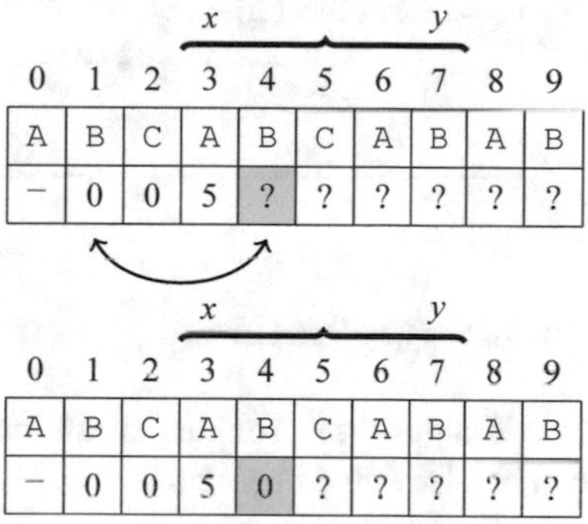

0	1	2	3	4	5	6	7	8	9
A	B	C	A	B	C	A	B	A	B
–	0	0	?	?	?	?	?	?	?

$\overbrace{}^{x} \qquad \overbrace{}^{y}$

0	1	2	3	4	5	6	7	8	9
A	B	C	A	B	C	A	B	A	B
–	0	0	5	?	?	?	?	?	?

Fig. 14.8 Scenario 2:
Calculating the value of z[4]

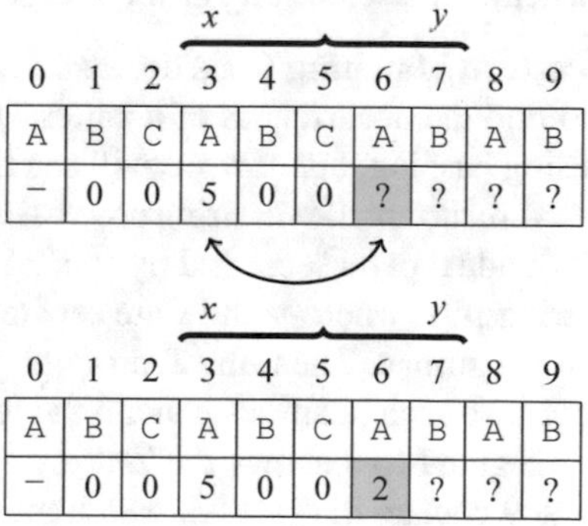

$\overbrace{}^{x} \qquad \overbrace{}^{y}$

0	1	2	3	4	5	6	7	8	9
A	B	C	A	B	C	A	B	A	B
–	0	0	5	?	?	?	?	?	?

0	1	2	3	4	5	6	7	8	9
A	B	C	A	B	C	A	B	A	B
–	0	0	5	0	?	?	?	?	?

Fig. 14.9 Scenario 3:
Calculating the value of z[6]

$\overbrace{}^{x} \qquad \overbrace{}^{y}$

0	1	2	3	4	5	6	7	8	9
A	B	C	A	B	C	A	B	A	B
–	0	0	5	0	0	?	?	?	?

0	1	2	3	4	5	6	7	8	9
A	B	C	A	B	C	A	B	A	B
–	0	0	5	0	0	2	?	?	?

Scenario 2: $y \geq k$ and $k + z[k - x] \leq y$. In this case, we know that $z[k] = z[k - x]$ because $s[0 \ldots y - x]$ and $s[x \ldots y]$ are equal, and we stay inside the $[x, y]$ range. For example, in Fig. 14.8, we conclude that $z[4] = z[1] = 0$.

Scenario 3: $y \geq k$ and $k + z[k - x] > y$. In this case, we know that $z[k] \geq y - k + 1$. However, since we do not have information after the position y, we have to compare substrings character by character starting at positions $y - k + 1$ and $y + 1$. For example, in Fig. 14.9, we know that $z[6] \geq 2$. Then, since $s[2] \neq s[8]$, it turns out that, in fact, $z[6] = 2$.

The resulting algorithm works in $O(n)$ time because always when two characters match when comparing substrings character by character, the value of y increases. Thus, the total work needed for comparing substrings is only $O(n)$.

In practice, we can implement the Z-algorithm as follows:

```
int x = 0, y = 0;
for (int i = 1; i < n; i++) {
    z[i] = (y < i) ? 0 : min(y-i+1,z[i-x]);
    while (i+z[i] < n && s[z[i]] == s[i+z[i]]) {
        z[i]++;
    }
    if (i+z[i]-1 > y) {
        x = i; y = i+z[i]-1;
    }
}
```

14.3.2 Applications

The Z-algorithm provides an alternative way to solve many string problems that can be also solved using hashing. However, unlike hashing, the Z-algorithm always works, and there is no risk of collisions. In practice, it is often a matter of taste whether to use hashing or the Z-algorithm.

Pattern Matching Consider again the pattern matching problem, where our task is to find the occurrences of a pattern p in a string s. We already solved the problem using hashing, but now we will see how the Z-algorithm handles the problem.

A recurrent idea in string processing is to construct a string that consists of multiple individual parts separated by special characters. In this problem, we can construct a string $p\#s$, where p and s are separated by a special character $\#$ that does not occur in the strings. Then, the Z-array of $p\#s$ tells us the positions where p occurs in s because such positions contain the length of p.

Figure 14.10 shows the Z-array for $s =$ ABCABABCA and $p =$ ABC. Positions 4 and 9 contain the value 3, which means that p occurs in positions 0 and 5 in s.

Finding Borders All borders of a string can be efficiently found using the Z-algorithm because a suffix at position k is a border exactly when $k + z[k] = n$ where n is the length of the string. For example, in Fig. 14.11, A, ABA and ABACABA are borders because $10 + z[10] = 11, 8 + z[8] = 11$, and $4 + z[4] = 11$.

Fig. 14.10 Pattern matching using the Z-algorithm

	0	1	2	3	4	5	6	7	8	9	10	11	12
	A	B	C	#	A	B	C	A	B	A	B	C	A
	–	0	0	0	3	0	0	2	0	3	0	0	1

Fig. 14.11 Finding borders using the Z-algorithm

0	1	2	3	4	5	6	7	8	9	10
A	B	A	C	A	B	A	C	A	B	A
$-$	0	1	0	7	0	1	0	3	0	1

14.4 Suffix Arrays

The *suffix array* of a string describes the lexicographic order of its suffixes. Each value in the suffix array is a starting position of a suffix. For example, Fig. 14.12 shows the suffix array of the string ABAACBAB.

It is often convenient to represent the suffix array vertically and also show the corresponding suffixes (Fig. 14.13). However, note that the suffix array itself only contains the starting positions of the suffixes and not their characters.

14.4.1 Prefix Doubling Method

A simple and efficient way to create the suffix array of a string is to use a prefix doubling construction, which works in $O(n \log^2 n)$ or $O(n \log n)$ time, depending on the implementation.[2] The algorithm consists of rounds numbered $0, 1, \ldots, \lceil \log_2 n \rceil$, and round i goes through substrings whose length is 2^i. During a round, each substring x of length 2^i is given an integer label $l(x)$ such that $l(a) = l(b)$ exactly when $a = b$ and $l(a) < l(b)$ exactly when $a < b$.

On round 0, each substring consists of only one character, and we can, for example, use labels A $= 1$, B $= 2$, and so on. Then, on round i, where $i > 0$, we use the labels for substrings of length 2^{i-1} to construct labels for substrings of length 2^i. To give a label $l(x)$ for a substring x of length 2^i, we divide x into two halves a and b of length 2^{i-1} whose labels are $l(a)$ and $l(b)$. If the second half begins outside the string, we assume that its label is 0. First, we give x an *initial* label that is a pair $(l(a), l(b))$. Then, after all substrings of length 2^i have been given initial labels, we sort the initial labels and give *final* labels that are consecutive integers 1, 2, 3, etc. The purpose of giving the labels is that after the last round, each substring has a *unique* label, and the labels show the lexicographic order of the substrings. Then, we can easily construct the suffix array based on the labels.

Figure 14.14 shows the construction of the labels for ABAACBAB. For example, after round 1, we know that $l(AB) = 2$ and $l(AA) = 1$. Then, on round 2, the initial label for ABAA is $(2, 1)$. Since there are two smaller initial labels $((1, 6)$ and $(2, 0))$, the final label is $l(ABAA) = 3$. Note that in this example, each label is unique already after round 2 because the first four characters of the substrings completely determine their lexicographical order.

---

[2]The idea of prefix doubling is due to Karp, Miller, and Rosenberg [20]. There are also more advanced $O(n)$ time algorithms for constructing suffix arrays; Kärkkäinen and Sanders [19] provide a quite simple such algorithm.

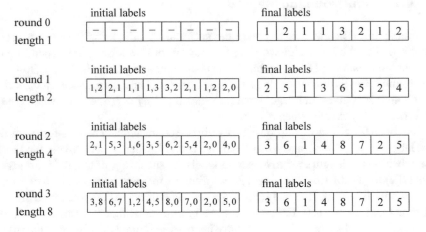

0   1   2   3   4   5   6   7

| 2 | 6 | 0 | 3 | 7 | 1 | 5 | 4 |

Fig. 14.12 Suffix array of the string ABAACBAB

0	2	AACBAB
1	6	AB
2	0	ABAACBAB
3	3	ACBAB
4	7	B
5	1	BAACBAB
6	5	BAB
7	4	CBAB

Fig. 14.13 Another way to represent the suffix array

round 0
length 1

initial labels

| – | – | – | – | – | – | – | – |

final labels

| 1 | 2 | 1 | 1 | 3 | 2 | 1 | 2 |

round 1
length 2

initial labels

| 1,2 | 2,1 | 1,1 | 1,3 | 3,2 | 2,1 | 1,2 | 2,0 |

final labels

| 2 | 5 | 1 | 3 | 6 | 5 | 2 | 4 |

round 2
length 4

initial labels

| 2,1 | 5,3 | 1,6 | 3,5 | 6,2 | 5,4 | 2,0 | 4,0 |

final labels

| 3 | 6 | 1 | 4 | 8 | 7 | 2 | 5 |

round 3
length 8

initial labels

| 3,8 | 6,7 | 1,2 | 4,5 | 8,0 | 7,0 | 2,0 | 5,0 |

final labels

| 3 | 6 | 1 | 4 | 8 | 7 | 2 | 5 |

Fig. 14.14 Constructing the labels for the string ABAACBAB

The resulting algorithm works in $O(n \log^2 n)$ time because there are $O(\log n)$ rounds and we sort a list of n pairs on each round. In fact, an $O(n \log n)$ implementation is also possible because we can use a linear-time sorting algorithm to sort the pairs. Still, a straightforward $O(n \log^2 n)$ time implementation just using the C++ `sort` function is usually efficient enough.

14.4.2 Finding Patterns

After constructing the suffix array, we can efficiently find the occurrences of any given pattern in the string. This can be done in $O(k \log n)$ time, where n is the length

0	2	AACBAB	0	2	AACBAB	0	2	AACBAB
1	6	AB	1	6	AB	1	6	AB
2	0	ABAACBAB	2	0	ABAACBAB	2	0	ABAACBAB
3	3	ACBAB	3	3	ACBAB	3	3	ACBAB
4	7	B	4	7	**B**	4	7	B
5	1	BAACBAB	5	1	**B**AACBAB	5	1	**BA**ACBAB
6	5	BAB	6	5	**B**AB	6	5	**BA**B
7	4	CBAB	7	4	CBAB	7	4	CBAB

Fig. 14.15 Finding the occurrences of BA in ABAACBAB using a suffix array

of the string and k is the length of the pattern. The idea is to process the pattern
character by character and maintain a range in the suffix array that corresponds to
the prefix of the pattern processed so far. Using binary search, we can efficiently
update the range after each new character.

For example, consider finding the occurrences of the pattern BA in the string
ABAACBAB (Fig. 14.15). First, our search range is [0, 7], which spans the entire suffix
array. Then, after processing the character B, the range becomes [4, 6]. Finally, after
processing the character A, the range becomes [5, 6]. Thus, we conclude that BA has
two occurrences in ABAACBAB in positions 1 and 5.

Compared to string hashing and the Z-algorithm discussed earlier, the advantage
of the suffix array is that we can efficiently process *several* queries that are related
to different patterns, and it is not necessary to know the patterns beforehand when
constructing the suffix array.

14.4.3 LCP Arrays

The *LCP array* of a string gives for its each suffix a *LCP value*: the length of the
longest common prefix of the suffix and the next suffix in the suffix array. Figure 14.16
shows the LCP array for the string ABAACBAB. For example, the LCP value of the
suffix BAACBAB is 2 because the longest common prefix of BAACBAB and BAB is
BA. Note that the last suffix in the suffix array does not have a LCP value.

Next, we present an efficient algorithm, due to Kasai et al. [21], for constructing
the LCP array of a string, provided that we have already constructed its suffix array.
The algorithm is based on the following observation: Consider a suffix whose LCP
value is x. If we remove the first character from the suffix and get another suffix,
we immediately know that its LCP value has to be at least $x - 1$. For example, in
Fig. 14.16, the LCP value of the suffix BAACBAB is 2, so we know that the LCP value
of the suffix AACBAB has to be at least 1. In fact, it happens to be exactly 1.

We can use the above observation to efficiently construct the LCP array by calculating the LCP values in decreasing order of suffix length. At each suffix, we calculate
its LCP value by comparing the suffix and the next suffix in the suffix array character

Fig. 14.16 LCP array of the
string ABAACBAB

0	1	AACBAB
1	2	AB
2	1	ABAACBAB
3	0	ACBAB
4	1	B
5	2	BAACBAB
6	0	BAB
7	–	CBAB

by character. Now, we can use the fact that we know the LCP value of the suffix that has one more character. Thus, the current LCP value has to be at least $x - 1$, where x is the previous LCP value, and we do not need to compare the first $x - 1$ characters of the suffixes. The resulting algorithm works in $O(n)$ time because only $O(n)$ comparisons are done during the algorithm.

Using the LCP array, we can efficiently solve some advanced string problems. For example, to calculate the number of distinct substrings in a string, we can simply subtract the sum of all values in the LCP array from the total number of substrings, i.e., the answer to the problem is

$$\frac{n(n + 1)}{2} - c,$$

where n is the length of the string and c is the sum of all values in the LCP array. For example, the string ABAACBAB has

$$\frac{8 \cdot 9}{2} - 7 = 29$$

distinct substrings.

14.5   String Automata

An *automaton*[3] is a directed graph whose nodes are called *states* and edges are called *transitions*. One of the states is a *start state*, marked with an incoming edge, and there can be any number of *accept states*, marked with double circles. Each transition is assigned a character.

We can use an automaton to check if a string has a required format. To do that, we begin at the start state and then process the characters from left to right and move

---

[3]More precisely, we focus on *deterministic finite automata*, also called *DFA*'s.

Fig. 14.17 An automaton
that accepts all AB-strings
whose first and last character
are different

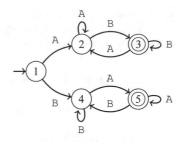

through the transitions. If the final state after processing the entire string is an accept
state, the string is accepted, and otherwise, it is rejected.

In automata theory, any set of strings can be called a *language*. The language of
an automaton consists of all strings it accepts. An automaton *recognizes* a language
if it is able to accept all strings in the language and reject all other strings.

For example, the automaton in Fig. 14.17 accepts all strings that consist of characters A and B and whose first and last character are different, i.e., the language of
the automaton is

$$\{\text{AB, BA, AAB, ABB, BAA, BBA}, \dots\}.$$

In this automaton, state 1 is the start state, and states 3 and 5 are accept states. When
the automaton is given the string ABB, it goes through states $1 \rightarrow 2 \rightarrow 3 \rightarrow 3$ and
accepts the string, and when the automaton is given the string ABA, it goes through
states $1 \rightarrow 2 \rightarrow 3 \rightarrow 2$ and rejects the string.

We assume that our automata are *deterministic*, i.e., there are no two transitions
from a state with the same character. This allows us to efficiently and unambiguously
process any string using an automaton.

14.5.1 Regular Languages

A language is called *regular* if there is an automaton that recognizes it. For example,
the set of AB-strings whose first and last character is different are a regular language
because the automaton in Fig. 14.17 recognizes it.

It turns out that a language is regular exactly when there is a *regular expression*
that describes the required format of the strings in the language. Regular expressions
have the following basic building blocks:

- A vertical bar | means that we can choose one of the options. For example, the
  regular expression AB | BA | C accepts the strings AB, BA, and C.
- Parentheses (and) can be used in grouping. For example, the regular expression
  A(A|B)C accepts the strings AAC and ABC.

- An asterisk * means that the preceding part can be repeated any number of times (including zero times). For example, the regular expression A(BC)* accepts the strings A, ABC, ABCBC, etc.

Here is a regular expression for the automaton in Fig. 14.17:

$$A(A|B)*B|B(A|B)*A$$

In this case, we have two options: either the string begins with A and ends with B or begins with B and ends with A. The part (A|B)* corresponds to any string consisting of characters A and B.

Intuitively, a language is regular if we can create an algorithm that goes through the input string from left to right once, uses a constant amount of memory and can detect if the string belongs to the language. For example, the language

$$\{AB, AABB, AAABBB, AAAABBBB, \dots\}$$

is not regular because we should remember the number of A's and then check that the number of B's is the same, but this is not possible for arbitrarily long strings using a constant amount of memory.

Note that regular expression implementations in programming languages often have extensions that allow them to recognize languages that actually are not regular and it is not possible to create automata for such languages.

14.5.2   Pattern Matching Automata

A *pattern matching automaton* can be used to efficiently detect all occurrences of a pattern in a string. The idea is to create an automaton that accepts a string exactly when the pattern is a suffix of the string. Then, when the automaton processes a string, it always moves to an accept state when it has found a pattern occurrence.

Given a pattern p of n characters, a pattern matching automaton consists of $n + 1$ states. The states are numbered $0, 1, \dots, n$, where state 0 is the start state and state n is the only accept state. When we are in state i, we have been able to match the prefix $p[0 \dots i - 1]$, i.e., the first i characters, of the pattern. Then, we either move to state $i + 1$ if the next input character is $p[i]$, or to some state $x \leq i$ otherwise.

For example, Fig. 14.18 shows a pattern matching automaton that detects occurrences of the pattern ABA. When the automaton processes the string ABABA, it moves through states $0 \rightarrow 1 \rightarrow 2 \rightarrow 3 \rightarrow 2 \rightarrow 3$. It reaches the accept state 3 two times, which corresponds to two pattern occurrences.

To construct the automaton, we should determine all transitions between the states. Let nextState[s][c] denote the state where we move from state s after reading character c. For example, in Fig. 14.18, nextState[1][B] = 2 because we move from state 1 to state 2 after reading B. It turns out that we can efficiently calculate the nextState values by first creating a *border array* for the pattern where border[i] denotes the length of the longest (proper) border of $p[0 \dots i]$. For example, Fig. 14.19

Fig. 14.18 A pattern
matching automaton for the
pattern ABA

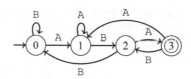

Fig. 14.19 Border array of
ABAABABAAA

0	1	2	3	4	5	6	7	8	9
A	B	A	A	B	A	B	A	A	A
0	0	1	1	2	3	2	3	4	1

shows the border array of ABAABABAAA. For example, border[4] = 2 because AB
is the maximum length border of ABAAB.

We can construct the border array in $O(n)$ time as follows:

```
border[0] = 0;
for (int i = 1; i < n; i++) {
    int k = border[i-1];
    while (k != 0 && p[k] != p[i]) {
        k = border[k-1];
    }
    border[i] = (p[k] == p[i]) ? k+1 : 0;
}
```

The algorithm calculates the values of border[i] using the previously calculated
values in the array. The idea is to go through the borders of $p[0 \dots i-1]$ and select
the longest border that can be extended by adding the character $p[i]$. The algorithm
works in $O(n)$ time because border[$i + 1$] $\leq$ border[i] + 1, so the total number
of iterations of the while loop is $O(n)$.

After constructing the border array, we can use the formula

$$\text{nextState}[s][c] = \begin{cases} s+1 & s < n \text{ and } p[s] = c \\ 0 & s = 0 \\ \text{nextState}[\text{border}[s-1]][c] & \text{otherwise} \end{cases}$$

to calculate the transitions. If we can extend our currently matched prefix, we move to
the next state. If we cannot and we are in state 0, we stay in that state. Otherwise, we
determine the longest border of our current prefix and follow a previously calculated
transition. Using this formula, the pattern matching automaton can be constructed in
$O(n)$ time assuming a constant alphabet.

The Knuth–Morris–Pratt algorithm [24] is a well-known pattern matching algorithm based on simulating a pattern matching automaton. It can be seen as an
alternative for the Z-algorithm (Sect. 14.3).

Fig. 14.20 A suffix automaton for the string BACA

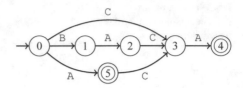

14.5.3   Suffix Automata

A *suffix automaton* [5] is an automaton that accepts all suffixes of a string and has the minimum amount of states. For example, Fig. 14.20 shows a suffix automaton for the string BACA. This automaton accepts the suffixes A, CA, ACA, and BACA.

Each state of a suffix automaton corresponds to a set of strings, meaning that if we are in that state, we have matched one of the strings. For example, in Fig. 14.20, state 3 corresponds to {C, AC, BAC}, state 5 corresponds to {A}. Let length[x] denote the maximum length of a string in state x. Using this notation, length[3] = 3 and length[5] = 1. It turns out that all strings in a state are suffixes of the longest string, and their lengths cover a contiguous interval. For example, in state 3, all strings are suffixes of BAC, and their lengths are 1 . . . 3.

Given a string s of length n, we can create its suffix automaton in $O(n)$ time by starting with an empty automaton that has only state 0 and adding all the characters one by one to the automaton. To do this, we also store for each state $x > 0$ a *suffix link* link[x] that points to a previous state in the automaton. We add a new character c to the automaton as follows:

1. Let x denote the current last state of the automaton, i.e., the state that has no outgoing transitions. We create a new state y and add a transition from x to y using c. Then, we set length[y] = length[x] + 1 and link[y] = 0.
2. We follow suffix links starting from x and add for each visited state a new transition to y using c, until we find a state s that already has a transition using c. If there is no such state s, we terminate when we reach state 0. Otherwise, we move to the next step.
3. Let u denote the state such that there is a transition from s to u using c. If length[s] + 1 = length[u], we set link[y] = u and terminate. Otherwise, we move to the next step.
4. We create a new state z by cloning state u (we copy all outgoing transitions from u to z and set link[z] = link[u]), add a transition from s to z using c and set length[z] = length[s] + 1. Then, we set link[u] = link[y] = z.
5. Finally, we follow suffix links starting from s. As long as the current state has a transition to state u using c, we replace u by z in that transition. When we find a state without a transition to state u using c, or when we reach state 0, we terminate.

Figure 14.21 shows the process that creates a suffix automaton for the string BACA. After adding the last character, we must create an additional state 5 by cloning state

Fig. 14.21 Suffix automaton
construction

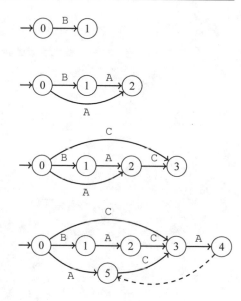

2. In this example, all suffix links point to state 0, expect that in the final automaton, there is a suffix link from state 4 to state 5 that is marked as a dashed edge. After creating the automaton, we can determine the accept states by starting at the last state and following the suffix links until we reach state 0. All states on that path (states 4 and 5 in the example) are accept states.

Note that suffix links tell us to which state we should move if we want to find shorter strings that are suffixes of the strings in our current state. In our example, state 4 corresponds to {CA, ACA, BACA}, and state 5 corresponds to {A}. Thus, the suffix link from state 4 to state 5 can be used to find the shorter suffix A. In fact, if we follow suffix links from state x to state 0, we will find *all* suffixes of the longest string in state x, and each suffix belongs to exactly one state.

After creating a suffix automaton, we can check in $O(m)$ if any given pattern of length m occurs in the string. By using dynamic programming, we can also find the number of times a pattern occurs, calculate the number of distinct substrings, etc. In general, suffix automata are an alternative for suffix arrays, and we can approach many string problems from a new viewpoint using them.

Additional Topics

15

This final chapter presents a selection of advanced algorithms and data structures. Mastering the techniques of this chapter may sometimes help you to solve the most difficult problem in a programming contest.

Section 15.1 discusses square root techniques for creating data structures and algorithms. Such solutions are often based on the idea of dividing a sequence of n elements into $O(\sqrt{n})$ blocks, each of which consists of $O(\sqrt{n})$ elements.

Section 15.2 further explores the possibilities of segment trees. For example, we will see how to create a segment tree that supports both range queries and range updates at the same time.

Section 15.3 presents the treap data structure which allows us to efficiently split an array into two parts and combine two arrays into a single array.

Section 15.4 focuses on optimizing dynamic programming solutions. First we will learn the convex hull trick which is used with linear functions, and after this we will discuss the divide and conquer optimization and Knuth's optimization.

Section 15.5 shows some ideas how we can optimize backtracking algorithms. First we improve an algorithm that counts paths in a grid by pruning the search tree, and after this we solve the 15 puzzle problem using the IDA* algorithm.

Section 15.6 deals with miscellaneous algorithm design techniques, such as meet in the middle and parallel binary search.

15.1 Square Root Techniques

A square root can be seen as a "poor man's logarithm": The complexity $O(\sqrt{n})$ is better than $O(n)$ but worse than $O(\log n)$. In any case, many data structures and algorithms involving square roots are fast and usable in practice. This section shows some examples of how square roots can be used in algorithm design.

© Springer Nature Switzerland AG 2020
A. Laaksonen, *Guide to Competitive Programming*, Undergraduate Topics
in Computer Science, https://doi.org/10.1007/978-3-030-39357-1_15

15.1.1 Data Structures

Sometimes we can create an efficient data structure by dividing an array into *blocks* of size $\sqrt{n}$ and maintaining information about array values inside each block. For example, suppose that we should process two types of queries: modifying array values and finding minimum values in ranges. We have previously seen that a segment tree can support both operations in $O(\log n)$ time, but next we will solve the problem in another simpler way where the operations take $O(\sqrt{n})$ time.

We divide the array into blocks of $\sqrt{n}$ elements and maintain for each block the minimum value inside it. For example, Fig. 15.1 shows an array of 16 elements that is divided into blocks of four elements. When an array value changes, the corresponding block needs to be updated. This can be done in $O(\sqrt{n})$ time by going through the values inside the block, as shown in Fig. 15.2. Then, to calculate the minimum value in a range, we divide the range into three parts such that the range consists of single value and blocks between them. Figure 15.3 shows an example of such a division. The answer to the query is either a single value or the minimum value inside a block. Since the number of single elements is $O(\sqrt{n})$ and the number of blocks is also $O(\sqrt{n})$, the query takes $O(\sqrt{n})$ time.

How efficient is the resulting structure in practice? To find this out, we conducted an experiment where we created an array of n random `int` values and then processed n random minimum queries. We implemented three data structures: a segment tree with $O(\log n)$ time queries, the square root structure described above with $O(\sqrt{n})$ time queries, and a plain array with $O(n)$ time queries. Table 15.1 shows the results of the experiment. It turns out that in this problem, the square root structure is quite efficient up to $n = 2^{18}$; however, after this, it requires clearly more time than a segment tree.

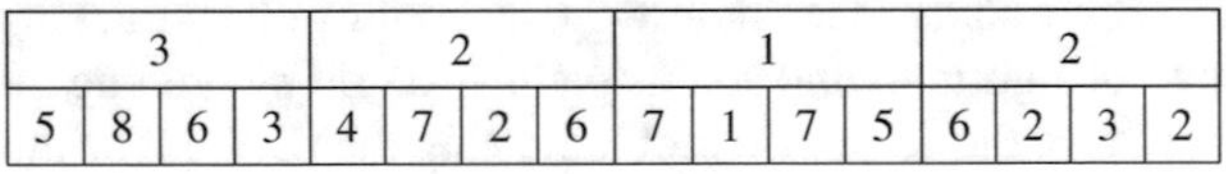

Fig. 15.1 Square root structure for finding minimum values in ranges

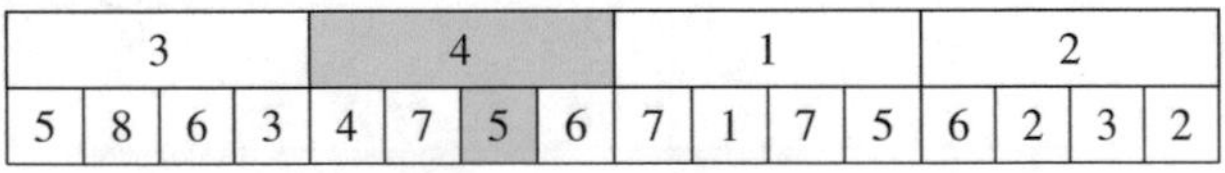

Fig. 15.2 When an array value is updated, the value in the corresponding block has to be also updated

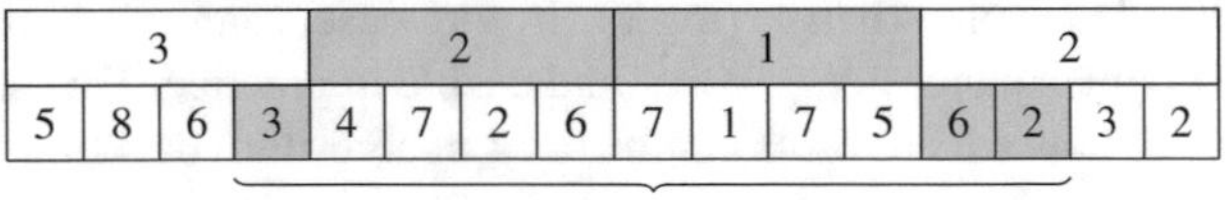

Fig. 15.3 To determine the minimum value in a range, the range is divided into single values and blocks

Table 15.1 Running times of three data structures for range minimum queries: a segment tree ($O(\log n)$), a square root structure ($O(\sqrt{n})$), and a plain array ($O(n)$)

Input size n	$O(\log n)$ Queries (s)	$O(\sqrt{n})$ Queries (s)	$O(n)$ Queries (s)
2^{16}	0.02	0.05	1.50
2^{17}	0.03	0.16	6.02
2^{18}	0.07	0.28	24.82
2^{19}	0.14	1.14	> 60
2^{20}	0.31	2.11	> 60
2^{21}	0.66	9.27	> 60

Fig. 15.4 Instance of the letter distance problem

A	C	E	A
B	D	F	D
E	A	B	C
C	F	E	A

15.1.2   Subalgorithms

Next we discuss two problems that can be efficiently solved by creating two *subalgorithms* that are specialized for different kinds of situations during the algorithm. While either of the subalgorithms could be used to solve the problem without the other, we get an efficient algorithm by combining them.

Letter Distances Our first problem is as follows: We are given an $n \times n$ grid whose each square is assigned a letter. What is the minimum Manhattan distance between two squares that have the same letter? For example, in Fig. 15.4 the minimum distance is 2 between the two squares with letter "D".

To solve the problem, we can go through all letters that appear in the grid, and for each letter c, determine the minimum distance between two squares with letter c. Consider two algorithms for processing a fixed letter c:

Algorithm 1: Go through all pairs of squares that contain the letter c, and determine the minimum distance pair among them. This algorithm works in $O(k^2)$ time, where k is the number of squares with letter c.

Algorithm 2: Perform a breadth-first search that simultaneously begins at each square with letter c. The search takes $O(n^2)$ time.

Both algorithms have certain worst-case situations. The worst case for Algorithm 1 is a grid where each square has the same color, in which case $k = n^2$ and the algorithm takes $O(n^4)$ time. Then, the worst case for Algorithm 2 is a grid where each square has a distinct color. In this case, the algorithm is performed $O(n^2)$ times, which takes $O(n^4)$ time.

However, we can *combine* the algorithms so that they function as subalgorithms of a single algorithm. The idea is to decide for each color c separately which algorithm to use. Clearly, Algorithm 1 works well if k is small, and Algorithm 2 is best suited

Fig. 15.5 Turn in the black
squares game. The minimum
distance from X to a black
square is 3

for cases where k is large. Thus, we can fix a constant x and use Algorithm 1 if k is
at most x, and otherwise use Algorithm 2.

In particular, by choosing $x = \sqrt{n^2} = n$, we get an algorithm that works in $O(n^3)$
time. First, each square that is processed using Algorithm 1 is compared with at most
n other squares, so processing those squares takes $O(n^3)$ time. Then, since there are
at most n colors that appear in more than n squares, Algorithm 2 is performed at
most n times and its total running time is also $O(n^3)$.

Black Squares As another example, consider the following game: We are given an
$n \times n$ grid where exactly one square is black and all other squares are white. On each
turn, one white square is chosen, and we should calculate the minimum Manhattan
distance between this square and a black square. After this, the white square is
painted black. This process continues for $n^2 - 1$ turns, after which all squares have
been painted black.

For example, Fig. 15.5 shows a turn in the game. The minimum distance from the
chosen square X to a black square is 3 (by going two steps down and one step right).
After this, the square is painted black.

We can solve the problem by processing the turns in *batches* of k turns. Before
each batch, we calculate for each square of the grid the minimum distance to a
black square. This can be done in $O(n^2)$ time using breadth-first search. Then,
when processing a batch, we keep a list of all squares that have been painted black
during the current batch. Thus, the minimum distance to a black square is either the
precalculated distance or a distance to one of the squares on the list. Since the list
contains at most k values, it takes $O(k)$ time to go through the list.

Then, by choosing $k = \sqrt{n^2} = n$, we get an algorithm that works in $O(n^3)$ time.
First, there are $O(n)$ batches, so the total time used for breadth-first searches is $O(n^3)$.
Then, the list of squares in a batch contains $O(n)$ values, so calculating minimum
distances for $O(n^2)$ squares also takes $O(n^3)$ time.

Tuning Parameters In practice, it is not necessary to use the exact square root
value as the parameter, but rather we can fine-tune the performance of an algorithm
by experimenting with different parameters and choosing the parameter that works
best. Of course, the optimal parameter depends on the algorithm and also on the
properties of the test data.

Table 15.2 shows the results of an experiment where the $O(n^3)$ time algorithm for
the black squares game was performed for different values of k when $n = 500$. The
order in which the squares were painted black was randomly selected. In this case,
the optimal parameter seems to be about $k = 2000$.

Table 15.2 Optimizing the value of the parameter k in the black squares algorithm

Parameter k	Running time (s)
200	5.74
500	2.41
1000	1.32
2000	1.02
5000	1.28
10000	2.13
20000	3.97

15.1.3 Integer Partitions

Suppose that there is a stick whose length is n and it is divided into some parts whose lengths are integers. For example, Fig. 15.6 shows some possible partitions for $n = 7$. What is the maximum number of *distinct* lengths in such a partition?

It turns out that there are at most $O(\sqrt{n})$ distinct lengths. Namely an optimal way to produce as many distinct lengths as possible is to include lengths $1, 2, \ldots, k$. Then, since

$$1 + 2 + \cdots + k = \frac{k(k+1)}{2},$$

we can conclude that k can be at most $O(\sqrt{n})$. Next we will see how this observation can be used when designing algorithms.

Knapsack Problem Consider a knapsack problem where we are given a list of integer weights $[w_1, w_2, \ldots, w_k]$ such that $w_1 + w_2 + \cdots + w_k = n$, and our task is to determine all possible weight sums that can be created. For example, Fig. 15.7 shows the possible sums using the weights $[3, 3, 4]$.

Using a standard knapsack algorithm (Sect. 6.2.3), we can solve the problem in $O(nk)$ time, so if $k = O(n)$, the time complexity becomes $O(n^2)$. However, since there are at most $O(\sqrt{n})$ distinct weights, we can actually solve the problem more efficiently by simultaneously processing all weights of a certain value. For example,

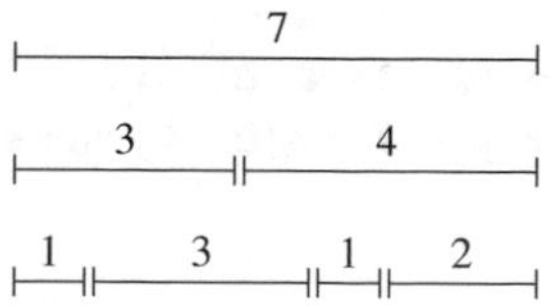

Fig. 15.6 Some integer partitions of a stick of length 7

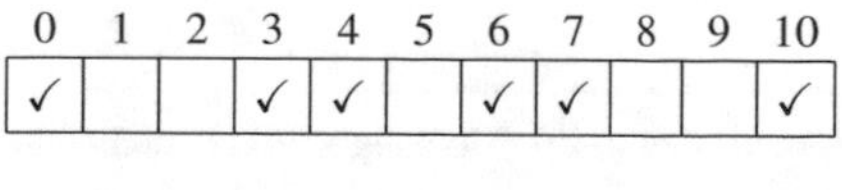

Fig. 15.7 Possible sums using the weights $[3, 3, 4]$

if the weights are [3, 3, 4], we first process the two weights of value 3, and then the weight of value 4. It is not difficult to modify the standard knapsack algorithm so that processing each group of equal weights only takes $O(n)$ time, which yields an $O(n\sqrt{n})$ time algorithm.

String Construction As another example, suppose that we are given a string of length n and a dictionary of words whose total length is m. Our task is to count the number of ways we can construct the string using the words. For example, there are four ways to construct the string ABAB using the words {A, B, AB}:

- A + B + A + B
- AB + A + B
- A + B + AB
- AB + AB

Using dynamic programming, we can calculate for each $k = 0, 1, \ldots, n$ the number of ways to construct a prefix of length k of the string. One way to do this is to use a trie that contains reverses of all the words in the dictionary, which yields an $O(n^2 + m)$ time algorithm. However, another approach is to use string hashing and the fact that there are at most $O(\sqrt{m})$ distinct word lengths. Thus, we can restrict ourselves to word lengths that actually exist. This can be done by creating a set that contains all hash values of words, which results in an algorithm whose running time is $O(n\sqrt{m} + m)$ (using `unordered_set`).

15.1.4 Mo's Algorithm

Mo's algorithm[1] processes a set of range queries on a *static* array (i.e., the array values do not change between the queries). Each query requires us to calculate something based on the array values in a range $[a, b]$. Since the array is static, the queries can be processed in any order, and the trick in Mo's algorithm is to use a special order which guarantees that the algorithm works efficiently.

The algorithm maintains an *active range* in the array, and the answer to a query concerning the active range is known at each moment. The algorithm processes the queries one by one and always moves the endpoints of the active range by inserting and removing elements. The array is divided into blocks of $k = O(\sqrt{n})$ elements, and a query $[a_1, b_1]$ is always processed before a query $[a_2, b_2]$ if

- $\lfloor a_1/k \rfloor < \lfloor a_2/k \rfloor$ or
- $\lfloor a_1/k \rfloor = \lfloor a_2/k \rfloor$ and $b_1 < b_2$.

---

[1] According to [6], Mo's algorithm is named after Mo Tao, a Chinese competitive programmer.

Fig. 15.8 Moving between
two ranges in Mo's algorithm

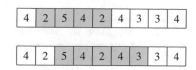

Thus, all queries whose left endpoints are in a certain block are processed one after another sorted according to their right endpoints. Using this order, the algorithm only performs $O(n\sqrt{n})$ operations, because the left endpoint moves $O(n)$ times $O(\sqrt{n})$ steps, and the right endpoint moves $O(\sqrt{n})$ times $O(n)$ steps. Thus, both endpoints move a total of $O(n\sqrt{n})$ steps during the algorithm.

Example Consider a problem where we are given a set of array ranges, and we are asked to calculate the number of *distinct* values in each range. In Mo's algorithm, the queries are always sorted in the same way, but the way the answer to the query is maintained depends on the problem.

To solve the problem, we maintain an array count where count[x] indicates the number of times an element x occurs in the active range. When we move from one query to another query, the active range changes. For example, consider the two ranges in Fig. 15.8. When we move from the first range to the second range, there will be three steps: The left endpoint moves one step to the right, and the right endpoint moves two steps to the right.

After each step, the array count needs to be updated. After adding an element x, we increase the value of count[x] by 1, and if count[x] = 1 after this, we also increase the answer to the query by 1. Similarly, after removing an element x, we decrease the value of count[x] by 1, and if count[x] = 0 after this, we also decrease the answer to the query by 1. Since each step requires $O(1)$ time, the algorithm works in $O(n\sqrt{n})$ time.

15.2 Segment Trees Revisited

A segment tree is a versatile data structure that can be used to solve a large number of problems. However, so far we have only seen a small part of the possibilities of segment trees. Now is the time to discuss some more advanced variants of segment trees that allow us to solve more advanced problems.

Until now, we have implemented the operations of a segment tree by walking *from bottom to top* in the tree. For example, we have used the following function (Sect. 9.2.2) to calculate the sum of values in a range [a, b]:

```
int sum(int a, int b) {
    a += n; b += n;
    int s = 0;
    while (a <= b) {
        if (a%2 == 1) s += tree[a++];
        if (b%2 == 0) s += tree[b--];
        a /= 2; b /= 2;
    }
    return s;
}
```

However, in advanced segment trees, it is often necessary to implement the operations *from top to bottom* as follows:

```
int sum(int a, int b, int k, int x, int y) {
    if (b < x || a > y) return 0;
    if (a <= x && y <= b) return tree[k];
    int d = (x+y)/2;
    return sum(a,b,2*k,x,d) + sum(a,b,2*k+1,d+1,y);
}
```

Using this function, we can calculate the sum in a range $[a, b]$ as follows:

```
int s = sum(a,b,1,0,n-1);
```

The parameter k indicates the current position in `tree`. Initially k equals 1, because we begin at the root of the tree. The range $[x, y]$ corresponds to k and is initially $[0, n - 1]$. When calculating the sum, if $[x, y]$ is outside $[a, b]$, the sum is 0, and if $[x, y]$ is completely inside $[a, b]$, the sum can be found in `tree`. If $[x, y]$ is partially inside $[a, b]$, the search continues recursively to the left and right half of $[x, y]$. The left half is $[x, d]$, and the right half is $[d + 1, y]$ where $d = \lfloor \frac{x+y}{2} \rfloor$.

Figure 15.9 shows how the search proceeds when calculating the value of $\text{sum}_q(a, b)$. The gray nodes indicate nodes where the recursion stops and the sum can be found in `tree`. Also in this implementation, operations take $O(\log n)$ time, because the total number of visited nodes is $O(\log n)$.

15.2.1 Lazy Propagation

Using *lazy propagation*, we can build a segment tree that supports *both* range updates and range queries in $O(\log n)$ time. The idea is to perform updates and queries from top to bottom and perform updates *lazily* so that they are propagated down the tree only when it is necessary.

The nodes of a lazy segment tree contain two types of information. Like in an ordinary segment tree, each node contains the sum, minimum value, or some other values related to the corresponding subarray. In addition, a node may contain in-

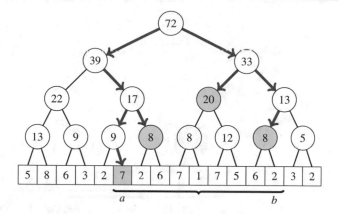

Fig. 15.9 Traversing a segment tree from top to bottom

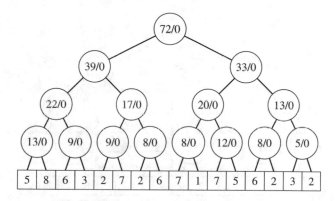

Fig. 15.10 Lazy segment tree for range updates and queries

formation about a lazy update which has not been propagated to its children. Lazy segment trees can support two types of range updates: Each array value in the range is either *increased* by some value or *assigned* some value. Both operations can be implemented using similar ideas, and it is even possible to construct a tree that supports both operations at the same time.

Let us consider an example where our goal is to construct a segment tree that supports two operations: increasing each value in $[a, b]$ by a constant and calculating the sum of values in $[a, b]$. To achieve this goal, we construct a tree where each node has two values s/z: s denotes the sum of values in the range, and z denotes the value of a lazy update, which means that all values in the range should be increased by z. Figure 15.10 shows an example of such a tree, where $z = 0$ in all nodes, meaning that there are no ongoing lazy updates.

We implement the tree operations from top to bottom. To increase the values in a range $[a, b]$ by u, we modify the nodes as follows: If the range $[x, y]$ of a node is completely inside $[a, b]$, we increase the z value of the node by u and stop. Then, if

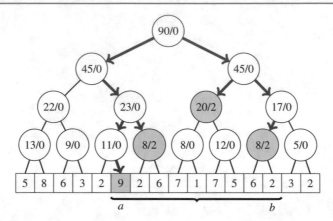

Fig. 15.11 Increasing the values in the range $[a, b]$ by 2

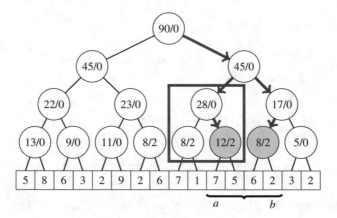

Fig. 15.12 Calculating the sum of values in the range $[a, b]$

$[x, y]$ partially belongs to $[a, b]$, we continue our walk recursively in the tree, and after this calculate the new s value for the node. As an example, Fig. 15.11 shows our tree after increasing the range $[a, b]$ by 2.

In both updates and queries, lazy updates are propagated downward when we move in the tree. Always before accessing a node, we check if it has an ongoing lazy update. If it has, we update its s value, propagate the update to its children, and then clear its z value. For example, Fig. 15.12 shows how our tree changes when we calculate the value of $\text{sum}_a(a, b)$. The rectangle contains the nodes whose values change when a lazy update is propagated downward.

Polynomial Updates We can generalize the above segment tree so that it is possible to update ranges using polynomials of the form

$$p(u) = t_k u^k + t_{k-1} u^{k-1} + \cdots + t_0.$$

In this case, the update for a value at position i in $[a, b]$ is $p(i - a)$. For example, adding the polynomial $p(u) = u + 1$ to $[a, b]$ means that the value at position a increases by 1, the value at position $a + 1$ increases by 2, and so on.

To support polynomial updates, each node is assigned $k + 2$ values, where k equals the degree of the polynomial. The value s is the sum of the elements in the range, and the values $z_0, z_1, \ldots, z_k$ are the coefficients of a polynomial that corresponds to a lazy update. Now, the sum of values in a range $[x, y]$ equals

$$s + \sum_{u=0}^{y-x} (z_k u^k + z_{k-1} u^{k-1} + \cdots + z_1 u + z_0),$$

and the value of such a sum can be efficiently calculated using sum formulas. For example, the term z_0 corresponds to the sum $z_0(y - x + 1)$, and the term $z_1 u$ corresponds to the sum

$$z_1(0 + 1 + \cdots + y - x) = z_1 \frac{(y - x)(y - x + 1)}{2}.$$

When propagating an update in the tree, the indices of $p(u)$ change, because in each range $[x, y]$, the values are calculated for $u = 0, 1, \ldots, y - x$. However, we can easily handle this, because $p'(u) = p(u + h)$ is a polynomial of equal degree as $p(u)$. For example, if $p(u) = t_2 u^2 + t_1 u + t_0$, then

$$p'(u) = t_2(u + h)^2 + t_1(u + h) + t_0 = t_2 u^2 + (2h t_2 + t_1)u + t_2 h^2 + t_1 h + t_0.$$

15.2.2 Dynamic Trees

An ordinary segment tree is static, which means that each node has a fixed position in the segment tree array and the structure requires a fixed amount of memory. In a *dynamic segment tree*, memory is allocated only for nodes that are actually accessed during the algorithm, which can save a large amount of memory.

The nodes of a dynamic tree can be represented as structs:

```
struct node {
    int value;
    int x, y;
    node *left, *right;
    node(int v, int x, int y) : value(v), x(x), y(y) {}
};
```

Here `value` is the value of the node, $[x, y]$ is the corresponding range, and `left` and `right` point to the left and right subtree. Nodes can be created as follows:

```
// create a node with value 2 and range [0,7]
node *x = new node(2,0,7);
// change value
x->value = 5;
```

Sparse Segment Trees A dynamic segment tree is a useful structure when the under-
lying array is *sparse*, i.e., the range $[0, n - 1]$ of allowed indices is large, but most
array values are zeros. While an ordinary segment tree would use $O(n)$ memory,
a dynamic segment tree only uses $O(k \log n)$ memory, where k is the number of
operations performed.

A *sparse segment tree* initially has only one node $[0, n - 1]$ whose value is zero,
which means that every array value is zero. After updates, new nodes are dynamically
added to the tree. Any path from the root node to a leaf contains $O(\log n)$ nodes, so
each segment tree operation adds at most $O(\log n)$ new nodes to the tree. Thus, after
k operations, the tree contains $O(k \log n)$ nodes. For example, Fig. 15.13 shows a
sparse segment tree where $n = 16$, and the elements at positions 3 and 10 have been
modified.

Note that if we know all elements that will be updated during the algorithm
beforehand, a dynamic segment tree is not necessary, because we can use an ordinary
segment tree with index compression (Sect. 9.2.3). However, this is not possible when
the indices are generated during the algorithm.

Persistent Segment Trees Using a dynamic implementation, we can also create a
persistent segment tree that stores the *modification history* of the tree. In such an
implementation, we can efficiently access all versions of the tree that have existed
during the algorithm. When the modification history is available, we can perform

Fig. 15.13 Sparse segment
tree where the elements at
positions 3 and 10 have been
modified

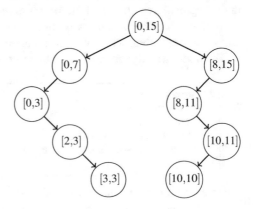

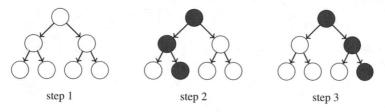

Fig. 15.14 Modification history of a segment tree: the initial tree and two updates

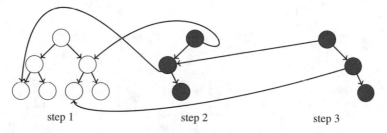

Fig. 15.15 Compact way to store the modification history

queries in any previous tree like in an ordinary segment tree, because the full structure of each tree is stored. We can also create new trees based on previous trees and modify them independently.

Consider the sequence of updates in Fig. 15.14, where marked nodes change and other nodes remain the same. After each update, most nodes of the tree remain the same, so a compact way to store the modification history is to represent each historical tree as a combination of new nodes and subtrees of previous trees. Figure 15.15 shows how the modification history can be stored. The structure of each previous tree can be reconstructed by following the pointers starting at the corresponding root node. Since each operation adds only $O(\log n)$ new nodes to the tree, it is possible to store the full modification history of the tree.

15.2.3   Data Structures in Nodes

Instead of single values, the nodes of a segment tree can also contain *data structures* that maintain information about the corresponding ranges. As an example, suppose that we should be able to efficiently count the number of occurrences of an element x in a range $[a, b]$. To do this, we can create a segment tree where each node is assigned a data structure that can be asked how many times any element x appears in the corresponding range. After this, the answer to a query can be calculated by combining the results from nodes that belong to the range.

The remaining task is to choose a suitable data structure for the problem. A good choice is a map structure whose keys are array elements and values indicate how many times each element occurs in a range. Figure 15.16 shows an array and the

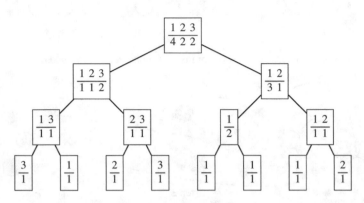

Fig. 15.16 Segment tree for calculating the number of occurrences of an element in an array range

corresponding segment tree. For example, the root node of the tree tells us that element 1 appears 4 times in the array.

Each query in the above segment tree works in $O(\log^2 n)$ time, because each node has a map structure whose operations take $O(\log n)$ time. The tree uses $O(n \log n)$ memory, because it has $O(\log n)$ levels, and each level contains n elements that have been distributed in the map structures.

15.2.4   Two-Dimensional Trees

A *two-dimensional segment tree* allows us to process queries related to rectangular subarrays on a two-dimensional array. The idea is to create a segment tree that corresponds to the columns of the array and then assign each node of this structure a segment tree that corresponds to the rows of the array.

For example, Fig. 15.17 shows a two-dimensional segment tree that supports two queries: calculating the sum of values in a subarray and updating a single array value. Both the queries take $O(\log^2 n)$ time, because $O(\log n)$ nodes in the main segment tree are accessed, and processing each node takes $O(\log n)$ time. The structure uses a total of $O(n^2)$ memory, because the main segment tree has $O(n)$ nodes, and each node has a segment tree of $O(n)$ nodes.

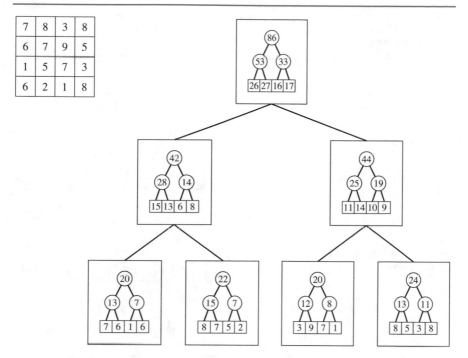

Fig. 15.17 Two-dimensional array and the corresponding segment tree for calculating sums of rectangular subarrays

15.3 Treaps

A *treap* is a binary tree that can store the contents of an array in such a way that we can efficiently split an array into two arrays and merge two arrays into an array. Each node in a treap has two values: a *weight* and a *value*. Each node's weight is smaller or equal than the weights of its children, and the node is located in the array *after* all nodes in its left subtree and *before* all nodes in its right subtree.

Figure 15.18 shows an example of an array and the corresponding treap. For example, the root node has weight 1 and value D. Since its left subtree contains three nodes, this means that the array element at position 3 has value D.

15.3.1 Splitting and Merging

When a new node is added to the treap, it is assigned a *random* weight. This guarantees that the tree is balanced (its height is $O(\log n)$) with high probability, and its operations can be performed efficiently.

Fig. 15.18 Array and the corresponding treap

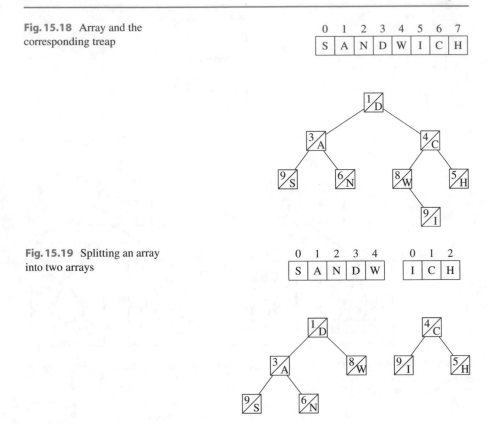

Fig. 15.19 Splitting an array into two arrays

Splitting The splitting operation of a treap creates two treaps which divide the array into two arrays so that the first k elements belong to the first array and the rest of the elements belong to the second array. To do this, we create two new treaps that are initially empty and traverse the original treap starting at the root node. At each step, if the current node belongs to the left treap, the node and its left subtree are added to the left treap, and we recursively process its right subtree. Similarly, if the current node belongs to the right treap, the node and its right subtree are added to the right treap, and we recursively process its left subtree. Since the height of the treap is $O(\log n)$, this operation works in $O(\log n)$ time.

For example, Fig. 15.19 shows how to divide our example array into two arrays so that the first array contains the first five elements of the original array and the second array contains the last three elements. First, node D belongs to the left treap, so we add node D and its left subtree to the left treap. Then, node C belongs to the right treap, and we add node C and its right subtree to the right treap. Finally, we add node W to the left treap and node I to the right treap.

Merging The merging operation of two treaps creates a single treap that concatenates the arrays. The two treaps are processed simultaneously, and at each step, the treap whose root has the smallest weight is selected. If the root of the left treap has the

Fig. 15.20 Merging two arrays into an array, before merging

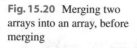

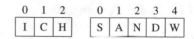

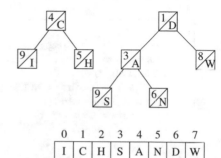

Fig. 15.21 Merging two arrays into an array, after merging

0	1	2	3	4	5	6	7
I	C	H	S	A	N	D	W

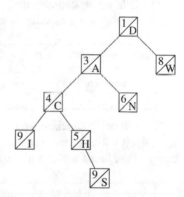

smallest weight, the root and its left subtree are moved to the new treap and its right subtree becomes the new root of the left treap. Similarly, if the root of the right treap has the smallest weight, the root and its right subtree are moved to the new treap and its left subtree becomes the new root of the right treap. Since the height of the treap is $O(\log n)$, this operation works in $O(\log n)$ time.

For example, we may now swap the order of the two arrays in our example scenario and then concatenate the arrays again. Figure 15.20 shows the arrays before merging, and Fig. 15.21 shows the final result. First, node D and its right subtree are added to the new treap. Then, node A and its right subtree become the left subtree of node D. After this, node C and its left subtree become the left subtree of node A. Finally, node H and node S are added to the new treap.

15.3.2 Implementation

Next we will learn a convenient way to implement a treap. First, here is a struct that stores a treap node:

```
struct node {
    node *left, *right;
    int weight, size, value;
    node(int v) {
        left = right = NULL;
        weight = rand();
        size = 1;
        value = v;
    }
};
```

The field `size` contains the size of the subtree of the node. Since a node can be `NULL`, the following function is useful:

```
int size(node *treap) {
    if (treap == NULL) return 0;
    return treap->size;
}
```

The following function `split` implements the splitting operation. The function recursively splits the treap `treap` into treaps `left` and `right` so that the left treap contains the first k nodes and the right treap contains the remaining nodes.

```
void split(node *treap, node *&left, node *&right, int k) {
    if (treap == NULL) {
        left = right = NULL;
    } else {
        if (size(treap->left) < k) {
            split(treap->right, treap->right, right,
                    k-size(treap->left)-1);
            left = treap;
        } else {
            split(treap->left, left, treap->left, k);
            right = treap;
        }
        treap->size = size(treap->left)+size(treap->right)+1;
    }
}
```

Then, the following function `merge` implements the merging operation. This function creates a treap `treap` that contains first the nodes of the treap `left` and then the nodes of the treap `right`.

```
void merge(node *&treap, node *left, node *right) {
    if (left == NULL) treap = right;
    else if(right == NULL) treap = left;
    else {
        if (left->weight < right->weight) {
            merge(left->right, left->right, right);
            treap = left;
        } else {
            merge(right->left, left, right->left);
            treap = right;
        }
        treap->size = size(treap->left)+size(treap->right)+1;
    }
}
```

For example, the following code creates a treap that corresponds to the array [1, 2, 3, 4]. Then it divides it into two treaps of size 2 and swaps their order to create a new treap that corresponds to the array [3, 4, 1, 2].

```
node *treap = NULL;
merge(treap, treap, new node(1));
merge(treap, treap, new node(2));
merge(treap, treap, new node(3));
merge(treap, treap, new node(4));
node *left, *right;
split(treap, left, right, 2);
merge(treap, right, left);
```

15.3.3 Additional Techniques

The splitting and merging operations of treaps are very powerful, because we can freely "cut and paste" arrays in logarithmic time using them. Treaps can be also extended so that they work almost like segment trees. For example, in addition to maintaining the size of each subtree, we can also maintain the sum of its values, the minimum value, and so on.

One special trick related to treaps is that we can efficiently *reverse* an array. This can be done by swapping the left and right child of each node in the treap. For example, Fig. 15.22 shows the result after reversing the array in Fig. 15.18. To do this efficiently, we can introduce a field that indicates if we should reverse the subtree of the node and process swapping operations lazily.

Fig. 15.22 Reversing an
array using a treap

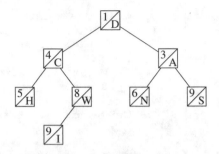

15.4 Dynamic Programming Optimization

This section discusses techniques for optimizing dynamic programming solutions. First, we focus on the convex hull trick, which can be used to efficiently find minimum values of linear functions. After this, we discuss two other techniques that are based on properties of cost functions.

15.4.1 Convex Hull Trick

The *convex hull trick* allows us to efficiently find the minimum function value at a given point x among a set of n linear functions of the form $f(x) = ax + b$. For example, Fig. 15.23 shows functions $f_1(x) = x + 2$, $f_2(x) = x/3 + 4$, $f_3(x) = x/6 + 5$ and $f_4(x) = -x/4 + 7$. The minimum value at point $x = 4$ is $f_2(4) = 16/3$.

Fig. 15.23 Minimum
function value at point $x = 4$
is $f_2(4) = 16/3$

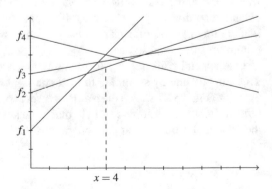

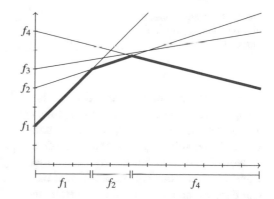

Fig. 15.24 Ranges where f_1, f_2, and f_4 have the minimum value

   The idea is to divide the x-axis into ranges where a certain function has the minimum value. It turns out that each function will have at most one range, and we can store the ranges in a sorted list that will contain at most n ranges. For example, Fig. 15.24 shows the ranges in our example scenario. First, f_1 has the minimum value, then f_2 has the minimum value, and finally f_4 has the minimum value. Note that f_3 never has the minimum value.

   Given a list of ranges, we can find the minimum function value at point x in $O(\log n)$ time using binary search. For example, since point $x = 4$ belongs to the range of f_2 in Fig. 15.24, we immediately know that the minimum function value at point $x = 4$ is $f_2(4) = 16/3$. Thus, we can process a set of k queries in $O(k \log n)$ time. Moreover, if the queries are given in increasing order, we can process them in $O(k)$ time by just iterating through the ranges from left to right.

   Then, how to determine the ranges? If the functions are given in decreasing order of their slopes, we can easily find the ranges, because we can maintain a stack that contains the ranges, and the amortized cost for processing each function is $O(1)$. If the functions are given in an arbitrary order, we need to use a more sophisticated set structure and processing each function takes $O(\log n)$ time.

Example Suppose that there are n consecutive concerts. The ticket for concert i costs p_i euros, and if we attend the concert, we get a discount coupon whose value is d_i ($0 < d_i < 1$). We can later use the coupon to buy a ticket for $d_i p$ euros where p is the original price. It is also known that $d_i \geq d_{i+1}$ for all consecutive concerts i and $i + 1$. We definitely want to attend the last concert, and we can also attend other concerts. What is the minimum total price for this?

   We can easily solve the problem using dynamic programming by calculating for each concert i a value u_i: the minimum price for attending the concert i and possibly some previous concerts. A simple way to find the optimal choice for the previous concert is to go through all previous concerts in $O(n)$ time, which results in an $O(n^2)$ time algorithm. However, we can use the convex hull trick to find the optimal choice in $O(\log n)$ time and get an $O(n \log n)$ time algorithm.

   The idea is to maintain a set of linear functions, which initially only contains the function $f(x) = x$, which means that we do not have a discount coupon. To calculate

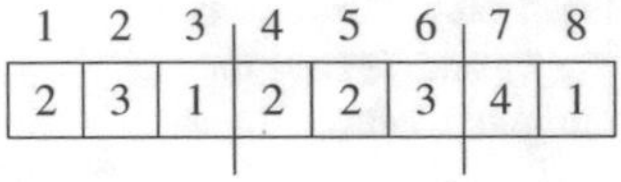

Fig. 15.25 Optimal way to
divide a sequence into three
blocks

1	2	3	4	5	6	7	8
2	3	1	2	2	3	4	1

the value u_i for a concert, we find a function f in our set that minimizes the value of
$f(p_i)$, which can be done in $O(\log n)$ time using the convex hull trick. Then, we add
a function $f(x) = d_i x + u_i$ to our set, and we can use it to attend another concert
later. The resulting algorithm works in $O(n \log n)$ time.

Note that if it is additionally known that $p_i \leq p_{i+1}$ for all consecutive concerts
i and $i + 1$, we can solve the problem more efficiently in $O(n)$ time, because we
can process the ranges from left to right and find each optimal choice in amortized
constant time instead of using binary search.

15.4.2 Divide and Conquer Optimization

The *divide and conquer optimization* can be applied to certain dynamic programming
problems where a sequence $s_1, s_2, \ldots, s_n$ of n elements has to be divided into k
subsequences of consecutive elements. A cost function $\text{cost}(a, b)$ is given, which
determines the cost of creating a subsequence $s_a, s_{a+1}, \ldots, s_b$. The total cost of a
division is the sum of the individual costs of the subsequences, and our task is to find
a division that minimizes the total cost.

As an example, suppose that we have a sequence of positive integers and
$\text{cost}(a, b) = (s_a + s_{a+1} + \cdots + s_b)^2$. Figure 15.25 shows an optimal way to divide a sequence into three subsequences using this cost function. The total cost of
the division is $(2 + 3 + 1)^2 + (2 + 2 + 3)^2 + (4 + 1)^2 = 110$.

We can solve the problem by defining a function $\text{solve}(i, j)$ which gives the
minimum total cost of dividing the first i elements $s_1, s_2, \ldots, s_i$ into j subsequences.
Clearly, $\text{solve}(n, k)$ equals the answer to the problem. To calculate a value of
$\text{solve}(i, j)$, we have to find a position $1 \leq p \leq i$ that minimizes the value of

$$\text{solve}(p - 1, j - 1) + \text{cost}(p, i).$$

For example, in Fig. 15.25, an optimal choice for $\text{solve}(8, 3)$ is $p = 7$. A simple
way to find an optimal position is to check all positions $1, 2, \ldots, i$, which takes
$O(n)$ time. By calculating all values of $\text{solve}(i, j)$ like this, we get a dynamic
programming algorithm that works in $O(n^2 k)$ time. However, using the divide and
conquer optimization, we can improve the time complexity to $O(nk \log n)$.

The divide and conquer optimization can be used if the cost function satisfies the
quadrangle inequality

$$\text{cost}(a, c) + \text{cost}(b, d) \leq \text{cost}(a, d) + \text{cost}(b, c)$$

for all $a \leq b \leq c \leq d$. Let $\text{pos}(i, j)$ denote the smallest position p that minimizes
the cost of a division for $\text{solve}(i, j)$. If the above inequality holds, it is guaranteed

that $pos(i, j) \leq pos(i + 1, j)$ for all values of i and j, which allows us to calculate the values of $solve(i, j)$ more efficiently.

The idea is to create a function $calc(j, a, b, x, y)$ that calculates all values of $solve(i, j)$ for $a \leq i \leq b$ and a fixed j using the information that $x \leq pos(i, j) \leq y$. The function first calculates the value of $solve(z, j)$ where $z = \lfloor (a + b)/2 \rfloor$. Then it performs recursive calls $calc(j, a, z - 1, x, p)$ and $calc(j, z + 1, b, p, y)$ where $p = pos(z, j)$. Here the fact that $pos(i, j) \leq pos(i + 1, j)$ is used to limit the search range. To calculate all values of $solve(i, j)$, we perform a function call $calc(j, 1, n, 1, n)$ for each $j = 1, 2, \ldots, k$. Since each such function call takes $O(n \log n)$ time, the resulting algorithm works in $O(nk \log n)$ time.

Finally, let us prove that the squared sum cost function in our example satisfies the quadrangle inequality. Let $sum(a, b)$ denote the sum of values in range $[a, b]$, and let $x = sum(b, c)$, $y = sum(a, c) - sum(b, c)$, and $z = sum(b, d) - sum(b, c)$. Using this notation, the quadrangle inequality becomes

$$(x + y)^2 + (x + z)^2 \leq (x + y + z)^2 + x^2,$$

which is equal to

$$0 \leq 2yz.$$

Since y and z are nonnegative values, this completes the proof.

15.4.3   Knuth's Optimization

Knuth's optimization[2] can be used in certain dynamic programming problems where we are asked to divide a sequence $s_1, s_2, \ldots, s_n$ of n elements into single elements using splitting operations. A cost function $cost(a, b)$ gives the cost of processing a sequence $s_a, s_{a+1}, \ldots, s_b$, and our task is to find a solution that minimizes the total sum of the splitting costs.

For example, suppose that $cost(a, b) = s_a + s_{a+1} + \cdots + s_b$. Figure 15.26 shows an optimal way to process a sequence in this case. The total cost of this solution is $19 + 9 + 10 + 5 = 43$.

We can solve the problem by defining a function $solve(i, j)$ which gives the minimum cost of dividing the sequence $s_i, s_{i+1}, \ldots, s_j$ into single elements. Then, $solve(1, n)$ gives the answer to the problem. To determine a value of $solve(i, j)$, we have to find a position $i \leq p < j$ that minimizes the value of

$$cost(i, j) + solve(i, p) + solve(p + 1, j).$$

---

[2] Knuth [23] used his optimization to construct optimal binary search trees; later, Yao [36] generalized the optimization to other similar problems.

Fig. 15.26 Optimal way to divide an array into single elements

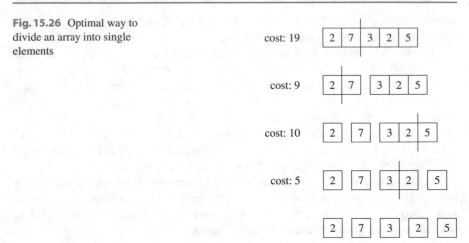

If we check all positions between i and j, we get a dynamic programming algorithm that works in $O(n^3)$ time. However, using Knuth's optimization, we can calculate the values of $\mathtt{solve}(i, j)$ more efficiently in $O(n^2)$ time.

Knuth's optimization is applicable if

$$\mathtt{cost}(b, c) \le \mathtt{cost}(a, d)$$

and

$$\mathtt{cost}(a, c) + \mathtt{cost}(b, d) \le \mathtt{cost}(a, d) + \mathtt{cost}(b, c)$$

for all values of $a \le b \le c \le d$. Note that the latter inequality is the quadrangle inequality that was also used in the divide and conquer optimization. Let $\mathtt{pos}(i, j)$ denote the smallest position p that minimizes the cost for $\mathtt{solve}(i, j)$. If the above inequalities hold, we know that

$$\mathtt{pos}(i, j - 1) \le \mathtt{pos}(i, j) \le \mathtt{pos}(i + 1, j).$$

Now we can perform n rounds $1, 2, \ldots, n$, and on round k calculate the values of $\mathtt{solve}(i, j)$ where $j - i + 1 = k$, i.e., we process the subsequences in increasing order of length. Since we know that $\mathtt{pos}(i, j)$ has to be between $\mathtt{pos}(i, j - 1)$ and $\mathtt{pos}(i + 1, j)$, we can perform each round in $O(n)$ time, and the total time complexity of the algorithm becomes $O(n^2)$.

15.5 Backtracking Techniques

This section shows some ideas how we can make backtracking algorithms work faster. We first consider a problem where we want to count the number of paths in a grid and can improve the algorithm by pruning the search tree. After that, we solve the 15 puzzle problem using the IDA* algorithm and heuristic functions.

15.5.1 Pruning the Search Tree

We can improve many backtracking algorithms by *pruning* the search tree: If we notice that a partial solution cannot be extended to a complete solution, it is no use to continue the search.

Let us consider the problem of calculating the number of paths in a 7×7 grid from the upper-left corner to the lower-right corner such that the path visits each square exactly once. Figure 15.27 shows one such path, and it turns out that the total number of paths is 111712.

We begin with a simple backtracking algorithm and then optimize it step by step using observations of how the search can be pruned. After each optimization, we measure the running time of the algorithm and the number of recursive calls to see the effect of each optimization on the efficiency of the search.

Basic Algorithm The first version of the algorithm does not contain any optimizations. We simply use backtracking to generate all possible paths from the upper-left corner to the lower-right corner and count the number of such paths.

- running time: 483 s
- number of recursive calls: $76 \cdot 10^9$

Optimization 1 In any solution, we first move one step down or right, and there are two paths that are symmetric about the diagonal of the grid. For example, the paths in Fig. 15.28 are symmetric. Hence, we can decide that we always first move one step down (or right) and finally multiply the number of solutions by two.

Fig. 15.27 Path from the upper-left corner to the lower-right corner

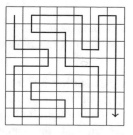

Fig. 15.28 Two symmetric paths about the diagonal of the grid

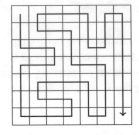

Fig. 15.29 We reach the lower-right square before visiting all other squares

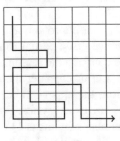

Fig. 15.30 Path splits the grid into two parts that contain unvisited squares

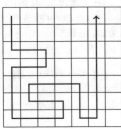

- running time: 244 s
- number of recursive calls: $38 \cdot 10^9$

Optimization 2 If the path reaches the lower-right square before visiting all other squares of the grid, it will clearly not be possible to complete the solution. An example of this is shown in Fig. 15.29. Using this observation, we can terminate the search immediately if we reach the lower-right square too early.

- running time: 119 s
- number of recursive calls: $20 \cdot 10^9$

Optimization 3 If the path touches a wall and can turn either left or right, the grid splits into two parts that contain unvisited squares. For example, the path in Fig. 15.30 can turn either left or right. In this case, we cannot visit all squares anymore, so we can terminate the search. This optimization is very useful:

Fig. 15.31 More general situation where the path splits the grid into two parts

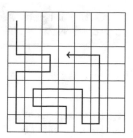

- running time: 1.8 s
- number of recursive calls: $221 \cdot 10^6$

Optimization 4 The idea of the previous optimization can be generalized: If the path cannot continue forward but can turn either left or right, the grid splits into two parts that both contain unvisited squares. Figure 15.31 shows an example of such a case. It is clear that we cannot visit all squares anymore, so we can terminate the search. After this optimization, the search is very efficient:

- running time: 0.6 s
- number of recursive calls: $69 \cdot 10^6$

Conclusion Now is a good point to stop optimizing the algorithm and see what we have achieved. The running time of the original algorithm was 483 s, and after the optimizations, the running time is only 0.6 s. Thus, the algorithm became nearly 1000 times faster thanks to the optimizations.

This is a usual phenomenon in backtracking, because the search tree is usually large and even simple observations can effectively prune the search. Especially useful are optimizations that occur during the first steps of the algorithm, i.e., at the top of the search tree.

15.5.2 Heuristic Functions

In some backtracking problems, we want to find an optimal solution, such as a sequence of moves that contains the minimum number of moves. In such problems, we can improve the search by using a *heuristic function* that estimates the distance from a search state to a final state.

In the 15 puzzle problem, we are given a 4×4 grid that contains 15 tiles (numbered $1, 2, \ldots, 15$) and an empty square. On each move, we can choose any tile adjacent to the empty square and move it to the empty square. We want to find the minimum number of moves that produces the final grid shown in Fig. 15.32.

To solve the problem, we use an algorithm called IDA* that consists of several backtracking searches. Each search attempts to find a solution where the number of

Fig. 15.32 Final grid in the
15 puzzle problem

1	2	3	4
5	6	7	8
9	10	11	12
13	14	15	

Fig. 15.33 Minimum
number of moves in this grid
is 61

11	3	12	9
8	15	6	5
14		10	2
7	13	1	4

moves is at most k. The initial value of k is 0, and we increase k by 1 after each search until a solution is found.

The algorithm uses a heuristic function that estimates the remaining number of moves needed to reach the final grid. The heuristic function must be *admissible* which means that it never overestimates the number of moves. Thus, we get a lower bound for the number of moves using the function.

As an example, we consider the grid shown in Fig. 15.33. It turns out that the minimum number of moves in this grid is 61. Since each search state has 2–4 possible moves, depending on the position of the empty grid, a simple backtracking algorithm would take too much time. Fortunately, the IDA* algorithm includes a heuristic function that can make the search much faster.

We next consider several heuristic functions and measure the running time of the algorithm and the number of recursive calls. In all heuristics, we implement the backtracking so that it never cancels the previous move, because this would not lead to an optimal solution.

Heuristic 1 A simple heuristic is to calculate for each tile the Manhattan distance from its current position to the final position. The Manhattan distance is calculated using the formula $|x_c - x_f| + |y_c - y_f|$ where (x_c, y_c) is the current position of a tile and (x_f, y_f) is its final position. We get a lower bound for the number of moves by summing all such distances, because each move changes the horizontal or vertical position of a single tile by one.

- running time: 126 s
- number of recursive calls: $1.5 \cdot 10^9$

Heuristic 2 We can create a better heuristic by focusing on tiles that are already in the correct row or column. As an example, consider tiles 6 and 8 in our example puzzle. They are already in the correct row but their order is wrong. We have to move one of them vertically to change their order, which creates two extra moves.

Thus, we can improve our heuristic as follows: We first calculate the sum of Manhattan distances but then add two extra moves for each row/column where two tiles are in the correct row/column in the wrong order.

- running time: 22 s
- number of recursive calls: $1.43 \cdot 10^8$

Heuristic 3 We can further improve the previous heuristic: If there are more than two tiles that are in the correct row/column, we may be able to add more than two extra moves. For example, consider tiles 5, 6, and 8 in our example puzzle. Since they are in the reverse order, we have to move at least two of them vertically which produces four extra moves.

More precisely, if there are c_1 tiles in the correct row/column and there are c_2 tiles in a maximum size subset of them where the order is correct, we can add $2(c_1 - c_2)$ extra moves.

- running time: 39 s
- number of recursive calls: $1.36 \cdot 10^8$

Conclusion What happened? We created a better heuristic but it increased the running time of the algorithm from 22 s to 39 s.

A good heuristic function has two properties: It gives a lower bound that is close to the real distance, and it can be calculated efficiently. Our last heuristic is more accurate than the previous heuristic but it is difficult to calculate, so a simpler heuristic seems to be a better choice in this case.

15.6 Miscellaneous

This section presents a selection of miscellaneous algorithm design techniques. We discuss the meet in the middle technique, a dynamic programming algorithm for counting subsets, the parallel binary search technique, and an offline solution to the dynamic connectivity problem.

15.6.1 Meet in the Middle

The *meet in the middle* technique divides the search space into two parts of about equal size, performs a separate search for both of the parts, and finally combines the results of the searches. Meet in the middle allows us to speed up certain $O(2^n)$ time algorithms so that they work in only $O(2^{n/2})$ time. Note that $O(2^{n/2})$ is much faster than $O(2^n)$, because $2^{n/2} = \sqrt{2^n}$. Using an $O(2^n)$ algorithm we can process inputs where $n \approx 20$, but using an $O(2^{n/2})$ algorithm the bound is $n \approx 40$.

Suppose that we are given a set of n integers and our task is to determine whether the set has a subset with sum x. For example, given the set $\{2, 4, 5, 9\}$ and $x = 15$, we can choose the subset $\{2, 4, 9\}$, because $2 + 4 + 9 = 15$. We can easily solve the problem in $O(2^n)$ time by going through every possible subset, but next we will solve the problem more efficiently in $O(2^{n/2})$ time using meet in the middle.

The idea is to divide our set into two sets A and B such that both sets contain about half of the numbers. We perform two searches: the first search generates all subsets of A and stores their sums to a list S_A, and the second search creates a similar list S_B for B. After this, it suffices to check if we can choose one element from S_A and another element from S_B such that their sum is x, which is possible exactly when the original set contains a subset with sum x.

For example, let us see how the set $\{2, 4, 5, 9\}$ is processed. First, we divide the set into sets $A = \{2, 4\}$ and $B = \{5, 9\}$. After this, we create lists $S_A = [0, 2, 4, 6]$ and $S_B = [0, 5, 9, 14]$. Since S_A contains the sum 6 and S_B contains the sum 9, we conclude that the original set has a subset with sum $6 + 9 = 15$.

With a good implementation, we can create the lists S_A and S_B in $O(2^{n/2})$ time in such a way that the lists are sorted. After this, we can use a two pointers algorithm to check in $O(2^{n/2})$ time if the sum x can be created from S_A and S_B. Thus, the total time complexity of the algorithm is $O(2^{n/2})$.

15.6.2   Counting Subsets

Let $X = \{0 \ldots n - 1\}$, and each subset $S \subset X$ is assigned an integer value$[S]$. Our task is to calculate for each S

$$\text{sum}(S) = \sum_{A \subset S} \text{value}[A],$$

i.e., the sum of values of subsets of S.

For example, suppose that $n = 3$ and the values are as follows:

- value$[\emptyset] = 3$
- value$[\{0\}] = 1$
- value$[\{1\}] = 4$
- value$[\{0, 1\}] = 5$

- value$[\{2\}] = 5$
- value$[\{0, 2\}] = 1$
- value$[\{1, 2\}] = 3$
- value$[\{0, 1, 2\}] = 3$

In this case, for example,

$$\text{sum}(\{0, 2\}) = \text{value}[\emptyset] + \text{value}[\{0\}] + \text{value}[\{2\}] + \text{value}[\{0, 2\}]$$
$$= 3 + 1 + 5 + 1 = 10.$$

Next we will see how to solve the problem in $O(2^n n)$ time using dynamic programming and bit operations. The idea is to consider subproblems where it is limited which elements may be removed from S.

Let $\texttt{partial}(S, k)$ denote the sum of values of subsets of S with the restriction that only elements $0 \dots k$ may be removed from S. For example,

$$\texttt{partial}(\{0, 2\}, 1) = \texttt{value}[\{2\}] + \texttt{value}[\{0, 2\}],$$

because we only may remove elements $0 \dots 1$. Note that we can calculate any value of $\texttt{sum}(S)$ using $\texttt{partial}$, because

$$\texttt{sum}(S) = \texttt{partial}(S, n - 1).$$

To use dynamic programming, we have to find a recurrence for $\texttt{partial}$. First, the base cases are

$$\texttt{partial}(S, -1) = \texttt{value}[S],$$

because no elements can be removed from S. Then, in the general case we can calculate the values as follows:

$$\texttt{partial}(S, k) = \begin{cases} \texttt{partial}(S, k - 1) & k \notin S \\ \texttt{partial}(S, k - 1) + \texttt{partial}(S \setminus \{k\}, k - 1) & k \in S \end{cases}$$

Here we focus on the element k. If $k \in S$, there are two options: We can either keep k in the subset or remove it from the subset.

Implementation There is a particularly clever way to implement a dynamic programming solution using bit operations. Namely we can declare an array

```
int sum[1<<N];
```

that will contain the sum of each subset. The array is initialized as follows:

```
for (int s = 0; s < (1<<n); s++) {
    sum[s] = value[s];
}
```

Then, we can fill the array as follows:

```
for (int k = 0; k < n; k++) {
    for (int s = 0; s < (1<<n); s++) {
        if (s&(1<<k)) sum[s] += sum[s^(1<<k)];
    }
}
```

This code calculates the values of $\texttt{partial}(S, k)$ for $k = 0 \dots n - 1$ to the array sum. Since $\texttt{partial}(S, k)$ is always based on $\texttt{partial}(S, k - 1)$, we can reuse the array sum, which yields a very efficient implementation.

Fig. 15.34 Instance of the
road building problem

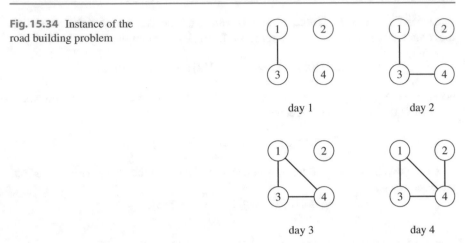

15.6.3   **Parallel Binary Search**

Parallel binary search is a technique that allows us to make some binary search-based
algorithms more efficient. The general idea is to perform several binary searches
simultaneously, instead of doing the searches separately.

As an example, consider the following problem: There are n cities numbered
$1, 2, \ldots, n$. Initially there are no roads between the cities. Then, during m days, each
day a new road is built between two cities. Finally, we are given k queries of the form
(a, b), and our task is to determine for each query the earliest moment when cities a
and b are connected. We can assume that all requested pairs of cities are connected
after m days.

Figure 15.34 shows an example scenario where there are four cities. Suppose that
the queries are $q_1 = (1, 4)$ and $q_2 = (2, 3)$. The answer for q_1 is 2, because cities 1
and 4 are connected after day 2, and the answer for q_2 is 4, because cities 2 and 3
are connected after day 4.

Let us first consider an easier problem where we have only one query (a, b). In
this case, we can use a union-find structure to simulate the process of adding roads
to the network. After each new road, we check if cities a and b are connected and
stop the search if they are. Both adding a road and checking if cities are connected
takes $O(\log n)$ time, so the algorithm works in $O(m \log n)$ time.

How could we generalize this solution to k queries? Of course we could process
each query separately, but such an algorithm would take $O(km \log n)$ time, which
would be slow if both k and m are large. Next we will see how we can solve the
problem more efficiently using parallel binary search.

The idea is to assign each query a range $[x, y]$ which means that the cities are
connected for the first time no earlier than after x days and no later than after y
days. Initially, each range is $[1, m]$. Then, we simulate $\log m$ times the process of
adding all roads to the network using a union-find structure. For each query, we check
at moment $u = \lfloor (x + y)/2 \rfloor$ if the cities are connected. If they are, the new range

becomes $[x, u]$, and otherwise the range becomes $[u + 1, y]$. After $\log m$ rounds, each range only contains a single moment which is the answer to the query.

During each round, we add m roads to the network in $O(m \log n)$ time and check whether k pairs of cities are connected in $O(k \log n)$ time. Thus, since there are $\log m$ rounds, the resulting algorithm works in $O((m + k) \log n \log m)$ time.

15.6.4 Dynamic Connectivity

Suppose that there is a graph of n nodes and m edges. Then, we are given q queries, each of which is either "add an edge between nodes a and b" or "remove the edge between nodes a and b." Our task is to efficiently report the number of connected components in the graph after each query.

Figure 15.35 shows an example of the process. Initially, the graph has three components. Then, the edge 2–4 is added, which joins two components. After this, the edge 4–5 is added and the edge 2–5 is removed, but the number of components remains the same. Then, the edge 1–3 is added, which joins two components, and finally, the edge 2–4 is removed, which divides a component into two components.

If edges would only be added to the graph, the problem would be easy to solve using a union-find data structure, but the removal operations make the problem much more difficult. Next we will discuss a divide and conquer algorithm for solving the offline version the problem where all queries are known beforehand, and we are allowed to report the results in any order. The algorithm presented here is based on the work by Kopeliovich [25].

The idea is to create a timeline where each edge is represented by an interval that shows the insertion and removal time of the edge. The timeline spans a range $[0, q + 1]$, and an edge that is added on step a and removed on step b is represented by an interval $[a, b]$. If an edge belongs to the initial graph, $a = 0$, and if an edge is never removed, $b = q + 1$. Figure 15.36 shows the timeline in our example scenario.

To process the intervals, we create a graph that has n nodes and no edges and use a recursive function that is called with range $[0, q + 1]$. The function works as follows for a range $[a, b]$: First, if $[a, b]$ is completely inside the interval of an edge, and the edge does not belong to the graph, it is added to the graph. Then, if the size of $[a, b]$ is 1, we report the number of connected components, and otherwise we recursively process ranges $[a, k]$ and $[k, b]$ where $k = \lfloor (a + b)/2 \rfloor$. Finally, we remove all edges that were added at the beginning of processing the range $[a, b]$.

Always when an edge is added or removed, we also update the number of components. This can be done using a union-find data structure, because we always remove the edge that was added last. Thus, it suffices to implement an *undo* operation for the union-find structure, which is possible by storing information about operations in a stack. Since each edge is added and removed at most $O(\log q)$ times and each operation works in $O(\log n)$ time, the total running time of the algorithm is $O((m + q) \log q \log n)$.

Note that in addition to counting the number of components, we may maintain any information that can be combined with the union-find data structure. For example,

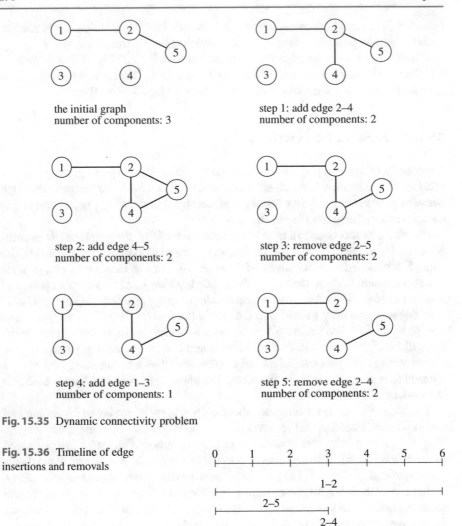

the initial graph
number of components: 3

step 1: add edge 2–4
number of components: 2

step 2: add edge 4–5
number of components: 2

step 3: remove edge 2–5
number of components: 2

step 4: add edge 1–3
number of components: 1

step 5: remove edge 2–4
number of components: 2

Fig. 15.35 Dynamic connectivity problem

Fig. 15.36 Timeline of edge
insertions and removals

we may maintain the number of nodes in the largest component or the bipartiteness
of each component. The technique can also be generalized to other data structures
that support insertion and undo operations.

Correction to: Range Queries

16

Correction to:
Chapter 9 in: A. Laaksonen, *Guide to Competitive*
***Programming*, Undergraduate Topics in Computer Science,**
https://doi.org/10.1007/978-3-030-39357-1

The original version of the book was inadvertently published with an incomplete code in Chap. 9 and it has been updated.

The chapter has been updated with the change and the correct presentation is given here;

The following function calculates the value of sum $_q (a, b)$:

```
int sum (int a, int b) {
a += n; b += n;
int s = 0;
while (a <= b) {
if (a%2 == 1) s += tree [a++];
if (b%2 == 0) s += tree [b–];
a /= 2; b /= 2;
}
return s;
}
```

The updated version of this chapter can be found at
https://doi.org/10.1007/978-3-030-39357-1_9

© Springer Nature Switzerland AG 2020
A. Laaksonen, *Guide to Competitive Programming*, Undergraduate Topics
in Computer Science, https://doi.org/10.1007/978-3-030-39357-1_16

Appendix
Mathematical Background

A.1 Sum Formulas

Each sum of the form

$$\sum_{x=1}^{n} x^k = 1^k + 2^k + 3^k + \ldots + n^k,$$

where k is a positive integer, has a closed-form formula that is a polynomial of degree $k + 1$. For example,[1]

$$\sum_{x=1}^{n} x = 1 + 2 + 3 + \ldots + n = \frac{n(n+1)}{2}$$

and

$$\sum_{x=1}^{n} x^2 = 1^2 + 2^2 + 3^2 + \ldots + n^2 = \frac{n(n+1)(2n+1)}{6}.$$

An *arithmetic progression* is a sequence of numbers where the difference between any two consecutive numbers is constant. For example,

$$3, 7, 11, 15$$

is an arithmetic progression with constant 4. The sum of an arithmetic progression can be calculated using the formula

$$\underbrace{a + \cdots + b}_{n \text{ numbers}} = \frac{n(a+b)}{2}.$$

---

[1] There is even a general formula for such sums, called *Faulhaber's formula*, but it is too complex to be presented here.

© Springer Nature Switzerland AG 2020
A. Laaksonen, *Guide to Competitive Programming*, Undergraduate Topics in Computer Science, https://doi.org/10.1007/978-3-030-39357-1

where a is the first number, b is the last number and n is the amount of numbers. For example,

$$3 + 7 + 11 + 15 = \frac{4 \cdot (3 + 15)}{2} = 36.$$

The formula is based on the fact that the sum consists of n numbers and the value of each number is $(a + b)/2$ on average.

A *geometric progression* is a sequence of numbers where the ratio between any two consecutive numbers is constant. For example,

$$3, 6, 12, 24$$

is a geometric progression with constant 2. The sum of a geometric progression can be calculated using the formula

$$a + ak + ak^2 + \cdots + b = \frac{bk - a}{k - 1}$$

where a is the first number, b is the last number and the ratio between consecutive numbers is k. For example,

$$3 + 6 + 12 + 24 = \frac{24 \cdot 2 - 3}{2 - 1} = 45.$$

This formula can be derived as follows. Let

$$S = a + ak + ak^2 + \cdots + b.$$

By multiplying both sides by k, we get

$$kS = ak + ak^2 + ak^3 + \cdots + bk,$$

and solving the equation

$$kS - S = bk - a$$

yields the formula.

A special case of a sum of a geometric progression is the formula

$$1 + 2 + 4 + 8 + \ldots + 2^{n-1} = 2^n - 1.$$

A *harmonic sum* is a sum of the form

$$\sum_{x=1}^{n} \frac{1}{x} = 1 + \frac{1}{2} + \frac{1}{3} + \ldots + \frac{1}{n}.$$

An upper bound for a harmonic sum is $\log_2(n) + 1$. Namely, we can modify each term $1/k$ so that k becomes the nearest power of two that does not exceed k. For example, when $n = 6$, we can estimate the sum as follows:

$$1 + \frac{1}{2} + \frac{1}{3} + \frac{1}{4} + \frac{1}{5} + \frac{1}{6} \leq 1 + \frac{1}{2} + \frac{1}{2} + \frac{1}{4} + \frac{1}{4} + \frac{1}{4}.$$

This upper bound consists of $\log_2(n) + 1$ parts ($1, 2 \cdot 1/2, 4 \cdot 1/4$, etc.), and the value of each part is at most 1.

A.2 Sets

A *set* is a collection of elements. For example, the set

$$X = \{2, 4, 7\}$$

contains elements 2, 4 and 7. The symbol $\emptyset$ denotes an empty set, and $|S|$ denotes the size of a set S, i.e., the number of elements in the set. For example, in the above set, $|X| = 3$. If a set S contains an element x, we write $x \in S$, and otherwise we write $x \notin S$. For example, in the above set, $4 \in X$ and $5 \notin X$.

New sets can be constructed using set operations:

- The *intersection* $A \cap B$ consists of elements that are in both A and B. For example, if $A = \{1, 2, 5\}$ and $B = \{2, 4\}$, then $A \cap B = \{2\}$.
- The *union* $A \cup B$ consists of elements that are in A or B or both. For example, if $A = \{3, 7\}$ and $B = \{2, 3, 8\}$, then $A \cup B = \{2, 3, 7, 8\}$.
- The *complement* $\bar{A}$ consists of elements that are not in A. The interpretation of a complement depends on the *universal set*, which contains all possible elements. For example, if $A = \{1, 2, 5, 7\}$ and the universal set is $\{1, 2, \ldots, 10\}$, then $\bar{A} = \{3, 4, 6, 8, 9, 10\}$.
- The *difference* $A \setminus B = A \cap \bar{B}$ consists of elements that are in A but not in B. Note that B can contain elements that are not in A. For example, if $A = \{2, 3, 7, 8\}$ and $B = \{3, 5, 8\}$, then $A \setminus B = \{2, 7\}$.

If each element of A also belongs to S, we say that A is a *subset* of S, denoted by $A \subset S$. A set S always has $2^{|S|}$ subsets, including the empty set. For example, the subsets of the set $\{2, 4, 7\}$ are

$$\emptyset, \{2\}, \{4\}, \{7\}, \{2, 4\}, \{2, 7\}, \{4, 7\} \text{ and } \{2, 4, 7\}.$$

Some often used sets are $\mathbb{N}$ (natural numbers), $\mathbb{Z}$ (integers), $\mathbb{Q}$ (rational numbers) and $\mathbb{R}$ (real numbers). The set $\mathbb{N}$ can be defined in two ways, depending on the situation: either $\mathbb{N} = \{0, 1, 2, \ldots\}$ or $\mathbb{N} = \{1, 2, 3, \ldots\}$.

There are several notations for defining sets. For example,

$$A = \{2n : n \in \mathbb{Z}\}$$

consists of all even integers, and

$$B = \{x \in \mathbb{R} : x > 2\}$$

consists of all real numbers that are greater than two.

A.3 Logic

The value of a logical expression is either *true* (1) or *false* (0). The most important logical operators are $\neg$ (*negation*), $\wedge$ (*conjunction*), $\vee$ (*disjunction*), $\Rightarrow$ (*implication*) and $\Leftrightarrow$ (*equivalence*). Table A.1 shows the meanings of these operators.

Table A.1 Logical operators

A	B	$\neg A$	$\neg B$	$A \wedge B$	$A \vee B$	$A \Rightarrow B$	$A \Leftrightarrow B$
0	0	1	1	0	0	1	1
0	1	1	0	0	1	1	0
1	0	0	1	0	1	0	0
1	1	0	0	1	1	1	1

The expression $\neg A$ has the opposite value of A. The expression $A \wedge B$ is true if both A and B are true, and the expression $A \vee B$ is true if A or B or both are true. The expression $A \Rightarrow B$ is true if whenever A is true, also B is true. The expression $A \Leftrightarrow B$ is true if A and B are both true or both false.

A *predicate* is an expression that is true or false depending on its parameters. Predicates are usually denoted by capital letters. For example, we can define a predicate $P(x)$ that is true exactly when x is a prime number. Using this definition, $P(7)$ is true but $P(8)$ is false.

A *quantifier* connects a logical expression to the elements of a set. The most important quantifiers are $\forall$ (*for all*) and $\exists$ (*there is*). For example,

$$\forall x (\exists y (y < x))$$

means that for each element x in the set, there is an element y in the set such that y is smaller than x. This is true in the set of integers, but false in the set of natural numbers.

Using the notation described above, we can express many kinds of logical propositions. For example,

$$\forall x ((x > 1 \wedge \neg P(x)) \Rightarrow (\exists a (\exists b (a > 1 \wedge b > 1 \wedge x = ab))))$$

means that if a number x is larger than 1 and not a prime number, then there are numbers a and b that are larger than 1 and whose product is x. This proposition is true in the set of integers.

A.4 Functions

The function $\lfloor x \rfloor$ rounds the number x down to an integer, and the function $\lceil x \rceil$ rounds the number x up to an integer. For example,

$$\lfloor 3/2 \rfloor = 1 \text{ and } \lceil 3/2 \rceil = 2.$$

The functions $\min(x_1, x_2, \ldots, x_n)$ and $\max(x_1, x_2, \ldots, x_n)$ give the smallest and largest of values $x_1, x_2, \ldots, x_n$. For example,

$$\min(1, 2, 3) = 1 \text{ and } \max(1, 2, 3) = 3.$$

The *factorial* $n!$ can be defined by

$$\prod_{x=1}^{n} x = 1 \cdot 2 \cdot 3 \cdot \ldots \cdot n$$

or recursively

$$0! = 1$$
$$n! = n \cdot (n - 1)!$$

The *Fibonacci numbers* arise in many situations. They can be defined recursively as follows:

$$f(0) = 0$$
$$f(1) = 1$$
$$f(n) = f(n - 1) + f(n - 2)$$

The first Fibonacci numbers are

$$0, 1, 1, 2, 3, 5, 8, 13, 21, 34, 55, \ldots$$

There is also a closed-form formula for calculating Fibonacci numbers, which is sometimes called *Binet's formula*:

$$f(n) = \frac{(1 + \sqrt{5})^n - (1 - \sqrt{5})^n}{2^n \sqrt{5}}.$$

A.5 Logarithms

The *logarithm* of a number x is denoted $\log_b(x)$, where b is the base of the logarithm. It is defined so that $\log_b(x) = a$ exactly when $b^a = x$. The *natural logarithm* $\ln(x)$ of a number x is a logarithm whose base is $e \approx 2.71828$.

A useful property of logarithms is that $\log_b(x)$ equals the number of times we have to divide x by b before we reach the number 1. For example, $\log_2(32) = 5$ because 5 divisions by 2 are needed:

$$32 \rightarrow 16 \rightarrow 8 \rightarrow 4 \rightarrow 2 \rightarrow 1$$

The logarithm of a product is

$$\log_b(xy) = \log_b(x) + \log_b(y),$$

and consequently,

$$\log_b(x^n) = n \cdot \log_b(x).$$

In addition, the logarithm of a quotient is

$$\log_b\left(\frac{x}{y}\right) = \log_b(x) - \log_b(y).$$

Another useful formula is

$$\log_u(x) = \frac{\log_b(x)}{\log_b(u)},$$

using which it is possible to calculate logarithms to any base if there is a way to calculate logarithms to some fixed base.

A.6 Number Systems

Usually, numbers are written in base 10, which means that the digits $0, 1, \ldots, 9$ are used. However, there are also other number systems, like the base 2 binary system that has only two digits 0 and 1. In general, in a base b system, the integers $0, 1, \ldots, b-1$ are used as digits.

We can convert a base 10 number to base b by dividing the number by b until it becomes zero. The remainders in reverse order correspond to the digits in base b. For example, let us convert the number 17 to base 3:

- $17/3 = 5$ (remainder 2)
- $5/3 = 1$ (remainder 2)
- $1/3 = 0$ (remainder 1)

Thus, the number 17 in base 3 is 122. Then, to convert a base b number to base 10, it suffices to multiply each digit by b^k, where k is the zero-based position of the digit starting from the right, and sum the results together. For example, we can convert the base 3 number 122 back to base 10 as follows:

$$1 \cdot 3^2 + 2 \cdot 3^1 + 2 \cdot 3^0 = 17$$

The number of digits of an integer x in base b can be calculated using the formula $\lfloor \log_b(x) + 1 \rfloor$. For example, $\lfloor \log_3(17) + 1 \rfloor = 3$.

References

R. K. Ahuja, T. L. Magnanti, and J. B. Orlin, *Network Flows: Theory, Algorithms, and Applications*, (Pearson, 1993)

A.M. Andrew, Another efficient algorithm for convex hulls in two dimensions. Inf. Process. Lett. **9**(5), 216–219 (1979)

M. A. Bender and M. Farach-Colton, The LCA problem revisited. Lat. Am. Symp. Theor. Inform. 88–94, 2000

J. Bentley and D. Wood, An optimal worst case algorithm for reporting intersections of rectangles. IEEE Trans. Comput. C-29(7):571–577, 1980

A. Blumer et al., The smallest automation recognizing the subwords of a text. Theoret. Comput. Sci. **40**, 31–55 (1985)

Codeforces: On "Mo's algorithm", http://codeforces.com/blog/entry/20032

T. H. Cormen, C. E. Leiserson, R. L. Rivest, and C. Stein, *Introduction to Algorithms*, 3rd edn. (MIT Press, 2009)

K. Diks et al., *Looking for a Challenge?* (The Ultimate Problem Set from the University of Warsaw Programming Competitions, University of Warsaw, 2012)

J. Edmonds, R. Karp, Theoretical improvements in algorithmic efficiency for network flow problems. J. ACM. **19**(2), 248–264 (1972)

D. Fanding, A faster algorithm for shortest-path - SPFA. Journal of Southwest Jiaotong University **2**, (1994)

P. M. Fenwick, A new data structure for cumulative frequency tables. *Software: Practice and Experience*, **24**(3), 327–336, 1994

J. Fischer and V. Heun, Theoretical and practical improvements on the RMQ-problem, with applications to LCA and LCE. *17th Annual Symposium on Combinatorial Pattern Matching*, 36–48, 2006

F. Le Gall, Powers of tensors and fast matrix multiplication. *39th International Symposium on Symbolic and Algebraic Computation*, 296–303, 2014

A. Grønlund and S. Pettie, Threesomes, degenerates, and love triangles. *55th Annual Symposium on Foundations of Computer Science*, 621–630, 2014

D. Gusfield, *Algorithms on Strings*, Trees and Sequences, Comput. Sci. Comput. Biol. (Cambridge University Press, 1997)

S. Halim and F. Halim, *Competitive Programming 3: The New Lower Bound of Programming Contests*, (2013)

The International Olympiad in Informatics Syllabus, https://people.ksp.sk/~misof/ioi-syllabus/

© Springer Nature Switzerland AG 2020   303
A. Laaksonen, *Guide to Competitive Programming*, Undergraduate Topics
in Computer Science, https://doi.org/10.1007/978-3-030-39357-1

D. Johnson, Efficient algorithms for shortest paths in sparse networks. J. ACM **24**(1), 1–13 (1977)

J. Kärkkäinen and P. Sanders, Simple linear work suffix array construction. *International Colloquium on Automata, Languages, and Programming*, 943–955, 2003

R. M. Karp, R. E. Miller, and A. L. Rosenberg, Rapid identification of repeated patterns in strings, trees and arrays. *4th Annual ACM Symposium on Theory of Computing*, 125–135, 1972

T. Kasai, G. Lee, H. Arimura, S. Arikawa, and K. Park, Linear-time longest-common-prefix computation in suffix arrays and its applications. *12th Annual Symposium on Combinatorial Pattern Matching*, 181–192, 2001

J. Kleinberg and É. Tardos, *Algorithm Design*, (Pearson, 2005)

D.E. Knuth, Optimum binary search trees. Acta Informatica **1**(1), 14–25 (1971)

D.E. Knuth, J.H. Morris Jr., V.R. Pratt, Fast pattern matching in strings. SIAM J. Comput. **6**(2), 323–350 (1977)

S. Kopeliovich, Offline solution of connectivity and 2-edge-connectivity problems for fully dynamic graphs. MSc thesis, Saint Petersburg State University, 2012

M.G. Main, R.J. Lorentz, An $O(n \log n)$ algorithm for finding all repetitions in a string. Journal of Algorithms **5**(3), 422–432 (1984)

J. Pachocki, J. Radoszewski, Where to use and how not to use polynomial string hashing. Olympiads in Informatics **7**(1), 90–100 (2013)

D. Pearson, A polynomial-time algorithm for the change-making problem. Oper. Res. Lett. **33**(3), 231–234 (2005)

27-Queens Puzzle: Massively Parallel Enumeration and Solution Counting. https://github.com/preusser/q27

M. I. Shamos and D. Hoey, Closest-point problems. *16th Annual Symposium on Foundations of Computer Science*, 151–162, 1975

S. S. Skiena, *The Algorithm Design Manual*, (Springer, 2008)

S.S. Skiena, M.A. Revilla, Programming Challenges: The Programming Contest Training Manual, (Springer, 2003)

D.D. Sleator, R.E. Tarjan, A data structure for dynamic trees. J. Comput. Syst. Sci. **26**(3), 362–391 (1983)

P. Stańczyk, Algorytmika praktyczna w konkursach Informatycznych. MSc thesis, University of Warsaw, 2006

V. Strassen, Gaussian elimination is not optimal. Numer. Math. **13**(4), 354–356 (1969)

F. F. Yao, Efficient dynamic programming using quadrangle inequalities. *12h Annual ACM Symposium on Theory of Computing*, 429–435, 1980

Index

© Springer Nature Switzerland AG 2020
A. Laaksonen, *Guide to Competitive Programming*, Undergraduate Topics
in Computer Science, https://doi.org/10.1007/978-3-030-39357-1

Printed in the United States
By Bookmasters